From Margins to Mainstream

From Margins to Mainstream

Feminism and Fictional Modes in Italian Women's Writing, 1968–1990

Carol Lazzaro-Weis

UNIVERSITY OF PENNSYLVANIA PRESS

Philadelphia

Copyright © 1993 by the University of Pennsylvania Press
All rights reserved
Printed in the United States of America

Library of Congress Cataloging-in-Publication Data
Lazzaro-Weis, Carol M., 1949–
    From margins to mainstream: feminism and fictional modes in Italian women's
writing, 1968–1990 / Carol Lazzaro-Weis.
        p.   cm.
    Includes bibliographical references and index.
    ISBN 0-8122-3195-3 (cloth). — ISBN 0-8122-1438-2 (paper)
    1. Italian fiction—Women authors—History and criticism.   2. Italian fiction—
20th century—History and criticism.   3. Feminism and literature—Italy.   4. Feminism in literature.   I. Title.
PQ4174.L39   1993
853'.914099287—dc20   93-10867
                                                                          CIP

For
Peter Josef Weis

Contents

Acknowledgments

The writing of this book was greatly aided in its early stages by a grant from the Council of Southern Universities in 1986 and a 1989 summer research grant from the South Central Modern Language Association. Research grants from The Fulbright Commission and The American Council of Learned Scholars in 1990–91 enabled me to spend most of the year in Rome to meet with many Italian women writers, critics, and publishers and to complete the manuscript.

Portions of Chapters 1 and 2 appeared in "From Margins to Mainstream: Some Perspectives on Women and Literature in Italy in the 1980s," in *Contemporary Women Writers in Italy: A Modern Renaissance*, ed. Santo Arico (Amherst: University of Massachusetts Press, 1990). Parts of Chapter 3 appeared in "Gender and Genre in Italian Feminist Literature in the Seventies," *Italica* 65 (1988); and portions of Chapter 4 appeared in an earlier version as "The Female *Bildungsroman*: Calling It into Question," *NWSA Journal* 2 (1990). Permission to use this material is gratefully acknowledged.

I am very grateful to Alice Ceresa, Lidia Ravera, Sandra Petrignani, Dacia Maraini, Francesca Sanvitale, Francesca Duranti, Rosetta Loy, Maria Schiavo, and Biancamaria Frabotta for meeting with me to discuss their works. Special thanks go to Maria Rosa Cutrufelli for the many interesting discussions we have had over the years and for her help in introducing me to the literary community in Rome. I would also like to thank Glauca Gambon from the Circolo della Rosa for allowing me to participate in their lecture series and discussions; Paola Bono, Nadia Fusini, and Novella Bellucci from the University of Rome; Bianca Pomeranzi, Rosanna Fiocchetto, Laura Caputo, and Maria Mosca from the Virginia Woolf Centro Culturale; Luciana Tufani, editor of *Leggere Donna*; Maria Luisa Moretti from the women's book store in Rome, *Al tempo ritrovato*; and the staffs at *Donnawomenfemme* research center and Mondadori, Garzanti, and Rizzoli for compiling the many book reviews on works published by their companies. Special thanks go to Ana Rueda for her suggestions for revision of the final chapter. Finally, I thank the editors of the University of Pennsylvania Press and the readers they chose for their careful readings of the manuscript and most helpful suggestions, without which this book would not have been possible.

Introduction

This book has two goals. First, it aims to examine the variety of relationships in the making between feminism, feminist theory, and contemporary Italian women's narrative prose. Second, it provides a literary framework through which one can appreciate the differences among contemporary Italian women writers and the innovations these differences introduce into the Italian literary tradition as these women create a tradition of their own. Therefore, although the primary focus is on narratives written in the last twenty years, for the purpose of comparison, some older works written by both men and women will be included. While some of the works analyzed here are written by proclaimed feminist writers, many others are not. Some are published by small feminist publishing houses, others by the larger, mainstream companies.

The idea for this book began to take form in 1984 while I was teaching a seminar on autobiography and society at the Universität Saarbrücken in what was then West Germany. In the seminar we examined how male writers of canonical autobiographies implemented literary themes, stereotypes, and forms to describe their selves, their writings, and their relationship to language and society. We concluded the seminar with some recent examples of Italian feminist autobiographical writings, expecting to find in them obvious examples of how these traditional generic forms could no longer function as explanatory patterns for female experience, behavior, or even ethics. However, as I showed in an article published in *Italica* in 1988 (which appears here as part of Chapter 3), literary techniques and generic conventions stubbornly reappeared in these feminist works as well, in such a way that it was not possible simply to argue that these conventions silenced or marginalized female voices the way patriarchal laws, written or unwritten, excluded women.[1] Dacia Maraini and Armanda Guiducci, the two writers under discussion, successfully used literary forms and conventions to give voice to themes specific to them as women in a distinct historical and political situation. Clearly, the relationship of women's writing to genre was not one of total helplessness or natural antago- nism, and it needed to be explored.

In *La letteratura emarginata*, a collection of essays published in 1978, Walter Pedullà writes that Italian feminism, the major political and cultural movement of the seventies, was born of an ideology of margin- ality.[2] This marginality, however, so essential to the revolutionary and challenging nature of feminism, was not considered strictly a charac- teristic of feminist or women's writing. In the same collection of essays, the writer, journalist, and critic Silvia Castelli pointed to marginality, alienation, failed revolt, and literary narcissism as the major themes of all writers in the seventies.[3] According to Castelli, during that time, men and women writers experienced a separation from their readers and a loss of their position as authoritative, speaking subjects; they became mere spectators speaking from the "banks of the river capable only of representing the moment that the world had killed them as writers" (122). Castelli does discuss women's texts under the separate rubric of *la gabbia e l'ombra* where *gabbia* refers to the oppressive social norms that women must overthrow. *Ombra* is a space for both men and women: men had inhabited this space during the fascist period that caused the phenomenon Castelli terms the "feminization of the text" (125). In the seventies, Castelli continues, the crisis in the patriarchy forces the *gabbia* into feminine space where both sexes unite and work toward annulling differences (133). Her own experimental novel *Pitonessa*, published in 1978, is written in unpunctuated sentences and arbitrary paragraphs. It exemplifies a type of body language identified by Biancamaria Frabotta as similar to that of Monique Wittig in *Le corps lesbien*, where the term "lesbian" indicates a genderless, political and social class rather than sexual preference.[4] The mysterious *bambine* or *esse* who constantly disrupt the story of a woman whose husband's first love is photography or who interfere with the inquiries of another lady concerning her soldier husband who had been killed in service in Africa represent the free zone in which children grow up outside socialized, rigidified, sexual difference.

Although avant-garde writers occupied this prestigious marginal space, sooner or later, warns Pedullà, they would have to abandon this stance of voluntary marginality in order to gain a wider audience for their works and to insure against the trivialization or loss of the revolu- tionary force of their writings. Once again, this challenge was not solely directed at women authors. At a 1984 symposium in Palermo on the meaning of literature, Italian critics, using Umberto Eco's popular success *Il nome della rosa* (1980) as an example, called for a more communicative type of writing that would include more pragmatic and known literary techniques to replace the "nihilistic earthquake of the 70's."[5] In an article published the previous year, Anna Nozzoli—author of a study on women's writing in the twentieth century which concludes with a detailed chapter on radical feminist literature in the 1970s—also speaks of a discernable return to known literary forms in the works of many Italian women writers in the early 1980s, in contrast to the seemingly formless and militant autobiographies of the previous decade. Rather than viewing this shift as an indication of passive conformism on the part of women writers, Nozzoli notes a "relationship in the making between traditional narrative fiction and feminism that should not be neglected."[6] Since I had already determined the presence of generic forms and conventions in many of the so-called formless feminist narratives, it appeared evident that a study of women's evolving relationships to generic forms was necessary, not only to analyze the relationship of their writings to society, language, and self but also to document their entry into the dangerous realm of the "literary mainstream."

The remainder of this book grew around the difficulties encountered in trying to map the nonlinear entry of women's writing into a constantly changing and, in some cases, disappearing mainstream and the partial discoveries made along the way. I use the word "partial" because the relationship of women to generic categories cannot be described in definitive or exhaustive terms; rather, it is constantly being recreated in response both to shifting concerns and influences within the feminist movement as well as to the evolution of literary forms themselves. Thus, in order to write this book, it was necessary not only to study the history of literary forms but also to analyze the fears, hopes, and desires of feminism in general, and Italian feminism in particular, and to determine how these sentiments and ideologies defined, helped, or hindered women's writing by making constant declarations on what women's writing should be or do.

Initially the use of generic categories to study contemporary women's writing appeared to clash with the categories that feminist critics typically privileged to ascribe value and importance to women's writing: its originality, its (gender) specificity and difference, and finally and most important, its revolutionary, oppositional quality. Feminist theory, however, so useful in unmasking the patriarchal basis of Western culture and in challenging that culture to reconceptualize its social hierarchies, differences, and ideologies, produced some problematic results when applied to the study of women's writings. Theories concerning difference in women's literature that are based in gender and defend a woman's right to express herself differently often end up prescribing limits and emphasizing sameness. Theories of the innate oppositionality of women's literature, whether they value experimental or traditional forms, end up ignoring differences among women writers and their individual innovations because the critic searches for general, communal types of oppositional strategies that fight the same, often undifferentiated, enemy. On the one hand, debates in feminist theory over the role of experience, female identity, and the subject's agency helped feminist critics illuminate important aspects of women's writing which had long been slighted, misunderstood, or simply ignored. On the other hand, emphasis on the moral, political, and subversive power of women's writings had the adverse effect of reinforcing perceptions of women's narratives, especially contemporary ones, as topical and interesting but for the most part ideologically charged and thus nonliterary. Although this is the case for many feminist texts, at a 1988 conference in Palermo dedicated entirely to defining women's literature and how it can be read, Italian writer and critic Maria Rosa Cutrufelli cited the need for a return to an analysis of contemporary women's literature that would take as its object of investigation the relationship between the formal structures of the text and the feminist themes included therein.[7] The generic theory presented in the second part of Chapter 1 is formulated in response to this call to view women's narrative prose in a literary framework without neglecting the importance of included feminist themes.

The change in attitude toward literature and form among Italian women critics and writers is related to the evolution of Italian feminist theories that are discussed in Chapter 2. Marxist theories of marginality and alienation in the sixties influenced many experimental, avant-garde texts, including those of Gruppo 63. Formal complexity and a total break with traditional literary forms and notions of representation were viewed as the means to criticize and refute bourgeois society and its values. This emphasis on the oppositional function of literature represented a rejection of Crocian or any other literary theory that placed literary genius in a mystical, quasi-transcendental realm accessible only to androgynous, solitary types.[8]

When the limits of the experimentalism of the Italian avant-garde in the sixties and early seventies and its revealed indifference to gender became evident, Italian feminist writers overwhelmingly rejected formal complexity and exalted a nonliterary, expressly communicative writing style that aimed to bring to a conscious level the fallacious beliefs about the nature, sexuality, and destiny of women imposed upon them by a paternalistic Church and Italian society. Nonetheless, Italian feminism is firmly grounded in Marxist theory and analysis, and even this rejection of form is traceable to the Italian Marxist tradition.

Antonio Gramsci wrote that everyone was an intellectual capable of making theory; however, these theories were repressed because they were not expressed in recognizable forms. Maurizio Viano suggests that Italian feminists take to logical extremes Gramsci's view that theory is produced by writing and practice from a specific, concrete position: if masculine theories and literary forms exclude women's individuality and difference, new theories and forms would naturally result from the expression of new feminist positions (*contenuti*).[9]

New *contenuti*, however, do not always replace the old forms and structures that both sexes use to shape their narratives. The confessional outpourings of feminist writers often portrayed female narrators helpless to change their oppressed state and doing exactly what they criticize. When narrators of feminist works began to demonstrate masculine or contradicting traits, Italian feminist theoreticians began to speak of complicity with the enemy and the need to establish an even more autonomous and separatist stance. The Italian feminist theories on sexual difference in the 1980s discussed in Chapter 2 argue for the necessity of a strong female subject capable of creating a world consonant with her materialist desires in the same way that men created theories, social systems, and values around male needs and desires which they have falsely posited as universal ones. The question of how to formulate a female symbolic is far from settled. Feminist philosopher and assistant director of the *Istituto Gramsci* Claudia Mancina points out that the greatest achievement of the theory of sexual difference is to have replaced feminism's themes of oppression and inequality with a powerful critique of the illusion of the neutrality of the laws, philosophies, governments, and value systems created by men.[10] By unmasking this illusion of neutrality, Italian feminists reaffirm their right to inscribe their own partial vision into politics and society, as the recent attempt to incorporate the theory of sexual difference into the official platform of the Communist party indicates.

The return to literature in Italian women writers is informed by their desire both to unmask literature's purported neutral structure and to add their vision to it. New forms result from this activity but attention must be given to form as a medium that can enhance rather than impede expression. Italian women writers are not returning to literature to tell the same stories as men, although they may be using common traditions and structures. Writing is more than a space that allows women to speak to one another of their sexual differences, as was perhaps always the case; it is a space in which they can modify the now obviously partial interpretations previously accorded to certain forms and motifs. All of the texts examined in this book include feminist ideas, motifs, and themes. In Chapter 3, the narratives categorized as romance include the themes of mediation, the omnipotent mother figure, and other subjects brought to the fore by feminist inquiries. In the *Bildungsroman*, the form that portrays "the reconciliation of a problematic individual, guided by his lived experience of the ideal, with social reality," references to theories on how the processes of social conditioning prevent women from achieving that goal are easily discernable.[11] The same is true for the historical and the detective novels, which include themes of female exclusion from official History and the problems associated with the concept of a neutral justice, respectively.

My reason for classifying the works in the following categories is not to show how generic forms militate for or unwittingly demonstrate the inadequacy of any specific theory, feminist or otherwise, because the latter is the usual result of the inclusion of ideas or ideologies into a literary form. In Chapter 3, the feminist theme of mediation predominates in those narratives categorized as romance, not only because it is a topical theme in Italian feminism, but also because mediation itself is a long-standing convention of romance. Debates over forms of representation, typicality, and indeterminacy which have always informed plot construction in the *Bildungsroman* continue to do so in the narratives discussed in Chapter 4. Likewise, the experiments with the different ways of writing women's experience into history I discuss in Chapter 5 will revolve around problematic representations of destiny and fate typical of the historical novel. Again, in Chapter 6, I show how women writers exploit the more rigid and codified conventions of detective and crime novels, genres often considered to be antagonistic toward women in general, to express their gendered viewpoints on the form's inherent themes. In the final chapter, "Mainstreaming," I examine women authors who combine various literary conventions and techniques to review feminist themes against the backdrop of older structural patterns, such as the Pygmalion myth and the myth of romantic love, and who present their views of the self in a society formed by the feminist movement.

Generic categories have been taken to task for denying individual differences among texts. However, by revealing the different ways women writers deal with recurring themes and traditions, the generic groupings I employ prevent the conclusion that all contemporary Italian women writers, especially when they incorporate feminist themes and ideas into their works, are saying the same thing as an ideological tract or as every other woman writer. The primary function of my heuristic groupings is to bring together very different texts to analyze how individual women writers who are from different generations, but are writing in essentially the same time frame, forge a relationship between their texts and others by shared usage of distinct literary structures and traditions. Therefore, these categories do not serve as predictors of what Italian women's writing will be in the future nor can they completely describe everything it has been in the past. Rather, the generic classification of a work is in itself an experiment that begins the inquiry into how many Italian women writers in the last twenty years are constructing, through similarity and difference, stories and traditions that reflect their concerns, victories, defeats, and, finally, the creation of themselves as writing subjects.

Notes

1. Carol Lazzaro-Weis, "Gender and Genre in Italian Feminist Literature in the Seventies," *Italica* 65,4 (1988): 293–307.

2. Walter Pedullà, *La letteratura emarginata* (Rome: Lerici, 1978), 76.

3. Silvia Castelli, "Miti, forme e modelli della narrativa nuova," in Pedullà, *La letteratura emarginata*, 113–203.

4. Biancamaria Frabotta, *Letteratura al femminile* (Bari: DeDonato, 1981), 137–138.

5. See Lucia Re, "The Debate on the Meaning of Literature in Italy Today," *Quaderni d'italianistica* 7, 1 (1986): 96–111.

6. Anna Nozzoli, "La donna e il romanzo negli anni Ottanta," Proceedings of the conference "La donna nella letteratura italiana del 900," *Rivista di cittadina*, ed. Sergio Gensini (Empoli, 1983), 45–57. See also Nozzoli, *Tabù e coscienza: La condizione femminile nella letteratura italiana del Novecento* (Florence: La Nuova Italia, 1978).

7. Maria Rosa Cutrufelli, "Scritture, scrittrici: L'esperienza italiana," in *Donne e scrittura*, ed. Daniela Corona (Palermo: La Luna, 1990), 241.

8. For a discussion of Gruppo 63, its ideology and its influence on male writers in the sixties and seventies, see Gregory Lucente, *Beautiful Fables: Self-Consciousness in Italian Narrative from Manzoni to Calvino* (Baltimore, MD: Johns Hopkins University Press, 1986), esp. 310–328. An exception to this politically committed view is Giorgio Manganelli, who, in his essay "La letteratura come menzogna," describes literature as a "distinct and special realm, an artifice that creates the order of an entire universe, sufficient unto itself with no necessary recourse to the world outside either for its sense or its authenticity" (*Beautiful Fables*), 312.

9. Maurizio Viano, "Sesso debole, pensiero debole," *Annali d'italianistica* 7 (1989): 394–422.

10. Claudia Mancina, "Praticare la differenza come categoria politica: Il caso delle donne nel PCI," *Passaggi* 1 (1989): 25–32.

11. Georg Lukacs, *The Theory of the Novel*, trans. Anna Bostock (Cambridge, MA: MIT Press, 1971), 132.

Chapter 1
Feminism and Its Literary Discontents

Feminist critics of many persuasions have generally regarded the concept of genre with suspicion, if not downright contempt. First, genre theory has traditionally been the domain of male critics, who used it to establish a primarily male literary canon. And, although rigid theories of generic classification have been, in Fredric Jameson's terms, "thoroughly discredited by modern literary theory and practice," attempts such as his own to historicize generic categories by linking them to evolutions in political systems have made no serious effort to include women's works.[1] Thus genre theory is often perceived as a facile means to construct and maintain unequal social and literary hierarchies, because the works of women writers were either judged as second-rate imitations of a given example of the genre written by a male or classified under rubrics deemed inferior. Nancy Miller uses two volumes of *Littérature française* (1984) to make these points.[2] In this revised anthology, which boasts of including more women's writings, these works are found in the chapter "Forms and Genres," a catch-all category used to group together secondary generic categories of short duration and limited audience such as the *roman des coeurs sensibles*. Such categorizations, argues Miller, render these women writers invisible by excluding their names from the table of contents and trivialize their activity by implying that these "hidden bodies" steal themes from the master and simplify them for their predominantly female audiences.

Although generic categories can be faulted for perpetrating judgments of women's writing as lacking in originality and creativity and relegating their writing to a separate and unequal space, theoreticians of women's literature have also attempted to define women's writing by assigning it to its own space and tradition. In *A Room of One's Own*, Virginia Woolf, a now mythical figure for many Italian women writers and critics, and after whom the first women's studies center in Italy is named, emphasized that women should not write like men but must use writing to emphasize their difference. In *The Female Imagination*, Patricia Meyer Spacks locates female difference in a heightened sensitivity to quotidian detail in contrast to male preoccupation with theory in narrative.[3] Spacks's study inspired other excellent analyses of how women's place in society and similar experiences with domesticity, isolation, and lack of education created a different sensibility among women writers whose viewpoint was indeed primarily directed toward the personal sphere.[4] Her study can also be regarded as an elegant, analytical defense of a long-noted and usually scorned characteristic of women's writing. In 1891, Italian woman writer Neera addressed a letter to Luigi Capuana arguing that the power of women's imaginative writing lay precisely in their attention to domestic detail.[5] The existence of commonly recurring images, themes, motifs, and structures in Western women's writing in the past three hundred years has been noted by Italian women critics as well.[6] Nonetheless, despite the uselessness of denying similarities in the writings of Western women in the past—resemblances no doubt attributable to similarities in their oppressed and isolated states in male-dominated cultures—theories that define women's writing as a genre that excels in the personal domain risk entrapping contemporary and future women writers and their works in the private sphere to which they had been condemned in the past.

Studies arguing for the existence of separate (but equal) traditions of women's writings are generally associated with Anglo-American feminist criticism.[7] In Italy, the debate over separatism that started in the late 1970s split the movement in the 1980s and will be discussed in detail in the following chapter. In the main, however, although the assumption prevailed that women's writing was necessarily different from that of men, propositions to study women's literature as a separate and independent entity elicited wary, if not totally negative, responses. Feminist writer, poet, and critic Biancamaria Frabotta criticized Anna Nozzoli's important study of women's literature in the twentieth century on the grounds that such an approach, when used for contemporary writers, could banish feminism and women's literature to an ineffectual, easily avoidable, and eventually self-destructing female ghetto.[8] In *Le donne e la letteratura*, Elisabetta Rasy criticized Elaine Showalter's conclusion that the genre best expressing women's writing is the Gothic novel and presented this theory as an example of the dangers of treating women's writing as a separate category.[9]

The question of the utility of genre criticism—whether of the type that compared women's writings (unfavorably) with those of men, or that created separate categories rooted in a different female epistemol-ogy—was not solved but rather displaced in the 1980s by conflicts among different schools of feminist theory. Although differing theo-ries on the construction of female identity, the role of experience in feminist theory, and the subject's agency were not primarily literary ones, they all included stances on what women's writing and feminist criticism should be and do, which affected the course of feminist liter-ary criticism. In the early eighties, feminists on both sides of the Atlan-tic started to take stock of their past accomplishments and to theorize themselves. Although, as Showalter states in her introduction to *Femi-nist Criticism: Essays on Women, Literature, and Theory*, the feminist critical revolution "flourished in combination with every other critical ap-proach from formalism to semiotics," the appearance of many an-thologies of feminist criticism, such as her own, were also indications of the disagreements developing as a result of the adoption of various methodologies.[10]

In critical overviews that divided feminist approaches by national-ities, the American variety was generally faulted for being theoretically naive and "essentialist"—naive because it expressed the belief that writing could truthfully represent the female experience, and essen-tialist because it assumed a stable, unchanging, even authentic female consciousness that needed to be liberated and could speak for all women.[11] For many American feminist critics doubtful of such meth-odologies and convinced of their restrictive power, the theories of Julia Kristeva and Luce Irigaray, which, as Rita Felski observes, shifted feminist critical attention "from the female self to the feminine text," seemed more fruitful than theories seeking to uncover a distinct and unified female consciousness that would regulate how women write.[12] Indeed, Kristeva's theory of a presymbolic feminine that disrupts mas-culine repressive desires for order and mastery by unleashing an un-differentiated erotic pleasure through linguistic play had the obvious advantage of liberating feminist criticism from defining precisely what the female body really was. For Kristeva, language reproduces values, and the oppression of women was the work of a (masculine) language that privileged identity, singularity, and linearity.[13] Kristeva called on feminist critics to engage in the deconstructionist project of disman-tling the humanist, Cartesian concept of the essentialist subject in order to render oppression impossible. To do this, however, women had to abandon rather than reassert their identities and join in the battle of semiotic politics. All previous feminisms were judged as atavis-tic reappearances of an oppressive outmoded humanism.[14]

The reaction to Kristeva's sentencing of those critics concerned with notions of identity and women's experience into cohorts of an anachronistic humanist crime was not entirely positive. Alice Jardine explains this response by arguing that although both feminist and postmodern theories strive to go beyond traditional concepts of the self, representation, and truth, the total decentering of the subject and the denial of the authenticity of experience attacks the most sacred tenet of the feminist movement which, "while infinite in its variations, is finally rooted in the belief that women's truth-in-experience-and-reality is and always has been different from men's."[15]

Although Jardine recommends that women embrace the postmodern quest despite its risks, her book is concerned precisely with the dangers of accepting a philosophy that is grounded in many misogynistic and tortuous visions of woman. In Italy, Frabotta responded to Kristeva's ideas on the liberating potential of losing the self by quoting Kristeva's own comment that such an attitude renders creativity impossible because "there is no creation without an affirmation of a new identity, which comes out of the human crucible of the preceding phases and assures a new language."[16] Although Frabotta shared Kristeva's distrust of purely political solutions to women's problems, she noted that Kristeva's semiotic politics left no alternative to feminists other than "individual dissidence, theoretical and ethical work to be done in isolation, in exile."[17]

Kristeva's semiotic poetics not only liberated feminist critics from trying to define a female self, it also made distinct recommendations on what women's writing should be and do. Kristeva's theory of semiotics is outlined in Rasy's *La lingua della nutrice*, published in 1978.[18] Kristeva wrote the introduction to *Lingua della nutrice*, in which she designates Rasy's essay as an example of the kind of women's writing she espouses: a revolutionary theoretical prose capable of destroying traditional gender divisions and sensitizing women to the task of reformulating a new, genderless logic of love. "Are women," she asks,

only the agents of radical refusal, eternal witches when they are not the followers of the doctrines of new masters of power or anti-power? Or can they contribute toward constructing a new legitimacy that includes their pleasure, an ethic guaranteed not by constraint but by a logic, a poly-logic of love? (9–10)

In contrast to the rediscovery approach prevalent in Anglo-American circles, Kristeva and other continental female critics searched for signs of repression of the "feminine" in language and ignored women's writings, especially those cast in more traditional forms, and judged these writings incapable of performing any revolutionary activity. Ann Rosalind Jones described Kristeva as being contemptuous of the whole endeavor.[19] In 1974, reports Jones, Kristeva dismissed women novelists for having narrow thematic concerns, the main one being the reinventing of family histories through which they construct a reassuring identity for themselves. Stylistically, women writers fail to carry out the systematic dissection of language that she admires in writers such as James Joyce; even the more experimental texts lack a concern for musical forms in composition.

In *Les Chinoises*, Kristeva argues further that women writers are less able to attack the "symbolic" because their psycho-cultural self-images depend on a vicarious relationship to it. In addition, women cannot afford to lose their psychic and cultural identity by returning to unconscious bonds with the mother, a return she claims has led to a paranoid and separatist feminist politics.

Criticisms of deconstruction by American female theoreticians in the 1980s were not without resemblance to Frabotta's early demurrer. Despite their respective differences, however, the American and the French schools of thought came together in their desire and/or need to claim oppositional power for whatever they defined as feminine. If feminism, as Silvia Benhabib and Drucilla Cornell remind us, has its roots in the anarchist, utopian-socialist, communitarian movements of the previous century, feminist criticism is the direct heir of such desires: "The point of feminist criticism," writes Patrocinio Schweickart, "is not merely to interpret literature in various ways; the point is to *change the world*."[20] Differences in the theories of women's writings revolved heavily around what was considered subversive: innovative techniques or autobiographical realism, indeterminacy of self or autonomy of self. Ironically, disagreements among feminists arose from their dissatisfaction with these same revolutionary claims.

In summing up the confrontation between textual "aesthetics" and textual "politics," Felski takes to task the continental, that is, French contingency, composed of Jacques Derrida, Jean-François Lyotard, Jean Baudrillard, Kristeva, and Irigaray, among others, for their privileging of experimental literature. Despite important insights afforded by the psychoanalytical bent of deconstructionists, their overestimation of the radical power of experimental literature leaves unclear "the nature of the relationship between the subversion of literary discourse and liberating transformation, whether on an individual or social level."[21] Felski also points out that, as feminist critics have found out the hard way, there is no direct connection between the experience of oppression or marginalization that these "radical" texts supposedly exemplify and the concrete experience of such by women. Felski credits American feminism for "its valuable reintroduction of political interests into the interpretation of literary texts" and for serving to "remind critics that literature does not only refer to itself, or to the workings of metaphor or metonymy, but is deeply embedded within existing social relations" (28–29). However, because American feminist literary criticism is experientially and biographically based and reduces "the complex meanings of literary texts to the single authenticating source of authorial consciousness," it is unable "to analyze intersubjective, intertextual conventions of signification which cannot be explained in terms of the gender of the writing subject"; furthermore, it cannot construct a theory to analyze "literature *as form* and to acknowledge the *aesthetic significance* of self-reflexive, consciously experimental examples of modern literature and art that cannot be dealt with in experiential terms" (29–30, emphasis added).

Felski's discussion of feminist writings, in which she expressly links genre theory to feminist ideological frameworks, will receive more detailed attention at other points in this chapter. As she and others do not fail to note, however, deconstruction was and continues to be a valuable tool for feminist critics engaged in demystifying and criticizing the symbolic economy and in challenging hierarchical and oppositional logic. Nonetheless, the ideology of experimentation that inspired continental feminist criticism, still the most prestigious theoretical variety, and rejected traditional forms, language, plot, and causal constructions is now being recognized as a historical and social phenomenon whose premises are not above scrutiny. American feminist critics expected deconstruction to lead to analyses of the mechanisms of sexist oppression and the construction of gender categories. Christie McDonald recognized early on that deconstruction's tenets of undecidability and negativity seriously undercut women's ability to oppose misogynistic tendencies in practice and not just in philosophical thought.[22] In a 1985 article, Barbara Johnson critiqued her own book, *The Critical Difference* (1980), to show how deconstruction in the Yale school ignored gender differences.[23] Linda Alcoff's 1988 article, entitled "Cultural Feminism versus Post-Structuralism: The Identity Crisis in Feminist Theory," maps out an insidious intersection between the nominalist position of deconstruction on the category of "woman" as a fiction—an absence or rupture in discourse that must be dismantled and dismissed—and the humanistic, liberal "generic human thesis" that we are all the same underneath.[24] Mary Poovey protests that by providing no tools for analyzing specificity, deconstruction does not provide a model of change:

If we cannot describe why a particular group came to occupy the position of "other" or how its tenure in that position differs from the effect such positioning has on other groups, we have no basis upon which to posit or by which to predict any other state of affairs. We have no basis, in other words, *for political analysis or action*.[25]

Calls for the "historicizing" of deconstruction and an examination of its politics resulted from the disturbing fact that when deconstruction's politics became visible they were almost always conservative (Poovey, 60). Rosi Braidotti attributes the troubled reception of French post-structuralist theories by American feminists to the fact that these theories were imported through the literary exponents of the philosophy such as Kristeva, Annie LeClerc, and Hélène Cixous, rather than philosophers of difference such as Irigaray, from whom all recent feminist philosophy on sexual difference in Italy claims to derive. "The fact that the theory of sexual difference was introduced by literary critics and not philosophers is significant," Braidotti writes,

> because it permitted those who wanted to oppose this new theorization of a female subject to play their interdisciplinary card to the limit and accuse the theoreticians of difference of not sufficiently taking into account the social, economic and materialist aspects of the question.[26]

Braidotti is not alone in advancing the argument that the problem with continental theory lies with those who misapply it. Years ago, Frank Lentricchia had defined Derrida's real project as historical. He claims Derrida wanted, first, to conclude the project of Friedrich Nietzsche to liberate the signifier from its dependence on the logos and concept of the truth, and second, to uncover the nonontological incarceration of the signifier within its cultural matrices, which though themselves subject to difference and change, nevertheless in their moment of power use the signifier to establish dominance, to create truth, and to claim for themselves universality.[27] This second historicizing tendency, continues Lentricchia, is often overlooked or displaced by the recurring emphasis in Derrida's writings on pleasure and hedonistic free play which reflect the influence of the Hegelian dream of absolute freedom on Derrida. Thus, Lentricchia places the blame for deconstruction's lack of historicism on Derrida's American epigones, who promulgated certain aspects of Derrida's work to the detriment of its historical base.

If, for some critics, Lentricchia's views absolve Derrida from all blame, articles by male theoreticians such as Berel Lang and John Carlos Rowe on the negative dead end of deconstruction parallel the case made by the American feminist critics mentioned earlier.[28] Lang suggests that the substitution of key words such as "pleasure" and "will" for the older critical tenets of truth and understanding have become doctrinaire strategies that themselves need to be deconstructed to show their continuity rather than their break with the past. Rowe's article, besides being a critique of the subversive power of the concept of marginality in the theories of Irigaray, Geoffrey Hartman, and Edward W. Said, is a confession of his blind use of deconstructionist techniques in his book *Henry Adams and Henry James: The Emergence of Modern Consciousness* (1976). Rowe "confesses" that his fetishizing of Derridean free play as a distinctive characteristic of literary modernism serves as "the brighter figuration of a darker intention: the culture's preservation of its central governing power as indeterminate, as that metamorphic principle that absorbs differences without losing its 'essence'" (51). Although familiar ideas of deconstruction, such as Nietzschean irony, Irigaray's "woman," the aporia of language, and its undecidability that made communication impossible, do permit strategies of free play and laughter, Derrida's "dance" and Irigaray's "exstase" cannot escape their own mystification (44–46). In his conclusion, Rowe calls for the necessity of the critic to establish his or her own binary laws, that is, to expose his or her own prejudices through analysis, a necessary step in any study of cultural self-representations. Ironically, his final advice is directed at feminism, which must first "deconstruct its own internal coherence and self-sufficiency as a mode of political action" (67).

American feminist criticism at the end of the eighties is still trying to salvage the advantages of deconstruction's techniques and unite them with the insights concerning gender difference that cultural feminists continue to produce. Teresa de Lauretis notes, however, that in the attempt to wed deconstruction's nominalism to the promise of agency left over from liberal philosophy, American feminist critics are now almost totally engaged in the process of "typologizing, defining and branding various 'feminisms' along an ascending scale of theoretico-political sophistication where 'essentialism' weighs heavy at the lower end."[29] "Essentialists" linked experiential politics and experientially based writing to social change. Although deconstruction brought attention to previously marginalized groups and spoke of interlocking texts with other discourses, it dismissed any radical theory of difference based in the past historical experience of oppression and isolation of these groups, on the grounds that experientially based politics was inherently reactionary and incapable of recognizing its constant complicity with existing structures. As Jane Gallop explains, "The politics of experience is inevitably a conservative one since it cannot help but conserve ideological concerns which are not recognized as such but are taken for the 'real.'"[30]

In contrast to such arguments, de Lauretis proposes in her essay "Semiotics and Experience" that the real difficulty of feminist theory lies in the question of "how to theorize experience, which is at once social and personal, and how to construct the female subject from

[that] political and intellectual rage."[31] De Lauretis's goals and methods in redefining experience for feminist critics derive from Italian feminist practice in the seventies of self-analysis or *autocoscienza,* that is, "the practice of women reflecting politically on their condition" (185). In her essay, de Lauretis carefully redefines notions of the subject and experience to show that, far from being outmoded, they are, and have always been, an integral part of semiotics and feminist theory. She begins by pointing out, as does Jardine, how deconstruction's theoretical discourses deprive the interpretant of subjectivity and continue to exclude woman by objectifying her, and by making of her a "negative, semantic space of its [male] imaginary fantasy of coherence" (161). De Lauretis defines experience not in the "individualistic, idiosyncratic sense of something belonging to one and exclusively her own though others may have similar experiences"—a definition often associated with earlier American feminist theory and one totally denounced by deconstructionists—but rather as the "process by which subjectivity is constructed . . . by one's personal engagement in the practice, discourses and institutions that lend significance (value, meaning and affect) to the events of the world" (159). In other words, a theory of experience allows women to contemplate how we place ourselves or are placed in social reality, and what constitutes that which we perceive as subjective.

De Lauretis's theory is not based on the notion of an undivided self or an essential femaleness that needs to be liberated or uncovered. The subject is indeed divided and a product of social, psychological, or political constraints. De Lauretis contrasts Lacan's divided subject, who is produced by and in language, with C. S. Peirce's notion of a subject who *actively* receives and uses signs and who produces interpretants. Pierce's divided subject is divided by his relationship to a specific chain of interpretants that are neither true nor false. The process of interpretation or semiosis comes to a temporary stop when it intersects with a subject who is but provisionally there. De Lauretis's "experience" is, similar to Pierce's "complex of habits," that is, dispositions and perceptions that prepare one to act in a certain manner. She concludes that the examination of these habits or experiences, which result from the semiotic interaction of "outer and inner worlds," that is, the continuous engagement of the self or a subject in social reality, is the legitimate concern of feminist discourse.[32]

In her previously cited essay, Alcoff defends de Lauretis's shift away from the belief in the total power of language or textuality on the grounds that it correctly restores to woman the ability to interpret herself.[33] Predictably, Alcoff has been attacked for being "essentialist." According to Katrina Irving, Alcoff mistakenly attempts to retain agency by meshing two contradictory accounts of the subject.[34] Irving writes:

Alcoff rejects post-structuralism at the point where it seems to suggest that the subject is totally *written* by discourse. The notion of experience, as somehow prediscursive or extradiscursive, saves the notion of agency. To this she adds the idea of consciousness-raising (also drawn from de Lauretis). The way out of both an emphasis on the subjected subject and the dispersed and incoherent subject of post-structuralism is through a self-analyzing practice which alters discourse and in turn alters subjectivity. Alcoff can finally assert then that woman's identity is a product of her own interpretation, although that identity is provisional and the interpretation contingent on one's cultural and discursive context. Her final prescription for a feminist political stance is "positionally within a context," and she points out that women who have become feminists have not learned anything new about the world but merely learn to view those facts which they already possess through a different perspective (635).

As she is careful to state, Irving is not against Alcoff's attempt to retain agency. Rather she is opposed to her advocacy of a self-analyzing practice that still reflects a humanistic view of the subject free in some sense to mediate between experience and discourse, "a move no longer possible once you have granted, as Alcoff does, construction via discourse" (635). Experience cannot be placed outside of the realm of discourse, and discourse is the locus of all change. Therefore, Irving claims that "by stressing the role of conflicting discourses in the transformation of the subject rather than appealing to an experience free of discursive construction," feminist criticism finds a place for agency consonant with poststructuralist notions of subjectivity (637).

Thus, despite "theoretical differences," the feminist needs of de Lauretis, Alcoff, and Irving assure that they argue for the same goals. Irving describes the genesis of Mary Wollstonecraft's *A Vindication of the Rights of Women* as the result of the clash between two conflicting discourses of women's subordination and claims made for liberty and equality in the eighteenth century. Like de Lauretis, however, Irving believes that women's thought and action derive from the social as well as the linguistic contradictions with which they are confronted and which need to be theorized so that women, as subjects, can act upon changing their situation.

The debates over the role of experience and the subject's agency exacerbated the need of feminist literary critics to prove the revolutionary nature of women's writing; oppositionality eclipsed specificity or originality, although proof of the former would still imply the latter categories. American feminist critics interested in realistic genres, such as the nineteenth-century novel and variants of it like the *Bildungsroman*, used theories on experience, agency, and the subject to redefine techniques in women's narratives as revolutionary and subversive.[35] Although Kristeva ignored women's writings in general, other critics had expressed theories of literary form as oppression. In the early 1980s, American feminist critics such as Nancy Miller and Myra Jehlen defined the novel as a patriarchal discourse whose formal and linguistic conventions, encoded by men, condemned women novelists to viewing themselves as inferior beings.[36] To be sure, novels, especially when written in a more realistic vein, tend to represent the distance that still separates theoretical advances in knowledge and demands for change from actual mutations in society and cultural attitudes. Frabotta points to such discrepancies when she states that, in Italy, women's sexuality and writing are indeed at "antithetical poles" that somehow must be brought together.[37]

According to American critic Joanne Frye, this diametrical opposition in women's traditional prose narratives results from the fact that cultural ideology surrounds and encodes the actions of real women just as novelistic plots do. Frye argues, however, that the novel is an open form capable of self-criticism, incorporating evolving kinds of discourses and developing perceptions, and portraying both change and stasis. While representing the problems of progressive emancipation, the impact such change makes, and the regressive resistance engendered by such change, women's fictional prose can also portray female protagonists in the process of acting, writing, and transforming the cultural identities that seek to confine them. The constant return to representational genres in women's writing not only enacts a criticism of patriarchal values inherent in the act of writing itself but also reflects a feminist desire to share experience, develop a recognition of commonality in women's lives, and combat a sense of personal isolation (Frye, 1–12; 192–194). Frye is pragmatically suggesting that although feminist theory is experiencing difficulties with representation in women's writing, the common goals of the feminist movement itself necessitate studying these works and determining how the novel could better serve these goals. The novel is an important resource upon which to base a feminist poetics that would "be concerned with how the codes and conventions of the novel might be further broken down or refined to give expression to women's perceptions and to accommodate new possibilities in women's lives" (31).

For their part, Italian feminists were initially wary of the ability of traditional forms to communicate new feminist content. Italian feminist publishing houses, although they shared the goal of seeing more women's writings in print, were never in agreement as to what should constitute "women's writing." From its inception in 1976, Italian feminist publishing house Edizioni delle donne and others solved, or avoided, the problem by favoring the historical, psychological, and sociological studies concerning women or militant feminist tracts over fictional writings by Italian women.[38] One exception was a short, ironic *roman à clé, Tutti sanno,* by Maria Letizia Cravetta.[39] Far from praising the power or eloquence of women's fiction, however, Cravetta's "novel" defines it as the discourse most susceptible to subversion and incorporation into a patriarchal mainstream, although this mistrust is based on a fear of editorial rather than "formal" sabotage. *Tutti sanno* begins with a series of letters between fictitious French and Italian editors who are collaborating on the founding of a new series, Edipo Fiorito (The Flourishing Oedipus). Although the editors purported to introduce new semiotic and subversive writings to a more general public, as the title of their series implied, their real intention was to neutralize feminist writings. The introductory exchange of letters frames the interpolated tale of Donata, an Italian feminist, who had studied in Paris during the 1968 uprisings and who, after a series of failed relationships with men and writing, had withdrawn to the provinces to teach and live with her geraniums and cats. In the end, Donata realizes that her decision to leave the French capital had been an attempt to avoid writing and shield herself from illusions, disappointments, and suffering; she, therefore, vows to return to the battle of the pen. This traditionally written interpolated tale is part of a thesis written by a woman to illustrate the theories of a certain Professor de Verleau's as they appear in his seminal work *Histoire des considérations sur l'articulation critique du déséspoir.* When fictitious editor Emile Noget writes to his collaborator Alfredo Gasperotti, he insists on suppressing the scientific introduction to this work, arguing specifically that if the work were published as fiction, it would be easier to interpret its feminist message in a more modern, yet still patriarchal and conciliatory key (Cravetta 27).

In a 1986 article provocatively entitled "Il neo-femminismo in letteratura: Dove sono le ammazzoni?" (Neofeminism in Literature: Where Are the Amazons?), feminist critic and writer Adele Cambria claimed that with the exception of Elena Belotti's recent *Fiore dell'ibisco* (*The Hibiscus Flower,* 1985), feminism had made no inroads on women's fiction, which continued to exhibit conciliatory tendencies; again, Cambria blamed this tendency more on those editors who could be blocking women writers than on the repressive power of traditional language and form.[40] Belotti herself, a feminist psychologist, writer, and critic, appeared to agree more with Frye, however, when in response to Cambria she defined the novel as one of the main means of popularizing innovations and of "making them a part of the culture."[41] *Il fiore dell'ibisco* is written in traditional language and form and reflects the desire to share feminist knowledge and experiences. The encounter between a free-lance writer and Daniele, a boy whose governess the writer had been twenty years before, lends itself to the inclusion of such sensitive themes as nonbiological maternity and the development of sexual affection between an older woman and a younger man.[42] The text is a compendium of many psychoanalytical and feminist theories of the past thirty years. A digression on Daniele's mother and grandmother illustrates how and why suppressed and degraded women are unable to identify with one another. Chapters discussing the young protagonist's entry into what is now called the symbolic order, his discovery of his penis, and his attempt to seduce his governess recapitulate and popularize Freudian and Lacanian psychoanalytical theories of the male specular gaze.

Belotti also documents the superficiality of much social change. Daniele shows his former governess that he knows how to cook, and he proclaims himself a Leftist despite his rich bourgeois background. By expropriating certain "feminine" traits, Daniele feels he incarnates an androgynous vision that denies all differences between males and females who need to band together to fight political oppression. Yet the discussions between the two reveal that he still places himself at the center of any sexual relationship, believing that women should, or more precisely, must mirror his desires. Although the discussion of these theories results in a certain rapprochement between the former governess and her visitor, who act out their repressed sexual fantasies in a playful bath scene, the physical encounter that results is a disaster. Reality returns when Daniele admits their lovemaking was meant to avenge what he bitterly calls his girlfriend's "feminist" behavior. She had exploited him to become pregnant and then refused his marriage proposal. Significantly, however, the narrator does not regard this ruined liaison as a personal failure. Her marginal position as governess in an upper-class household had trained her to view things with a certain protective irony. She, in turn, destroys Daniele's cherished childhood illusion that she had once belonged to him alone by revealing that she had left her position to get an abortion. The battle of the sexes continues and, in the end, a saddened but not destroyed narrator contemplates the real changes produced by the cultural upheaval of the sixties and seventies.

Frye's argument for the novel as a locus of revolutionary discourse capable of effecting the goal of change desired by the feminist community is accompanied by a defense of the use of generic forms by women writers and critics. The main generic category Frye examines is the *Bildungsroman*. She agrees with Annis Pratt, Marianne Hirsch, Elizabeth Langland, and Elizabeth Abel that nineteenth- and early twentieth-century novelists used the form to portray the suppression and defeat of female autonomy, creativity, and maturity by patriarchal gender norms.[43] Frye argues, however, that it is these critics' definition of the genre as one that embodies a "belief in a coherent self (although not necessarily an autonomous one): [and] faith in the possibility of development," rather than the form itself, that forces them to seek images of failure in the female *Bildungsroman*. In her analysis of Alice Munro's *Lives of Girls and Women* and Toni Morrison's *The Bluest Eye*, Frye claims that the narrating "I" of both texts successfully challenges the idea of a coherent feminine self, which patriarchal society attempts to impose upon women, by representing the female protagonist engaged in multiple roles and formulating multiple self-definitions. Frye is not arguing that a coherent self could not exist. Women need to play multiple roles as part of the strategy to subvert the self imposed upon them from the outside and to move toward the development of an autonomous female identity.

Frye's informative analysis rests on the theory of multiple realities, that is, the assumption that each character can create and understand his or her own personal reality that is different from another's but equally valid. According to Frye, this contemporary theory is different from other, less useful ones because it allows her as a critic to interpret the female protagonists' actions as being more subversive than they originally seem. This same theory, however, is accompanied by some paradoxical limitations for the application of genre theory to women's literature. Jean Grimshaw convincingly argues that the real limitation of any theory based in the belief of the equal validity of all perspectives and realities, with the intention of claiming that understanding is determined by gender (that is, only women can understand certain experiences that are essentially incommunicable to men), is ultimately incapable of providing the means for conceptualizing the oppression and domination of one group by another.[44] In a literary study, such a theory inevitably serves to underline social and political stasis. Frye's dependency on the theory of multiple realities could explain why, on several occasions, her otherwise excellent arguments for the ability of the *Bildungsroman* protagonist to control her world take on the appearance of an apology for the fact that the text is representing exactly the opposite. Frye's *Bildungsroman* protagonists learn how to defend themselves, to take on a "protective coloring" while appearing to succumb to society's demands. To learn how to collaborate with the patriarchy publicly in order to achieve some measure of private success is not necessarily a new female strategy, or one that many feminists would applaud as progress. And, on a literary plane, stubbornly recurring generic conventions still function to stifle the female self at every turn, leaving women no other choice but to become the conniving, ambiguous, or indecisive stereotypes they had always been represented as in literature and society.

Although literary change becomes less obvious when novelistic action is compared with changes occurring in real life, Frye links novel writing and reading to social change by defining literary conventions as explanatory strategies, "matrices for the creation of a collective consciousness."[45] Frye envisages interpretive communities that can evaluate what will make women see their experiences differently rather than being trapped by them. Revised interpretations will, in turn, revise literary conventions since, as Jean Kennard states, "literary conventions change when their implications conflict with the vision of experience of a new interpretive community."[46]

In *Beyond Feminist Aesthetics,* Felski further develops the notions of feminist interpretive communities and the relationship of women's writing to genre. Like Frye, Felski argues that literature is a medium that can influence individual and cultural self-understanding in the sphere of everyday life by charting the changing preoccupations of social groups and the symbolic fictions by which they make sense of experience (7). Felski denies any a priori connection of feminism to literature: a link between the two can only be established if a text addresses themes in some way relevant to feminist concerns (12). Women's literature exists as a separate category due to the cultural phenomenon of women's explicit self-identification as an oppressed group which is, in turn, thematically articulated in literary texts (1). A feminist textual theory must be able to account for the levels of mediation between literary and social domains, in particular the diverse and often contradictory ideological and cultural forces that shape the processes of literary production and reception (8). Literary texts and social structures interact in a "feminist public sphere," an oppositional discursive arena within the society of late capitalism structured around the ideal of a *communal gendered identity* perceived to unite all participants. This discursive community, grounded in a necessary and often problematic commitment to a shared gender identity, determines the discursive presuppositions and the formal and thematic structures of the literary genre under analysis (9–10).

The linking of the revolutionary, critical force of women's writing to its "explanatory" power, however, has its own limitations and contradictory results. In her review of several recent works of feminist literary criticism in an article entitled "Feminism and Literature," Helen Vendler writes that the most conspicuous successes of feminist critics have been in the realms of history and sociology, because the information they make known to the public has real "explanatory power" concerning the changing positions of women in different societies.[47] In her essay, Vendler specifically challenges Felski's use of literary genre (the confession and the *Bildungsroman*) to clarify the relationship between feminism and the fictional writings of various contemporary English-speaking French and German women writers. Vendler's objection is that even if Felski argues that such works reflect a change in women's consciousness she is, in her own words, constructing a feminist social theory rather than a literary one that analyzes what women are writing. Since Felski, like Frye, admits the impossibility of definitively determining the influence of literary structures on social ones, Vendler argues that Felski's endeavor to make a connection between literature and life, the theory of literature and its practice, is merely a new version of an old problem and should be termed "sociology of literature."

Vendler's views, rather than tolling the death knell for relationships between feminist theory and literature, reflect her unease with feminist literary theories that claim moral and critical value for the text, but in so doing tend to reinforce prejudices that these works are indeed inferior as literature. Vendler blames this circumstance more on the theory than on the texts themselves. She counters Felski by pointing out that feminist critics are now aware that women do not view their oppression (the factor Felski claims unifies them) in the same way, and with the emergence of differences among members of the female sex, some women writers and critics are even questioning if gender is the difference one needs to center on in their writing.[48] Significantly, Vendler ends her critique with a quote from Italian writer Natalia Ginzburg, who flatly denies the influence of gender or even nationality on her writing: "You sit down, you write, you are not a woman, or an Italian. You are a writer" (21).

The relationship of feminist theory to literature was one of the main themes at a recent women's studies conference in Italy dedicated to the subject of women's literature (and not politics, psychoanalysis, history, or sociology) held in Palermo in July 1988. In the published proceedings of this convention, one finds that many familiar topics are raised, such as what women's writing is, how to define women's responsibility as writers, how to describe women's relationship to the written word, and so forth; the varied answers show that a consensus on any of these questions has not yet been reached.[49] Some writers and critics persist in defining autobiography as the type of writing best suited for women. Some continue to claim revolutionary transformational power for the female word, whereas others such as Spanish writer Anna Maria Moix flatly deny this potential: "A novel, a poem, a piano concert, a painting have never changed the world" (136). For Moix, feminism may produce feminist masterpieces, but "literature is something else." Frabotta addresses some of the contradictory restrictions feminist theory imposes on writers, specifically those theories positing that women have to write like "a woman." She argues that one writes not to know oneself but rather to experience the other: "The empirical I firmly rooted in psychology and history, in the act of writing . . . tires of itself and its limits . . . even those certifiable on one's birth record such as gender."[50]

Despite disagreements among the participants, however, Eleonora Chiavetta's review of the conference proceedings notes abundant calls for a more "professional" and more "literary" type of women's writing as well as a more literary method of reading women's works. Writer and feminist critic Maria Rosa Cutrufelli puts the personal quality of women's writing into a historical perspective: the commonality of women's writing across ages and cultures may have been that literature was a forum for women to talk about sexual difference. If the personal genres of earlier writings were historically determined, the gaze of contemporary women has necessarily shifted to the outside world, and Cutrufelli emphasizes that a good part of contemporary women's literature follows some sort of political choice. To be sure, a feminist poetics would have to respond to a different set of needs and desires, which contemporary feminist critics and women writers alike are searching to understand and clarify. Nonetheless, she argues, in order to prevent these works from vanishing or being relegated to a simple momentary social or political function, women critics need to develop a more literary method of reading women's writing. Cutrufelli asks for criteria based on more than empathy and the identification of feminist themes: the method must consist of "an eye trained to pick out the formal characteristics of the text and one capable of showing how the new themes are reflected in the *structural choices made in the work*."[51]

In her review of a recent Italian translation of Canadian writer Nicole Broussard's work, Cutrufelli makes further recommendations on how to bring feminist theory and women's writing closer together:

It is not a question here of the eternal quest to find out if there exists masculine or feminine qualities in writing: a quest so construed remains ambiguous, even impossible to fulfill unless we banalize the whole thing and start arguing that writing is neutral and writers are androgynes. It is necessary instead to concentrate on if and how the experience of the single body of the one writing becomes word and at the same time to take into account the "historical experience" of the writer's gender.[52]

For Cutrufelli, it is important to show how feminine sexuality and difference become part of *il mondo delle parole*, the world of words. The heightened awareness women writers today have of their difference and their conviction to assume and express that difference has been

formed and valorized by feminism; its expression, however, will necessarily be shaped by the form of the narrative in which it is found.
Broussard does this with an experimental narrative. Cutrufelli herself
explores how feminine sexuality and difference become part of the
world of language in her more traditionally cast historical novel, to be
discussed in Chapter 5.

Although the limitations feminist theory imposes on women's writing motivate Cutrufelli's literary theory of re-reading, connections
obviously exist between Italian women's narratives and the radical
theories of difference and separatism emanating from Italy today,
which will be discussed in Chapter 2. Calls for a more literary type of
writing and a feminist literary criticism that would emphasize the role
of formal structures are motivated by the desire of Italian women
critics and writers to come to terms with those conventions, images,
and motifs that suppressed their difference and to use these images to
communicate their differences in writing. As Italian women's writing
emerges from the margins, it is empowered by a tradition that refuses
to continue to be isolated or assimilated by the mainstream in any
traditional sense. In order to analyze such works, however, it is necessary to consider fully the role generic forms and literary conventions
can play in shaping expression and narratives. The following section
addresses the refusal of most feminist literary critics to contend with
the question of the structuring power of communal literary forms and
their influence on the writer, even in more recent critical analyses that
speak of form. The result is that structure is the recurring variable that
not only points to limits and weaknesses in any socio-literary theory but
also prevents critics from acknowledging women writers as artists in
their own right. The story of the entry of women writers into a mainstream they are helping to create is also the story of women's experience in and with formal conventions and structures that belong to
neither gender.

Generic categories, wrote Northrop Frye shortly before his death,
belong to that "intermediate order between the internal context of the
individual work and an external context outside of literature; an
order . . . external to the individual but not to literature as a whole."[53]
To analyze this procedure we need a concept of genre that is not based
on a necessary oppositionality between women and literature or assumes that hidden or overt structures can only suppress the female
voice. If women writers are indeed creating new themes and plots and
changing the interpretation of ancient myths in their writings, they do
so by recombining, challenging, and exploiting old structures to their
purposes. Although genre criticism has in the past offended certain
sensibilities, some contemporary theories on genre indicate ways to

create a literary framework to examine women's literary production and female difference—in Adena Rosmarin's terms, a framework that serves "the explanatory purpose of critical thought."[54]

First, however, we need to reexamine the ever-widening gap between current theory and practice in more general terms and to define the critical act in terms that enable us to perform it. We need a theory of genre that starts by validating women's writings in reference to works by other women and, at the same time, does not assume the separation from or innate oppositionality of women's writing to literary conventions. Feminist critics, like Felski, may be returning to formal analysis but they still use form as a means to contemplate what women's literature is not rather than to interpret what it is. This is due not only to problems within feminist theory but to contradictory movements in genre theory itself.

Genre, Women Writers, and the Feminist Critic

Genre study in the second half of this century received great impetus from the theories of the Russian formalists and the French structuralists. The formalists' commitment to studying literature systematically and scientifically and their contempt for evidence from extraliterary spheres naturally shifted the emphasis of their inquiry toward literary forms, their functions, and the process of literary change. In contrast to formalism's strict concentration on literature, structuralism applied its principles to all areas of human inquiry, from literary forms to forms of entertainment. Structuralists repeatedly drew attention toward those underlying themes and myths that conflicted with surface structures. Structuralists defined a literary type by its "underlying pattern—the rhetorical figure or the linguistic usage or even the type of discourse in ordinary life that it most resembles," as opposed to the classification of form by Chicago neo-Aristotelians according to overt and semantic characteristics such as the nature of the hero.[55] In *Structuralist Poetics*, Jonathan Culler claimed to speak for both these traditions when he argued for the preeminence of generic forms: just as linguistic utterances need to be interpreted in accordance with the rules of the determining *langue*, so must works be read in relationship to the literary form in which they are cast.[56]

Culler's introduction of continental theories to a resistant American critical audience met with much success, and his book was awarded the Modern Language Association's James Russell Lowell prize in 1975. According to Frank Lentricchia, this honor was bestowed on Culler not because he succeeded in making some formidable continental critical theories understandable to a skeptical group of scholars on this side of the Atlantic. Rather, Culler had defused these theories by removing the more radical challenges of structuralism from the picture.[57] Culler's definition of "literary competence" as the reader's ability to interpret literary and generic conventions substantially tamed two radical tenets of French structuralist thought: that the self is a construct of cultural systems over which the individual has no control, and that all form in a text is a result of a structured reading of a formless space. Culler

saves the notion of an individual self at its higher pitches of self-consciousness [who] can cut itself free of cultural determination and the meaning that is interpreted from a text is part of the ontological nature of the text itself. (108)

Lentricchia concludes that Culler brings us no farther than the generic critic Northrop Frye and again pushes literary criticism back into the isolationism of the New Critics, who insisted on the status of literature as a self-sufficient system that produced a specifically literary effect:

For by literary competence he [Culler] does not mean only to repeal the unobjectionable notion that to read literature successfully we need to acquire a training and a method different in some part from that demanded by other disciplines. When he speaks of literary competence as an "autonomous discipline" he means to posit, as Frye had done some twenty years earlier, that the conventions which we use to read literary texts derive from a conceptual framework uniquely compatible with the literary experience. Frye, we recall, eschews the help of Jungian psychology and neo-Kantian philosophy of symbolic forms, not by denying the obvious conceptual parallels from the work of Jung and Cassirer, but by suggesting that Jung and Cassirer are unnecessary because criticism as a scientific and systematic discipline can go it alone on its own conceptual basis, since the necessary concepts are intrinsic to the discipline. Like Frye, Culler denies the structuralist vision of an interdisciplinary methodology and the integration of various humanistic fields; he pushes literary criticism into the sort of isolationism which a variety of aesthetic idealisms since Kant (the New Criticism being only one instance) have declared as their primary theoretical intention. (108–109)

Northrop Frye's impressive *Anatomy of Criticism*, with its developmental system of modes and mythoi, had indeed exercised a strong hold over American criticism in the 1950s and 1960s. Naturally scholars were quick to determine lacunae and contradictions in the system, and attempts to improve upon Frye's categories were not lacking.[58] Lentricchia's criticism, however, for which he reserves a whole chapter in his book, is based not on contradictions within Frye's system but rather on the ideology that inspired it. For Lentricchia, Frye's systems fail because, like New Criticism, they reflect the "humanist idealism *in extremis*," a vision of the uncoerced, independent writer and critic that postmodernism eschews (26). Frye's assertions of an external order to which his theories, and, of course, his autonomous critical self, correspond then make him symbolic of a critical moment postmodernism strives to overcome.

Indeed, many of the most frequently reiterated debates of generic criticism center around those aspects that threaten to disturb postmodern sensibilities. The debate over whether genres are historical or prescriptive, or whether genres have determining characteristics at all, seems to hark back to the essentialism that deconstruction's ideology denies. Derrida argues, as could be expected, that all generic systems are untenable because all texts are indeterminate.[59] No one generic trait can possibly belong to only one genre: generic traits function as undoers of genre, they "belong without belonging" (64–65).

Champions of the concept of genre continue to defend it as a positive support for writer and reader alike. Quoting Claudio Guillen, Alistair Fowler maintains that genres operate as problem-solving models by inviting the writer to match experience and form "in a specific yet undetermined way."[60] Yet Fowler also attacks one of the oldest misapprehensions concerning genre, namely that it hides a hierarchic and retrogressive social philosophy. Indeed, on one level, genre seems to resist change; however, since it embodies long-standing values, its use may offset rather than reinforce the prejudices of a certain society. Thus Fowler wisely warns against a direct correlation of genres with their immediate social context, a correlation that implies genre is a more conservative force. Furthermore, genre is the basis of conventions that make communication possible.[61] At least one female (if not feminist) critic, Rosalie Colie, has shown how genre can positively assist cultural transfer and the spread of *nova reperta*.[62] The neglect of genre in modernist, experimental literature, Fowler suggests, has resulted in relegating many of these works to obscurity.

In his defense of genre in literature and literary theory, Fowler is careful to refute ideas of fixed generic categories and the hypostatization of genre, that is, the desire to define genres as sharply delimited objects in the "real world" (26–27). The argument that genres are not impenetrable categories is again advanced by Ralph Cohen, who also emphasizes the constructive role of the critic in the grouping of literary works.[63] Since the division into genres is a process established by the human need for distinction and interrelation and not innate textual traits, it is clear that the same texts can belong to different genres. Thus Cohen uses deconstruction's argument that a text has no innate traits to refute Michel Foucault and Derrida, who claim generic categories are not acceptable because we do not know how to understand texts as a class. Cohen develops what he terms a reader-centered historical genre theory that describes the hermeneutic consequences of classifying a work as a particular type (212).

Historical, descriptive, and theoretical genres alike come under attack in Rosmarin's theory of genre, which she describes as both reader centered and deconstructive. In *The Power of Genre*, Rosmarin proposes what she terms "an expressly deductive" genre criticism, that is, "one which simultaneously makes the reader aware of its premises and its explanatory power." The job of the critic is to act rhetorically and pragmatically, in other words, to exploit the invented nature of generic schemes. Genre is "a metaphoric and syllogistic way of talking," a critic's heuristic tool to convince a certain audience that his or her answer to a critical problem is correct (108). Rosmarin concludes that this new genre is correct not inherently but pragmatically, because it explains the outlined problem sufficiently well (50). She dismisses theories of historical genres such as Cohen's on the grounds that this method is another example of how a critic masks his or her first theoretical step and displaces the constitutive power from the critic's textualized act. Criticism, writes Rosmarin, does not derive power from what it is not—whether a text or a schema: "Rather, it engenders power by what it does" (49).

By "deconstructing" several contemporary genre critics, Rosmarin shows how their theories and many of the questions they set out to solve—whether the genre constitutes the particular or the particulars constitute the genre; whether genre is to be found in the text, in the reader's mind, or in the author's mind; whether genres are theoretical, historical, descriptive, or prescriptive—are all questions resulting from a basic contradiction between the nature of representation and genre criticism. Generic criticism, which is ineluctably deductive, always moving from general to particular, is necessarily at odds with representation, which only tolerates an inductive movement (33). Therefore, the only choice open to the generic critic is to concede the necessarily pragmatic and rhetorical nature of generic criticism instead of trying to ground it in an ultimately verifiable fact or horizon. Rosmarin argues that important generic critics such as E. D. Hirsch, Ronald Crane, Tzvetan Todorov, Northrop Frye, and Hans Robert Jauss, hide the purely rhetorical and suasive aspects of their work in a text or another previously existing system in order to make their arguments appear more "truthful": for example, Frye, at his best, is openly deductive, yet he often feels compelled to deny this procedure to prove the "truth" of his claims. For Rosmarin, the most convincing illusions of the natural and the truthful in art are results of technical achievements: "naturalness is a compliment paid to a successful illusion rather than an insight into its working" (12). Concerns such as whether or not the critic has uncovered the genre the author intended are purely representational worries. Genre's suasive power derives from its power to schematize in a way that works.

Rosmarin builds her deconstructive theory not only on a critique of more "traditional" critics who betray their outmoded concepts of representation and meaning. She starts her investigation by trying to answer why in our age of increased awareness of the constitutive power of our interpretive strategies, an awareness due to deconstruction, critics still deny this power when discussing genre and try to explain a text as if it were written without constraints or avoid admitting that they named the genre (8). For Rosmarin, one of the major conflicts in critical thought today is an increasing antagonism toward theory's "obvious futility as a practice—a practice, moreover, that paradoxically denies its status as such" (4). The Greeks defined theory as a mode of disinterested contemplation and viewing: the theorist was a spectator not an actor (4).[64] If traditional or representational theory conceives of itself as happening after the practice of criticism is finished, in other words, if we theorize about the truth we have inductively discovered, deconstruction likewise functions on the premise that pure theory is closest to pure truth, although it denies truth's existence or the possibility of reaching it. Paul de Man's romantic portrait of a man "trapped between the practical futility of his theoretical desire" (because to enact a theoretical program consistently is to research endlessly unanswerable questions) and his recognition that "to use language is to separate oneself from what we think about and thus get involved in practice" are classified by Rosmarin as symbolic images of deconstruction's conflict between theory and practice (5–6).

For Rosmarin, theory can be fruitfully united with practice only when theory initiates and informs the practice of criticism. Thus the goal of a rhetorical and pragmatic theory is not

the visualization or unearthing of something that already exists if only in "theory" but, rather, the performance of an act: the defining of a critical problem in such a way that its significance becomes obvious and its *solutions possible*. (20, emphasis added)

A rhetorical and pragmatic theory does not present itself as an after-the-fact contemplation, "a mirror-like correspondence to the not-itself to prove its validity." Rather theory is

an ongoing inquiry into what works. Far from being disinterested, ideally separated from practice it is manifestly interested in its practical or critical consequences, in articulating the ways in which theory and practice are and may be pragmatically joined. The pragmatic "ideal," in other words, is a theoretical criticism: a practice that explicitly argues the power of schemata or premises of its own devising to serve purposes of its own choosing. . . . Error and contradiction are integral parts and enabling conditions of such a criticism. Error makes classification possible and classification enables criticism to begin. (20–22)[65]

Rosmarin's theory relates to Cutrufelli's re-reading proposal first and foremost because it offers a possibility to ground a critical poetics of women's writing in something other than arguments for the utility or the transformative powers of its ideological content. Deconstruction disputes the power of genre because genre supposedly "works against the text's exalted structure . . . and its power to inquire into the stature and dynamics of its own writing" (7). Rosmarin's theoretical practice itself derives from deconstruction raising the critical act to the status of a more creative process on par with the literary act. But, whereas Roland Barthes redefined the critic as a creative reader who could free the text's semantic fields and free himself or herself from the obligation of simple paraphrasing, Rosmarin forms her definition to empower the critic *to justify the literary value of the text explained* through the demonstration of his or her logical and suasive prowess (49).[66] Therefore, although both theories admit the power of their self-constructed schemata, deconstruction denies the power of its schema to uncover or create anything but ambiguity and complexity, whereas Rosmarin emphasizes the interpretive, persuasive nature of her schema.

Rosmarin's line of argumentation also assists us in defining a deeper tension between feminist theory and the practice of generic criticism as part of the same tendency to separate theory from interpretive practice. This denial of interpretation causes Felski and Marianne Hirsch, both of whom evoke form and structures in their excellent analyses of women's writings, to dismiss their own findings concerning the role of forms and structures.[67]

In *Beyond Feminist Aesthetics*, Felski follows an essentially pragmatic, descriptive approach to analyze similarities in feminist writings that, although not written in the same language, share the same time frame. Her conclusions, however, are often determined more by her theoretical feminist goal to "draw out the enabling function of feminist literature as a critique of values and as a source of positive fictions of female identity" than by her critical act (182). Felski is careful to dispute that her generic approach is determined by the desire to uncover or rediscover embedded structures in the text, a theory implying that form and structure limit women writers. She subscribes to the idea that a text can participate in several genres at once, therefore no generic category can impose its recurring message on the writer. Because the formal structures she discusses derive from feminist theories rather than from any literary tradition, however, the usage of these forms gives rise to conflicting messages that Felski's explanatory act must justify. Contradictions are then blamed on the writer, feminist theory, society, or all three. Form and theory necessarily become an opposing force to which women must and will succumb. By repeating the postmodern denial of the power of the critical act, Felski subverts the validity of her own acute literary analysis of how women are constructing arguments.

Likewise Hirsch, in her diachronical study of women's fiction from the nineteenth-century realistic novel to modern feminist romances, writes in answer to a feminist question. She examines the intersection of familial structures and the structures of plotting with the aim of reframing "the familial structures basic to traditional narrative, and the narrative structures basic to traditional conceptions of the family, from the perspectives of the feminine and, more controversially, the maternal" (3). Hirsch maintains that the novel is polyvocal: it is a place where conflicting discourses interrogate dominant cultural codes and assumptions, a place where ideology is made and called into question. Hirsch is also careful to deny that she is speaking of any embedded, necessarily recurring structures, because repetition and timelessness in narrative have always been destructive for women (3).

Throughout her study, Hirsch innovatively and provocatively relates corresponding circuitous turns in narrative structures to evolving psychoanalytical and even mythical accounts of femininity and the mother's role in family and society. Her generic categories are defined thematically. The female "family romance" is based on Freud's description of the *Familienroman*; it is "an imaginary interrogation of origins, an interrogation which embeds the engenderment of narrative within the experience of the family" (9). The goal of the male protagonist in the family romance is to liberate himself from the family, something he usually does by imagining or finding out that he is an orphan. The male protagonist eliminates the mother only to realize later her indomitable spiritual strength; nineteenth-century women writers imitating this paradigm, however, come up with plots of "paternal protection and motherless freedom" (58). The only way the female protagonist can safeguard her position as a subject in the novel is to participate in a matricidal act: like Electra and Antigone she aligns herself with the brother or the understanding man who helps her to escape becoming a mother and an object. Matricides continue through what Hirsch classifies as fraternal plots and even Virginia Woolf's plots of "compulsory heterosexuality." And, disappointingly, Hirsch finds that matricide persists in the "feminist family romances," those stories influenced by postmodernist preoccupations with the maternal, pre-Oedipal attachment in language even though they are masked through processes of fantasy and projection.

In their analyses, both Hirsch and Felski wish to show that feminist theory is making a difference in women's narratives, and their findings show that thematically they do. Although both critics give excellent readings of how literary structures shape the expression of feminist or feminine themes, neither critic is satisfied with what she finds on a structural level where theory appears to make less of a difference. In answering the question of why, in women's narratives, the changes called for in feminist theory do not change literary structures, Felski presupposes a more autonomous woman writer who is perhaps less interested in effecting literary change than in constructing a strategy of moral criticism. Hirsch attributes the problem to the fact that maternal discourse is still a suppressed one; "so long as mothers remain the objects of exploration rather than psychological and linguistic subjects, the hold of tradition cannot be broken and new stories cannot be told" (161).

At several points in her discussion, however, Hirsch, like Felski, hints at possible formal issues in response to the inability of the texts to represent what they are looking for. In discussing why in feminist family romances the mother cannot speak, Hirsch writes:

The mother who possesses the recollection may well have to be eliminated as subject and maintained, in the position of the object of a "sustained quest" if the feminist family romance is to maintain, through fantasy, its imaginative and subversive vision of gender difference. (138)

Here ideology and literary structure reach a compromise that keeps the literary structure intact so that a story can be told. Indeed, the compromise shows insufficiencies and incoherences in feminist or any theory; it also shows how women are dealing with literary structures, topoi, and themes to tell stories and not just to propagate a certain ideology.

The purpose of this book is to discover how contemporary Italian women writers are constructing stories. Women are effecting changes in literary structures, but unless we understand how these structures work we are incapable of recognizing them and even less capable of understanding them. Both Hirsch and Felski offer invaluable insights into correspondences between feminist writings and literary structures and have inspired my own critical analyses, although in their works genre is still primarily a suppressing rather than shaping force. Some Italian women writers have also sustained a similar antagonistic relationship to generic forms. Nevertheless, this relationship is evolving into a more conscious exploitation of unchanging literary structures, as women writers build a different tradition. To learn to interpret ourselves without hiding theoretical prejudices may well be impossible. My theoretical step of categorizing selected narratives to interpret the work of many different Italian women writers today will reveal both similarities and differences among them. The similarities are undoubtedly due to goals women writers share, such as the improvement of women's lives, the disintegration of the barriers that caused their former isolation, and the desire to express the effects emancipation has had on their lives. The similarities are also probably due to the still unsatisfactorily defined concept of common gender. Primarily, however, they are due to my generic groupings which reveal similarity in the way that women's partial experience is being written into a more general and enduring tradition.

Hirsch interprets the ending of Toni Morrison's *Beloved* in a psychoanalytical, feminist, and then literary key:

Is this a reversion to oedipal meditations and triangulations, a return to the always already read? Or is it an affirmation of subjectivity which, even when it is maternal, can only emerge in and through human interconnection? Could it be the construction of a new plot which nevertheless emerges out of the reconstruction of old structures? (198)

Although these various interpretations express the different possibilities contemporary theory allows us to contemplate, the focus of this book is how Italian women writers are using traditional structures not just to create new plots, although this is often the result, but also to introduce the effect of their difference into those intermediary literary structures where meanings are made.

Notes

1. Fredric Jameson, *The Political Unconscious* (Ithaca, NY: Cornell University Press, 1981), 155.
2. Nancy Miller is speaking here of vol. 5 of *Littérature française: De Fénelon à Voltaire*, and vol. 6 *De l'Encyclopédie aux Méditations* (Paris: Arthaud, 1984). Her statements, originally part of a paper delivered at the 1986 Modern Language Association entitled "Authorized Versions," are repeated in several of her other articles: "Authorized Versions," *French Review* 61, 3 (1988): 405–413; "Feminist Writing and the History of the Novel," *Novel* 21, 2–3 (1988): 310–321; "Men's Reading, Women's Writing: Gender and the Rise of the Novel," *Yale French Studies* 75 (1988): 40–55.
3. Patricia Meyer Spacks, *The Female Imagination* (New York: Knopf, 1975).
4. A couple other examples would include Josephine Donovan, "Towards a Women's Poetics," *Tulsa Studies in Women's Literature* 3, 1–2 (1984): 99–110; and Jane Tompkins, *Sensational Designs: The Cultural Work of American Fiction* (New

York: Oxford University Press, 1985). In both of these works, the authors argue that a distinct female culture determines and shapes the difference in traditional novels written by women.

5. Neera [Anna Radius Zuccari], *Le idee di una donna e confessioni letterarie* (Florence: Vallecchi, 1977), 65. *Le idee di una donna* (*The Ideas of a Woman*) was first published in 1903. *Le confessioni letterarie* (*Literary Confessions*) first appeared in 1891.

6. Paola Blelloch, *Quel mondo dei guanti e delle stoffe* (Verona: Essedue Edizioni, 1987), Chap. 1, writes that bourgeois women writers, isolated in the home from other women, used their reading knowledge to get a better idea of those women similar to them since they could not experience this directly. Grazia Livi, in her book *Da una stanza all'altra* (Milan: Garzanti, 1984), notes that in all the pictorial images of women writing in centuries past "none of the women, a far as I can remember, was depicted at a desk with a pen between her fingers, in front of a window that opened up onto the magnitude of the world" ("Nessuna di loro, che io ricordi, è stata ritratta a uno scrittoio, con la penna tra le dita, davanti a una finestra spalancata sull'ampiezza del mondo" [13]).

7. For example, Elaine Showalter, *A Literature of Their Own* (Princeton, NJ: Princeton University Press, 1977) and Susan Gilbert and Sandra Gubar, *The Madwoman in the Attic* and *No Man's Land*, published by Yale University Press in 1979 and 1988, respectively.

8. Anna Nozzoli's book *Tabù e coscienza: La condizione femminile nella letteratura italiana del Novecento* (Florence: La Nuova Italia, 1978) includes analyses of women writers Gianni Manzini, Anna Banti, Fausta Cialente, and Elsa Morante and an essay on radical feminist literature of the seventies. Frabotta's criticism appears in her *Letteratura al femminile* (Bari: DeDonato, 1981), 5–6.

9. Elisabetta Rasy, *Le donne e la letteratura* (Rome: Riuniti, 1984), 32–34.

10. *Feminist Criticism: Essays on Women, Literature, and Theory*, ed. Elaine Showalter (New York: Pantheon, 1985), 3.

11. See, for example, Toril Moi, *Sexual/Textual Politics* (New York: Methuen, 1985). Similar views are expressed by Chris Weedon, *Feminist Practice and Poststructuralist Theory* (Oxford: Basil Blackwell, 1987).

12. Rita Felski, *Beyond Feminist Aesthetics: Feminist Literature and Social Change* (Cambridge, MA: Harvard University Press, 1989), 30.

13. Moi, *Sexual/Textual Politics*, 163–167.

14. In *Lingua della nutrice*, (Rome: Edizioni delle donne, 1978), 17, Rasy defines this strategy as a shift away from emancipationist feminism, essentially reformist in nature, and a step toward a radical and revolutionary liberation of the feminine.

15. Alice Jardine, *Gynesis: Configurations of Women in Modernity* (Ithaca, NY: Cornell University Press, 1985), 147.

16. Frabotta, *Letteratura al femminile*, 152–153: "Perché non c'è creazione senza quest'affermazione di un'identità nuova, uscita dal crogiolo mortale dalla frase precedente e che assicura un nuovo linguaggio." The quote comes from Kristeva's *La révolution du langage poétique* (Paris: Seuil, 1974), which was translated into Italian as *La rivoluzione del linguaggio poetico* (Padua: Marsilio, 1979).

17. "La dissidenza individuale, un lavoro di teoria e di etica da elaborarsi nell'isolamento, nell'esilio" (Frabotta, *Letteratura al femminile*, 152). For a similar interpretation in English, see Ann Rosalind Jones, "Julia Kristeva on Femininity: The Limits of a Semiotic Poetics," *Feminist Review* 18 (1984): 56–73.

18. In an essay published one year later, "Le temps des femmes," *Cahiers de recherche des sciences de textes et de documents* 5 (1979) (trans. Alice Jardine and Henry Blake, "Women's Time," *Signs* 7 [1981]: 20), Kristeva indicates Italy as a key participant in her new dimension of feminism. Part of Rasy's essay is translated in *Italian Feminist Thought: A Reader,* ed. Paola Bono and Sandra Kemp (Oxford: Blackwell, 1991), 76–81.

19. Jones, "Julia Kristeva on Femininity," 63.

20. Patrocinio Schweickart, "Reading Ourselves: Toward a Feminist Theory of Reading," repr. in *Speaking of Gender,* ed. Elaine Showalter (New York: Routledge, 1989), 24 (emphasis added).

21. Rita Felski, *Beyond Feminist Aesthetics: Feminist Literature and Social Change* (Cambridge, MA: Harvard University Press, 1989), 39.

22. Jacques Derrida and Christie McDonald, "Choreographies," *Diacritics* 12 (1982): 71. In this interview with Jacques Derrida, McDonald notes that "in an economy of a movement of writing that is always elusive, one can never decide properly whether the particular term implies complicity with or a break from the existent ideology."

23. Barbara Johnson, "Gender Theory and the Yale School," in *Rhetoric and Form: Deconstruction at Yale,* ed. Robert Con Davis and Ronald Schiefer (Oklahoma City: University of Oklahoma Press, 1985), repr. in *Speaking of Gender,* 45–55.

24. Linda Alcoff, "Cultural Feminism versus Post-Structuralism: The Identity Crisis in Feminist Theory," *Signs,* 13, 3 (1988): 418–422. Alcoff does specify that in the "liberal" view we all believe in certain truths, whereas in deconstruction underneath is just the same void."

25. Mary Poovey, "Feminism and Deconstruction," *Feminist Studies* 14 (1988): 61. More recently, Emily Apter, in the "The Story of I: Luce Irigaray's Theoretical Masochism," *NWSA Journal* 2, 2 (1990): 127–198, writes that, although as a graduate student in the late 1970s she embraced Irigaray's theories as "an inventive metaphorization of the female body politic rather than the result of a simplistic biological determinism exclusive of social constructionism," she is now more critical of the essentialism implicit in Irigaray's woman. Apter argues that Irigaray's irony is indeed self-entrapping. In the ongoing debate, Maggie Berg, in "Luce Irigaray's 'Contradictions': Poststructuralism and Feminism," *Signs* 17, 1 (1991): 52, defends Irigaray's strategic irony as being part of an explicit response to her main interlocutor, Jacques Lacan: "To redress the Irigaray-Lacan critical imbalance, I propose reading Irigaray's lips as a counterpart to Lacan's phallus, but without ignoring their irony, because I think the apparent contradictions in Irigaray's work are resolved by recognizing her ironic critique of Lacan."

26. Rosi Braidotti, "Il triangolo della differenza," *NoiDonne: Legendaria,* May 1990: 8.

27. Frank Lentricchia, *After the New Criticism* (Chicago: University of Chicago Press, 1980), 175ff.

28. Berel Lang, "Postmodernism and Philosophy: Nostalgia for the Future, Waiting for the Past," *New Literary History,* 18, 1 (1987): 209–224; John Carlos Rowe, "To Live Outside the Law, You Must Be 'Honest': The Authority of the Margin in Contemporary Theory," *Cultural Critique* 1 (1985–86): 35–68.

29. Teresa de Lauretis, "The Essence of the Triangle or, Taking the Risk of Essentialism Seriously: Feminist Theory in Italy, the U.S., and Britain," *Differences* 1, 2 (1990): 3–37.

30. Jane Gallop, "Quand nos lèvres s'écrivent: Irigaray's Body Politics," *Romanic Review* 74, 1 (1983): 83.

31. Teresa de Lauretis, *Alice Doesn't: Feminism, Semiotics, Cinema* (Bloomington: Indiana University Press, 1984), 166.

32. In her introductory essay to *Feminist Studies, Critical Studies* (Bloomington: Indiana University Press, 1986), de Lauretis reiterates her attack on "antihumanist feminists" and declares that "the relation of experience to discourse is what is at issue in the definition of feminism" (5).

33. In "Feminist Studies, Critical Studies: Issues, Terms, Contexts," de Lauretis writes: "The identity of a woman is the product of her own interpretation and reconstruction of her history, as mediated through the cultural discursive context to which she has access" (*Feminist Studies, Critical Studies*, 8–9).

34. Katrina Irving, "(Still) Hesitating on the Threshold: Feminist Theory and the Question of the Subject," *NWSA Journal* 1, 4 (1989): 630–643.

35. See, for example, Patricia Yaeger, *Honey-Mad Women: Emancipatory Strategies in Women's Writings* (New York: Columbia University Press, 1988).

36. In *The Heroine's Texts: Readings in the French and English Novel 1722–1781* (New York: Columbia University Press, 1980), 158, Nancy Miller concludes that until we experience great cultural change, women may have to stop reading novels. Myra Jehlen, in "Archimedes and the Paradox of Feminist Criticism," *Signs* 6, 4 (1981): 575–601, writes that because the novel has its base in the social structures of patriarchal society, it can be of little use to the feminist need for change.

37. Frabotta, *Letteratura al femminile*, 148.

38. Edizioni delle donne published radical pamphlets such as Valérie Solanas's *S.C.U.M.*, writings by Monique Wittig and Hélène Cixous, and radical feminist autobiographies such as German woman writer Verana Stefan's bestseller *Haütungen* (La pelle cambiata), the story of an attempt to escape sexual oppression through lesbian relationships.

39. Maria Letizia Cravetta, *Tutti sanno* (Rome: Edizioni delle donne, 1976).

40. Adele Cambria, "Il neo-femminismo in letteratura: Dove sono le ammazzoni?" in *Una donna, un secolo,* ed. Sandra Petrignani (Rome: Il Ventaglio, 1986), 141.

41. Elena Belotti, "Giovane scrittore, sì, giovane scrittrice, no," in *Una donna, un secolo*, ed. Petrignani, 151.

42. Belotti's book on relationships between older women and younger men in life and literature is called *Amore e pregiudizio: Il tabù dell'età nei rapporti sentimentali* (Milan: Mondadori, 1988). It was republished in 1990 in Mondadori's best-sellers series *Saggi*.

43. Annis Pratt, *Archetypal Patterns in Women's Fiction* (Bloomington: Indiana University Press, 1981); Elizabeth Abel, Marianne Hirsch, and Elizabeth Langland, eds., *The Voyage In: Fictions of Female Development* (Hanover, NH: University Press of New England, 1983). Abel, Hirsch, Langland maintain that twentieth-century novelists now use the form to expand and challenge its thematic limits to "emerge triumphant" (17).

44. Jean Grimshaw, *Philosophy and Feminism* (Minneapolis: University of Minnesota Press, 1986). Grimshaw makes no mention anywhere of deconstruction.

45. Frye adopts here Clifford Gertz's definition of ideologies. See Gertz, *The Interpretation of Cultures* (New York: Basic Books, 1973), 220.

46. Jean Kennard, "Convention Coverage or How to Read Your Own Life," *New Literary History* 13.1 (1981): 71–72.

47. Helen Vendler, "Feminism and Literature," *New York Review of Books*, May 30, 1990, 19–25.

48. Vendler quotes Christine di Stefano's essay "Dilemmas of Difference: Feminism, Modernity and Postmodernism," in Linda Nicholson's collection of essays *Feminism/Postmodernism* (New York: Routledge, 1990), where di Stefano states, "For some writers, gender is no more and perhaps not even as basic as poverty, class, ethnicity, race, sexual identity, and age in the lives of women who feel less divided from men as a group than for example, from white or bourgeois or Anglo or heterosexual men and women" (65). This book is also reviewed in her essay in a more positive light.

49. *Donne e scrittura*, Daniela Corona, ed., (Palermo: La Luna, 1990).

50. Biancamaria Frabotta, "L'identità dell'opera e l'io femminile," in *Donne e scrittura*, 44: "L'io empirico, quello ben radicato nella psicologia e nella storia, nell'atto dell'opera . . . presto si stanca di se stesso si disgusta dei suoi limiti . . . anche quelli certificabili all'anagrafe del sesso."

51. "Un occhio esercitato a cogliere da una parte le caratteristiche formali del testo, ma dall'altra anche le novità thematiche, e di come poi si rispecchino *nelle scelte strutturali dell'opera*," Maria Rosa Cutrufelli, "Scritture, scrittrici: L'esperienza italiana," in *Donne e scrittura*, ed. Corona, 241 (emphasis added).

52. Maria Rosa Cutrufelli, "Un mondo di parole che parte dal corpo," *NoiDonne: Legendaria*, June–August 1990, 6: "non si tratta dell'eterno quesito se esista o meno una 'qualità femminile' o una 'qualità maschile' della scrittura. Quesito che, così posto, risulta ambiguo e forse d'impossibile soluzione (a meno che non si voglia banalizzare il tutto, come pure spesso si fa, proclamando la neutralità della scrittura e l'androginia dello scrittore). Si tratta invece di capire se e come s'incarna nella scrittura l'esperienza del singolo corpo di chi scrive e, allo stesso tempo, l'esperienza storica del 'genere sessuale' a cui chi scrive appartiene."

53. Northrop Frye, "Varieties of Eighteenth Century Sensibility: Response," *Eighteenth Century Studies* 24, 2 (1990–91): 244.

54. Adena Rosmarin, *The Power of Genre* (Minneapolis: University of Minnesota Press, 1985), 25.

55. Heather Dubrow, *Genre* (New York: Methuen, 1983), 92.

56. Jonathan Culler, *Structuralist Poetics: Structuralism, Linguistics and the Study of Literature* (Ithaca, NY: Cornell University Press, 1975), 116ff.

57. Lentricchia, *After the New Criticism*, 103–112.

58. To attempt a complete bibliography of criticism on Frye would be impossible here. See Robert Scholes and Robert Kellogg, *The Nature of Narrative* (London: Oxford University Press, 1966). The latest series of essays on Frye is entitled *Visionary Poetics: Essays on Northrop Frye's Criticism*, ed. Robert Denham (New York: Peter Lang, 1991).

59. Jacques Derrida, "The Law of Genre," *Critical Inquiry* 7, 1 (1980): 64.

60. Alistair Fowler, *Kinds of Literature: An Introduction to the Theory of Genres and Modes* (Cambridge, MA: Harvard University Press, 1982), 31; Claudio Guillen, *Literature as System: Essays Toward the Theory of Literary History* (Princeton, NJ: Princeton University Press, 1971).

61. Fowler, *Kinds of Literature*, 36.

62. Rosalie Colie, *The Resources of Kind: Genre Theory in the Renaissance*, ed. Barbara Lewalski (Berkeley: University of California Press, 1973): 1–31.

63. Ralph Cohen, "History and Genre," *New Literary History* 17, 2 (1986): 203–218.

64. Feminist critics who have used this metaphor of a new feminist/female "theoretical gaze" include Italian critic Elisabetta Rasy, who in *Le Donne e la letteratura* argues for the need to develop "uno sguardo, un punto di vista che opera consapevolmente nei testi letterari femminili" (a gaze, a point of view that operates knowingly in women's literary texts [78]). See also German feminist theoretician Sigrid Wiegel's essay "Doppelblick," part of which has been translated into English by Harriet Anderson as "Double Focus: On the History of Women's Writing," in *Feminist Aesthetics*, ed. Gisela Ecker (London: The Women's Press, 1985, 59–80. Like Rosmarin, Laurie Fink, in "The Rhetoric of Marginality: Why I Do Feminist Theory," *Tulsa Studies in Women's Literature* 5, 2 (1986): 251–272, brings the word back to its original Greek meaning of "mode of speculation or vision" to discuss the relationship to theory feminist critics must maintain if they ever intend to do anything other than "deny the victimization of women or celebrate their domesticity" (266).

65. Although Rosmarin uses some of deconstruction's theoretical premises against themselves, her theoretical fathers are E. H. Gombrich and Hans Vaihinger. In his *Philosophy of "As If": A System of the Theoretical, Practical and Religious Fictions of Mankind* (trans. C. K. Ogden; London: Routledge and Keegan Paul, 1924), Vaihinger corrects Kant's categories (he terms them fictions) to emphasize that these schemata are "pragmatic": they are defined to serve the explanatory purpose of critical thought, not the reverse, and they necessarily contradict the topic of that thought (20). A critic's choice, therefore, is never between more or less "valid" interpretations but more or less useful ones, and "what we call truth, namely a conceptual world coinciding with the external world, is merely the most expedient error." Deconstruction certainly recognizes the inevitability of misreading, but whereas de Man and Harold Bloom lament this trajectory, Rosmarin argues that one must make the error as fruitful as possible. She argues against deconstruction when it denies its pragmatic and rhetorical premises, declares itself futile as an interpretive practice, and yearns for a theoretical identification with some pure essence, be it truth, language, or the body.

66. Roland Barthes, *Critique et vérité* (Paris: Seuil, 1966), esp. 45–79.

67. Marianne Hirsch, *The Mother-Daughter Plot: Narrative, Psychoanalysis, Feminism* (Bloomington: Indiana University Press, 1989).

Chapter 2
Separatism in Literature and Politics

In their introduction to *Italian Feminist Thought: A Reader*, Paola Bono and Sandra Kemp describe the Italian strain of feminism as one that "bridges the gap between institutional, theoretical and active/political feminism" (3). Consistently skeptical of a feminist literary aesthetic based on the idea of a repressed "feminine" in language, and far less integrated into the literary academy than their American counterparts, Italian feminists are thus presented as being in a position to challenge and complement their feminist sisters when the latter appear overly theoretical, institutionalized, or both. Contemporary Italian feminist theorizing, which has shifted from an emphasis on the analysis of the material and symbolic nature of women's oppression to the construction of purely feminine interpretative categories, appears to be following the more radical separatist and essentialist factions of early American feminist writers such as Mary Daly, Adrienne Rich, and Shulamith Firestone. Donald Meyer, however, describes Italian feminist separatism as a result of its own particular brand of "homelessness"; unable to establish its own base, Italian feminism was always "inside" a political party or movement that was not only condescending and indifferent, but often downright hostile.[1] Separatism and essential female difference are thus primarily strategic responses to the contradictory situations Italian feminism has had to contend with as it developed within its own traditions. In this chapter, we will focus on the changing functions and meanings of these concepts in the Italian context in order to paint a more detailed picture of the specificity of Italian feminism as well as its own theoretical and practical relationship to women's writings.[2]

Objections to reading women's literature as a separate entity and tradition, such as those advanced by Biancamaria Frabotta and Elizabetta Rasy at the end of the seventies, stemmed from a fear that such an approach would reinforce the existing tendency in Italian literary criticism to use the concept of "difference" in women's writings to separate and devalorize them. Italian women writers of Natalia Ginzburg's generation had rejected separate categorization, since to compare women writers only with each other or to anthologize them separately was understood as a reinforcement of their secondary status. Even when their readership was impressive, their status was not, as Anna Banti so poignantly describes in her autobiography, *Un grido lacerante*, published in 1982.[3] Anna Nozzoli characterizes Banti's rage in this book as a feminist rage and a sign, along with the appearance of Francesca Sanvitale's *Madre e figlia* in 1980, of the emerging relationship between traditionally written women's literature and feminist writings.[4] *Un grido lacerante* is the tale of Banti's courtship and married life with her professor and mentor, Roberto Longhi, a famous critic and head of the internationally recognized Fondazione di Studi di Storia dell'Arte Roberto Longhi (Roberto Longhi Foundation for Studies in Art History). Her description of the feelings of inadequacy and dependency which persisted in her despite her own successes, even after Longhi's death when she reluctantly took over the administration of his papers, delegating authority whenever she could, certainly demonstrates feminist theories that women's low self-image is determined by their subservient role to men. Banti makes it clear in this book and on several occasions, however, that her inferior self-image and rage also resulted from the denigration of those who classified her activity as a writer according to her sex, *una donna di lettere*. In her interview with Sandra Petrignani, Banti complains about this procedure of evaluating women writers: "They will say that she is great among women writers but they will not equate her to male writers."[5]

In Italy, as elsewhere, women writers have been no strangers to the novel. The more recent anthologies of Natalia Costa-Zalessow and Giuliana Morandini prove the extent to which Italian women were active in the genre, although until recently their works had been excluded from anthologies compiled by males.[6] The situation of Italian women novelists was particularly precarious since, unlike their American, French, or English sisters, these women were not writing in a clearly established or respected national tradition. In Italy, the novel has a troubled ancestry and a relatively short tradition. Sergio Pacifici attributes the rather late appearance of the Italian novel on the European scene, with Alessandro Manzoni's *I promessi sposi* in 1827, to a variety of social, political, and cultural conditions.[7] Many theoreticians have linked the realist novel and its rise in England to that country's democratic government and capitalistic endeavors. Pacifici supports these assumptions by arguing that regressive political conditions in

Italy and high illiteracy rates militated against an earlier appearance of the genre.[8] To these problems, Pacifici adds an almost endemic lack of interest in the genre among Italian intelligentsia, which he substantiates by noting that at the time of his work no good critical documentation of the Italian novel existed, a situation that has since changed.

Nonetheless, Pacifici's observations indicate the long-standing prejudices against the novel in Italian critical circles, where it was considered a much lower form of artistic expression than the poetry for which Italian literature was known and from which it derived its prestige. If supporters of the novel countered by pointing out that much Italian poetry was not read or understood outside of certain elitist circles, the question of the novel's public and its influence was also troubling. Thus even in 1991, Geno Pampaloni, in his introduction to the first volume of the narrative anthology *I giovani hanno riletto per voi: 40 anni di narrativa italiana (1940–1954)*, still feels an obligation to address this lingering preconception. Pampaloni writes that, although the novel with its too few readers is still "a relatively small part of modern culture," novels are important because they "mirror what is good and bad in society" and force us to reflect upon our deepest, darkest secrets.[9]

The anthology in question, a result of a collaborative project between the Fondazione Maria e Goffredo Bellonci in Rome and Mondadori publishing house, aims to correct the novel's inferior status by formulating a novelistic "canon" that is itself primarily formed by the reading public. For several years, Mondadori had provided students in selected high schools around Italy with various narrative texts or photocopies of them when these works (especially those of women) were out of print. The decision of which texts to include in the final version of the anthology was then based on favorable male and female student ratings. Pampaloni thus initially neutralizes possible accusations of interference from male-dominated editorial boards by describing the active participation of both sexes in a process of natural selection which allows the inclusion of more women writers in the anthology. He begins his introduction to the volume with a quote from writer Maria Bellonci calling for an undifferentiated and united appreciation of a common literary past:

Our books are the property of all of us, as they demonstrate the great human effort to understand and to make oneself understood. We would like to unite in the interest of saving these novels from indifference.[10]

Despite their candidacy for inclusion, however, women writers have a more spiritual than concrete presence in the first volume of this anthology. In his long introduction that follows Pampaloni's remarks, Walter

Pedullà mentions only Banti, Ginzburg, and Anna Maria Ortese briefly at the end. Although the scarce presence of women writers could be justified by the fact that this volume stops in 1954, the list of works being offered to students to choose from up until 1980 assures that women's contribution will remain limited. The maximum amount of women writers included on the list in any year is three: for most years there are only two; and, in years when female production in literature was well under way (1975–1977), the editors could find room for only one work. In 1978, a peak year in the production of feminist writings, no works by women writers are included. Furthermore, whereas every year the readers are exposed to different male writers, the women authors included remain the same: Banti, Bellonci, Ortese, Ginzburg, Lalla Romano, and Gina Lagorio. The inclusion of one book each by Dacia Maraini, Rosetta Loy, Laudammi Bonanni, and Rosanna Ombres may give the impression that a few more women are writing than before. Despite these attempts to rectify some past omissions, the anthology still reinforces the image of the woman writer as the unseen, self-sacrificing collaborator in a predominantly male enterprise. And, rather than reflecting the contribution of women to the formation of a new "canon," the anthology more accurately reflects the smaller female presence in mainstream presses.

In her article on women's writing in the eighties, Nozzoli acknowledged Frabotta's warning that separatism could be harmful to women's writing. She offered as evidence of its destructive effects the numbers attesting to a decreased acceptance of women's manuscripts by the larger, more established publishing concerns as the number of feminist editorial houses increased.[11] In May 1990, Anna Maria Crispino reviewed a decade of women's publishing and came to very different conclusions.[12] In the 1980s there was indeed an increase in the number of women writers who published in major publishing houses like Mondadori and Rizzoli, and their (male) directors rigorously deny making any distinction in accepting or marketing women's manuscripts. Franco Arnoldi from Rizzoli claims that the increased presence of women writers in their catalog is a natural result of the fact that women are in a stage of increased creativity and productivity. Paolo Caruso at Mondadori also denies that "affirmative action" in publishing is necessary since women writers are coming into their own and their books, when good, are naturally recognized as such and naturally compete with those of men. Crispino quickly unmasks this pretense of a neutral, unprejudiced, and asexual readership, however, by pointing out what is obvious to any reader of book review supplements in Italy: if women are publishing more, she asks, why is it that their books are ignored by male critics who rarely deign to review and thus publicize them? Publicity is the key word here, and Crispino cites the example of the United States university press system, where women's studies series are expanding. Although this tendency may seem "separatist," publishers of specialized series have the obvious advantage of being able to market their books more effectively to those interested. At a time when marketing procedures try to target every other minute difference and preference the reader could have, this feigned inattention to sexual difference minimizes and undermines women's literary presence. Crispino adds that women's books are reviewed more often in journals and newspapers in the United States than in Italy. The increased attention given to women's literature in the United States is, for Crispino, part of a valorizing procedure still lacking in Italy.

This acceptance of capitalist procedures along with suppositions of a pure and irreducible difference is the outcome of the failure of one political system in the eighties and the revealed shortcomings of the other. If Communism has definitely failed as an economic system, democracy has far from proved that its principles of equality and justice lead to something other than assimilation, homologation, and a persistently complementary and inferior concrete and mental status for women. Crispino's review of the present situation of women and publishing reveals the positive fruits of separatism. Women now oversee eleven publishing houses, six series, and twelve journals that are published regularly. Five *librerie delle donne* participate in a national network of distribution called Projetto Mappa to assure that women's works are available to researchers.[13] Crispino also mentions that some of the extremely small publishing houses have had substantial financial success and are marketing their works abroad; examples include recent translations into German and English of the cooperatively written *Non credere di avere dei diritti* (*Don't Think You Have Any Rights*) and the major film contract for *Mery per sempre* (written by a man) published by La Luna press, a small women-run operation founded in 1989. Crispino's argument for market separatism is based on her desire to see women reap the benefits of their increased popularity and creativity. The self-supported presses continue to present to the public more works written by women as well as offer fledgling women writers a place to hone their competitive skills.

The desire to compete is also the rationale given by Luisa Muraro for placing her new "quasi-collana" ("almost a series") in the nonfeminist, male-dominated Communist press *Riuniti*, although the books published in and written for the series are written by those who, like Muraro, argue for the necessity of separatist feminist interpretative categories. The first two books in the quasi-collana, Adriana Cavarero's *Nonostante Platone*—a series of re-readings of Greek myths in which the disempowerment and degradation of women by the patriarchy is retraced—and a translation of Mary Daly's *Beyond the Power of the Father*, hardly seem to indicate that Muraro intends to accompany her decision to reenter an integrated market with a less threatening and annoying comportment toward the male community.[14] Muraro hails the series as a radical feminist challenge to masculine universalizing thought. The (male) reviewer in *La repubblica*, however, views it as evidence that feminists are now "more tolerant." Their new attitude, he writes, is demonstrated by the fact that

feminists no longer theorize total separation of the sexes; they no longer consider themselves full-time militants; they no longer proclaim with Carla Lonzi in her pamphlet *Let's Spit on Hegel* that feminism is equal to existentialism; they no longer are tormented by their relationships with their mother (even if they say it is a fundamental one), nor with affectivity in language (even if they say it's important). Their mouths are no longer filled with the word "body." Above all, they no longer scream "I belong to myself alone."[15]

La repubblica's conciliatory article appeared in the wake of a heated exchange of newspaper articles culminating in a public debate, billed as "Eva versus Eva," at the Campo Marzio in October 1990 over an essay by Miriam Mafai, the well-known and respected Communist women's rights activist and former editor of the women's magazine *NoiDonne*. In the September issue of *MicroMega*, Mafai accused her separatist feminist colleagues seeking to legislate "feminine difference" of having become less tolerant and more ideological than their male comrades.[16] For Mafai, the present effort of Communist feminists to affirm and valorize sexual difference through the incorporation of a special charter for women in the Party platform and their suggested laws for reorganizing the work day around women's needs is, at best, a misguided attempt to apply Luce Irigaray's ideological and obscure theories on sexual difference (10). At worst, it represents a fanatical regression to Lenin's utopian ideal of a proletariat liberation that feminists now repropose in the name of their sex. Mafai concludes by saying she will continue to defend female difference in front of a justice that strives to be as neutral as possible (14).

To be sure, essential female difference is emphasized in the 1990 document prepared by the Women's Caucus of the Communist Party, the *Carta delle donne* (*Women's Charter*). The Carta begins by stating that conciliatory visions of the dual nature of the human race, which see one sex as being "complementary" to the other, are incompatible with feminism. Other incongruous ideas are: patriarchal modes of work, the idea of neutral equality, and the idea of a working class as a general class. The Carta declares that there are necessarily two sexes that must be recognized as essentially different and that men must recognize the value of what women say and do as equal subjects. Traditional harmonious visions of woman as complementary to man are responsible for reducing the necessary conflict between the sexes to a simple binary antagonism directed at eliminating the other. A feminist politics, practiced according to the tenets of the Carta, would assure female autonomy and women's right to produce political forms and contexts commensurate with their needs and desires.

In one of the many responses to Mafai's article, Maria Rosa Cutrufelli defends the Carta as a necessary strategy to "give political expression to a concrete historical moment" and not one that is meant to defend any feminine diversity metaphysically defined.[17] In her introduction to *Don't Think You Have Any Rights*, Teresa de Lauretis also writes that the concepts of essential difference and separatism inherent in the theory of sexual difference must be understood as part of a historical, materialist strategy to oppose the Marxist analysis of culture that had ignored the woman question: the theory of sexual difference is a critical *theory* of culture based on a *practice* of sexual difference (3). This refusal to separate theory from practice, so typical of Italian feminism in general, does not mean that such a juxtaposition is always clearly articulated, accepted, or understood. It is not completely true, as de Lauretis states, that separatism has a more positive connotation for Italians than for Americans. The concept is, however, basic to the movement (6).

For a brief time after the appearance of her article, Mafai seemed to stand alone against a reunited feminist community. Yet both the theory of sexual difference and its practice continue to be contested from within the feminist community, even in terms uncomfortably close to those of Mafai. Earlier in 1990, in the introduction to her interviews of the different separatist factions among Communist women, feminist Roberta Tatafiore questioned whether the theory of sexual difference and separatism are more products of Italian feminism's heritage than revolutionary stances: what if, she asks "feminism/communism are engaged in the final eschatological encounter of two totalitarianisms that are embracing even if they pretend to be fighting one another?"[18] This final statement does not denote a lack of support for feminist efforts on Tatafiore's part. Rather, it indicates the kind of self-scrutiny that is fanning the flames of the debates in contemporary Italian feminist theory as feminists seek to create new practical possibilities for women based on theories of non-negotiable difference, and, at the same time, to come to terms with their "common," yet mixed, past.

Feminism as Theory and Practice

Italian feminism grew out of two seemingly contradictory sources: Marxism (and the Communist Party) and Catholicism, or more precisely, the version of liberation theology propagated by Pope John XXIII.[19] Both of these components are now under attack.[20] In the past few years, Italian women have participated to an unprecedented extent in the debates concerning changes in the platform of the Italian Communist Party (Partito Communista Italiano), renamed in 1990 the Democratic Party of the Left (Partito Democratico della Sinistra). This is not to say that women have been unified in their approach. The male factions for and against platform changes had their equivalents in the groups of women who either voted to effect the politics of difference within the Party (*le donne del sì*) or advocated total separation based on an irresolvable inability to create feminine liberty within the Party structure if it were not totally reconstituted according to feminist guidelines (*le donne del no*). As Tatafiore's interviews of women from both groups show, however, although there are variations concerning how to include women's difference as a part of the dominant culture, most women agree on the basic tenet of the theory or thought of sexual difference (*il pensiero della differenza sessuale*). This tenet holds that there is an essential and original difference for everyone born female, a difference that is non-negotiable and must be explored in order to create a socio-symbolic order in which each woman can realize her individual and autonomous liberty without having to deny her female nature. Ida Dominijanni writes that the theory of sexual difference changes Simone de Beauvoir's famous dictum "One is not born a woman, one becomes one" into "One is born a woman, but one becomes different."[21]

Inspired in part by many of the more recent works of Luce Irigaray, especially *Sexes et parentés*, the theory and practice of sexual difference replace the former unifying category among women, that of belonging to an oppressed class, with a common gender identification.[22] According to proponents of this theory, women must stop defining themselves as an oppressed class since this definition, which leads to endless analyses of their misery (*miseria*) and alienation (*estraneità*), cannot result in a positive definition of their differences. Moreover, equality for women must be separated from the fiction of a neutral justice. Dominijanni denies any essentialism in the theory of non-negotiable sexual difference because the notion of gender determination in this theory has a specific function: to reveal the essentializing, generalizing gender schemes men use to describe women. She also discounts accusations of the undemocratic and illiberal nature of this theory, arguing that since the theory of sexual difference is born out of woman's desire to free herself from male dominion, it necessarily has as its primary goal the constitution of an order of justice and equality that allows women to be different from men and, even more significantly, from one another. The two enabling principles for Dominijanni are, first, Luisa Muraro and Adriana Cavarero's concept of a female genealogy to transmit knowledge and empower women and, second, a political separatist context from which a new female epistemology will derive.[23]

Tensions between women and the Italian Communist Party date back to the frustrated efforts of women intellectuals in the earlier part of the century to discuss *la questione femminile* in terms other than that of the liberation of the worker. Although Antonio Gramsci, founder of the Italian Communist Party in 1921, attributed great importance to cultural questions such as religion, family, and education, the Communists, as Judith Hellman explains, continued to see women's emancipation in terms of their economic independence.[24] If originally the Party showed less interest in the nonworking woman, after World War II, the creation of UDI (Unione Donne Italiane) was part of a general strategy of the Communist Party to increase its membership among nonworking women. UDI focused women on questions that pertained to the personal sphere, while the Communist Party still publicly maintained that women needed to enter the "productive" world of work. To be sure, the Communist Party valorized the social value of motherhood and fought for many women's benefits such as paid housework and maternal and paternal leaves. Yet theories concerning women's oppression in social relationships and in the home were noticeably lacking except when the party line insisted that women's liberation in the home would, as in the marketplace, result naturally from the emancipatory effects of the proper application of technology and not the redistribution of labor.

This inability or refusal to theorize on personal issues had its pragmatic explanations. Communists looking for votes needed to present themselves as being at least as family-oriented as the conservative Christian Democrats. Thus, arguments on both the abortion and divorce issues were never woman-centered. Divorce was presented as an antifascist and progressive legislation needed to strengthen the family since many already dissolved families were unable to function due to fascist laws. On the abortion issue limitations proposed by the Christian Democrats were also accepted. In both cases and elsewhere, there was no room to criticize the oppressed status of the traditional wife and mother.

Feminists and the new Left initially joined together in 1968 out of a desire to criticize the Italian Communist Party's "undemocratic discouragement of dissenting views," such as the Party's reluctance to speak out against Soviet action in Czechoslovakia. They adopted Pope John's emphasis on conscience, his willingness to reinterpret doctrine, and his utopian belief in the possibility of creating a new and different world order.[25] Elisabetta Rasy's description of the shift in Italian feminism in the late 1970s in terms of an opposition between *femminista* and *femminile*—where the term *femminista* means liberation, understood as a critical analysis of the personal and psychological sphere of women's lives as opposed to the enforcement of the juridical concept of emancipation—owes as much to liberation philosophy as it does to the influence of other forms of feminism.[26] Although this critique was assisted somewhat by preexisting institutional structures, such as the publication of a series of titles on women by the Party press *Riuniti*, and the appearance of more articles on sexism and feminist interests in Leftist journals, in many ways, says Hellman, it was still business as usual. The Communist Party appropriated and incorporated certain feminist arguments in much the manner denounced by Maria Letizia Cravetta in her ironic novel. Still, however, "separate" critical spaces were being jointly created by men and women. *Il manifesto*, considered today as a Communist newspaper and certainly one with the most prominent and radical contingent of women journalists, was founded in 1971 by Rossana Rossanda and Lidia Menapace along with male journalists who had been expelled from the Party for their critical views.

Although feminist inspiration had roots in liberation theology, as indicated by key words and concepts such as *autocoscienza* (consciousness-raising), demystification of authority, and personal autonomy (nobody can speak for anyone else), feminism's method of criticism in the seventies and eighties still owed much to Marxism. In the radio dialogues at the end of the seventies, Rossanda demonstrated some uneasiness with the recurrent use of the word "liberty" by feminists and argued that "equality" was still preferable because it suggested liberating everyone. Rossanda defined feminism as "a movement born under the sign of separatism, jealous of itself, with a tormented itinerary and still on the road of transformation." Nevertheless, she remained sympathetic to both the goals and the strategies of separatism since, as she points out, Gramsci had defined separatism as a necessary, preliminary step that would enable participants in a liberation movement to emerge with a strong affirmation of self.[27]

Feminism in Italy originally considered itself to be a discourse aimed at explaining and eradicating oppression.[28] However, Italian feminists took a communal view of oppression: Birnbaum records one early criticism of the American movement by Lidia Menapace in which she expresses her uneasiness with "their unhealthy preoccupation solely

with personal emancipation" (83). The importance of working together and forming cooperatives carries through into Italian feminism
today although the tendency of such groups to stifle dissent and creativity is now being examined.[29] Women's existential sense of alienation
and unease was analyzed according to Gramsci's secular answer to the
Pauline paradox, which is how to explain discrepancies between what
one does and what one says. According to Gramsci, discrepancies occur
when the oppressed come to identify with their oppressor. In feminist
terms, Dacia Maraini explains, women have internalized men's desire
for them to be fragile, dependent, masochistic, voluble, and incapable
and they thus tend to repress their own need for autonomy and independence.[30]

Even the insistence on the pragmatic relationship of theory and
practice is traceable to Gramsci, whose comment that relationships
between men and women would not change until women would learn
to play a different role is often quoted by Italian feminists. Practice is
what produces theory, and the "theorizing of experience" in feminist
thought called for by de Lauretis is firmly rooted in this tradition.
Although Italian feminists, like Kristeva and French feminist philosophers, expressed doubts that traditionally conceived politics could
solve their problems, obviously they never left the political scene or
abandoned their hopes to unite theory and political practice. Theoretical research proceeds through and affirms itself in different political
actions. Hence de Lauretis's remark in her introduction to *Non credere
di avere dei diritti*: "If putting a political practice into words is the same
thing as theorizing, then this is a book of theory, because the relations
between women were the subject matter of this book" (3).

In retracing the shared trajectory of Marxism and feminism in the
1970s, the feminist philosopher, critic, and, most recently, politician (*le
donne del no*) Maria Luisa Boccia emphasizes that both philosophies
look for cohesion between thought and action, theory and practice,
and believe that the transformation of objective reality in any given
situation results from the production of subjectivity.[31] Boccia reviews
three feminist works to show how Italian feminist theory evolved within a Marxist framework to its present theoretical and practical stances
on sexual difference. She begins with *La coscienza di sfruttata* (*The Exploited Consciousness* [1972], ed. Luisa Abba, Gabriella Ferri, Giorgia
Lazzaretto, Elena Medi, and Silvia Motta), a series of feminist essays
written by various women which focuses on the material condition of
women in a masculine society to discover "what every woman has in
common with one another" (44). A basic assumption in these earlier
essays is that woman's inferior status must come from something outside of herself; therefore, when woman isolates the origins of her

unease and brings them into question, she will know what needs to be destroyed so that she can be liberated. The authors conclude that, whereas Marxism and capitalism are two systems that enable men to liberate themselves and achieve individuality, the exclusion of women from productive roles through the appropriation and denial of women's sexuality make it impossible for women to achieve the same. Although she agrees with the authors' critique of Marxist production theory, Boccia argues that the main drawback of the collection is the search for a unified female identity based on a theoretical confusion resulting from the conflation of sex and class. This procedure produces false definitions of a collective social female identity (43).

The second work Boccia discusses is Lea Melandri's *L'infame originaria: Facciamola finita col cuore e con la politica* (*The Ultimate Infamy: Let's Wipe Out Romance and Politics*, 1977). Melandri analyzes how female dependency and alienation are the result of patriarchal ideology that separates the personal from the political, sentiment from reason, politics of the mind from that of the heart. These separations parallel the fallacious separation of sexual relationships from those of production and reproduction (49). According to Boccia, Melandri's main contribution is her change in focus. Instead of retracing the relationship between the sexes back to a socio-economic foundation, as happened in previous analyses where women were regarded in terms of their economic function, Melandri emphasizes how women have been cancelled from the socio-symbolic order through the expropriation of their sexuality and autonomous desires (49).

Boccia then reviews a third work, which develops in detail how women have been removed from society and history. This influential essay, *Sputiamo su Hegel*, by feminist philosopher and art critic Carla Lonzi, first circulated privately in 1971.[32] Lonzi develops her philosophical standpoint in opposition to Hegel's definition of woman's essential difference. Hegel defined woman's essence as a divine principle destined to preside over the conservation of the species; the male essence was a human principle deriving from a political ethos that develops through social relationships. Hegel's definition shows how man develops his individuality and creates the forms of his liberty through social relationships. Woman, defined as a general, ahistorical, and divine being, is thus left out of the picture. This theory, Lonzi argues, which gives ontological status to women's material oppression, is reproduced in theories from Marx through Freud, where woman is viewed as an enemy of civilization, to Lacan, where she still has no place.

If Hegel's spiritual definition of woman only allowed him to ignore the human origins of women's oppression, Marxist theories of history and power further contributed to removing women from the social sphere. Women cannot enter into any history conceived of as the struggle for power or which entertains a dialectic between the human masculine and the divine feminine, both principles being based on the suppression of female sexuality. Lonzi attributes women's ambiguous and fearful relationship to power to their acceptance of these male-defined world views. Not only do women refuse to seize power for themselves, they also persist in viewing power as the cause of their alienation (Lonzi, 20). Since these and all other female attitudes are culturally acquired, Lonzi recommends total deculturization through the practice of *autocoscienza*. When women progressively liberate themselves from the idea that they are complementary, naturally subservient entities to men, they will be able to engage in power struggles and competition with an equal but different masculine subject: "Woman does not refute man's subjective status but rather his absolute one" ("la donna non rifiuta l'uomo come soggetto, ma lo rifiuta come assoluto," Lonzi, 4).

Indeed, the Carta and the theory of sexual difference is as firmly based in Lonzi's work as in that of Irigaray.[33] Lonzi also rejects emancipatory thought and strategies because they condemn women to taking on the identity of a victim who alternates between two unsatisfactory behavioral modes: lamenting her fate or begging men for rights. Lonzi recommends that women openly contrast their existential, nontranscendental nature to the male tendency to theorize and accord her divine power over his origins and death. In fact, many feminist narratives in the seventies and eighties contrasted the masculine narcissistic death wish to a more positive, primordial, feminine attitude in ways similar to those of French feminist theoreticians when they reacted negatively to definitions of women in poststructuralist and deconstructionist theories as an absent, mysterious space. In a 1976 essay often quoted by Italian feminists entitled "Le sexe ou la tête," Hélène Cixous defines women's writing as a place to express a desire that affirms life and eradicates (metaphoric) death: "It is man who teaches woman (because man is always the master, as well) to be aware of lack, to be aware of absence, aware of death."[34] In Ginevra Bompiani's *Specie del sonno* (*A Kind of Sleep*, 1975), Eros explains to Psyche that death lurks behind everything he seeks, behind men, women, his work, and the search for a daughter in his own image (38). The female protagonist Sophie of Bompiani's *Mondanità* (*Worldliness*, 1980), a work I will discuss in Chapter 4 in the *Bildungsroman* category, is abandoned by her husband in an Istanbul mosque during their vacation when he realizes she represents for him the primeval woman who denies death and consequently denies both transcendence and meaning:

Because you are the woman who offers to death the sacrifice of presence . . . I want to find my death, not my life. You robbed me of it [death, thus meaning] the first time being my wife; a second time being the mother of my child; the third time being yourself. (82–83)

In an essay entitled "Le marché des femmes" in *Ce sexe qui n'en est pas un*, Irigaray bases her analysis of the rapport between the sexes on the exchange economy that Claude Lévi-Strauss had defined as the very foundation of culture.[35] In "Le Sexe ou la tête," Cixous also links the narcissistic male desire for death, which continues in modern philosophical theories of language, to the bourgeois concepts of possession, acquisition and consummation-consumption of the product woman.[36]

In Maria Schiavo's *Macellum: Storia violentata e romanzata di donne e di mercato* (*Macellum: A Violent Fictionalized Version of Women and the Marketplace*, 1979), a series of essays that show how language masks the basic oppression of woman and her status as an object to be possessed and consumed, females again refuse to represent death and meaning for men. Schiavo does not claim to write a historical account of women's oppression. Rather, through a series of encounters with historical and literary figures, she seeks to find relationships in language between women's oppression and patriarchal theories on such topics as the male preoccupation with death, the incest taboo, the Oedipal myth, and castration. One recurring figure who facilitates such explorations is Don Juan. Schiavo depicts him as the man who glorifies death as transcendence. Søren Kierkegaard's spiritual Don Juan idealizes women and makes of them his specular image to deny their presence. Schiavo quotes Don Juan's comments on the abandoned Cordelia in *Diary of a Seducer*: "Cordelia loves me and hates me. What does a young girl fear? The spirit. Why? Because the spiritual represents the negation of her entire feminine existence" (27). When Don Juan abandons Cordelia, she cannot return to the marketplace because she has no existence outside of the rapport of ownership (*appartenenza*) and dependency that the author is investigating. Yet Cordelia exercises some power on the linguistic level. When Marie Magdalene comes to resuscitate her, she flatly declines. By refusing the spiritual afterlife, Cordelia affirms her independent existence. Schiavo had previously quoted Lucretius to argue that the afterlife was a concept created in order to strengthen concepts of dependency and belonging.

Rosa Rossi's *L'ultimo capitolo* (*The Last Chapter*, 1984) is another example of the confluence of theories in this feminist polemic on the male death wish.[37] The male protagonist is an archeologist who retreats to his summer house after his wife's death in the hope that his nocturnal writings will ward off depression and his strong desire to commit suicide. The book's title is a reference to the last chapter of the gospel of Luke, when the angels ask the women searching for Christ's body why they seek the living among the dead. In his writings, the narrator also searches for someone among the deceased, namely his wife, whose image he had constructed as a specular reflection of his own desire. The archeologist only recovers from his inability to name things, including his wife, when he realizes that he cannot fix his wife's identity even in death; he must face the uncontrollable "forza del nulla" (the force of nothingness) with human fear and respect (124).

In Lonzi's system of thought, separatism is the only way to assure that woman would discontinue her complicity with the patriarchy and concentrate on forming her own subjectivity. This subjectivity is not based on rediscovering or revalorizing anything that came before, because woman is only now realizing herself in thought and practice as an autonomous, different subject. Revolutions based on the conflation of the masculine and feminine ("un impasto di femminile e di maschile"), such as the hippie movement, inevitably fail because this procedure turns revolutionary spaces into training grounds for the return to patriarchy (Lonzi, 43). Lonzi cites the early mother-son bond as another example of how working together reduces women to aiding in their own defeat. By joining with the son to defeat the father, the mother merely schools her child in the ways of patriarchal power struggles, a struggle in which only the son can later participate.

Lonzi's capital text is discussed again in Francesca Molfino's article on the relationship of psychoanalysis to Italian feminism.[38] According to Molfino, Lonzi's "political and theoretical pamphlet," which was inspired by the works of American radical feminists such as Eva Figes, Germaine Greer, Shulamith Firestone, Kate Millet, and Betty Friedan, opposed Lea Melandri's call to substitute a more psychoanalytically based *pratica dell'inconscio* (practice of the unconscious) for the practice of *autocoscienza*. Lonzi argued along the lines of the radical American feminists that psychoanalysis was a bourgeois instrument that had been invented and used to oppress women. Despite this disagreement, however, most Italian feminists at the end of the seventies shared a belief in some sort of specific female subjectivity that could emerge given certain conditions: a philosophy based on the materiality of the body, understanding of the female unconscious, political activism, and a deeper understanding of relationships among women (72).

All of these themes are present in Silvia Montefoschi's article published in the late seventies entitled "Maternity and Social Identity: Reflections on the Women's Movement and Psychoanalysis," another example of the continued close relationship between psychoanalysis and politics, theory and practice in Italian feminist thought.[39] It also contains the seeds of the present debate over the limits of gender in feminist political analysis, which will be discussed later in this chapter. Montefoschi begins by emphasizing that psychoanalysis does indeed have a repressive, normalizing side. This repressive side comes from its *theoretical* base, developed apart from psychoanalytical *practice* (144–145). In psychoanalytical theory the object of research is conceived as a "real object," that is, as an object existing independently from the socio-historical situation in which the process of perception operates (143). As a practice, however, psychoanalysis utilizes the dialectical method derived from the social sciences, where it is assumed that the object under observation is a "rational object" that the subject himself or herself posits. The "object" only exists in relationship to the subject and will change as he or she does. This latter practice can provide a valid instrument for transforming and liberating consciousness, and it is this dialectic that Montefoschi proposes to "theorize" (144–146).

Montefoschi takes apart both the Freudian-Lacanian psychoanalytical school (which she terms the "masculine psychologies") and American object relations ("feminine" theories), put forth by D. W. Winnicott, W. R. D. Fairbairn, and Melanie Klein, to show that, in both patriarchal systems of thought, the role of the mother is to cooperate in the creation and perpetuation of the dependency and individual lack of responsibility which have led to the crisis in capitalist and socialist political systems. Although the Freudian-Lacanian theories exclude women from participating in any productive social process by philosophically proving her nonexistence, Montefoschi considers the object-relations school (which claims to be empowering women) even more insidious since it grounds the stereotypical, ahistorical image of the mother as a passive nurturer in her biological status. Winnicott, Fairbairn, and Klein, despite their individual differences, cast the mother in the role of the all-powerful source of life and satisfier of needs. If she cannot refuse this role without becoming a monster, neither can she realistically fulfill it, as demonstrated by subsidiary theories on childhood frustration, where the mother is held responsible for everything that could and does go wrong with his or her formative years. This is so because, especially for Winnicott, the mother's ability to love is based not on any intentionality but rather on concepts of duty and religious devotion similar to those that, in many earlier societies, obliged vestal virgins and women in the family to renounce the personalization of Eros and to experience all erotic feelings as the execution of a sacred rite.

Montefoschi thus links the present-day cult of the mother to the ancient Great Mediterranean Mother myth, which Hegel again redefined to justify women's exclusion in political and economic areas. Woman can only find the meaning for her existence through total identification with her role as nourisher of her child's and society's needs. The woman-mother, who based her feelings of self-worth on the proper fulfillment of her role as a permanent satisfier of needs, comes to believe that she is indispensable to her child's survival and subsequently nurtures the narcissistic and dependent, irresponsible behavior in her (male) child, since this behavior functions to reinforce her only possible image of self-worth.

Montefoschi formulates her theoretical stance in order to answer concretely the question of why the stereotypical mother, a nurturing, self-sacrificing nonentity, raises her son to be, among other things, a bad lover and her daughter to despise or ignore her.[40] Images of Latin mothers who express frustrated sexual desires through a need to constantly feed their sons, who consider themselves irreplaceable in their son's eyes and cannot tolerate any competition—in other words, the mother (or mother-in-law) who can only be kept at bay by being made a grandmother if she lacks the civic decency and religious piety to die young and get out of the picture—abound in Italian literature and film, where they have been represented and interpreted as both tragic and comic stereotypical figures.[41]

Montefoschi's solution is to develop a dialectic based on Jungian analysis. She accepts Jung's division of attitudes into the masculine Logos (activity, rationality, and the capacity for control and self-determination) and the feminine Eros (receptivity, passiveness, availability, helpfulness, and piety), since Jung does not attribute these differences to corresponding ones in the psyche but classifies them as general human attitudes present in every man and woman. Jung's division of internal imaginative forces in people into the Anima for men and the Animus for women allow these forces, at least on a sublimal level, to inspire us, although on a social level we may choose to cooperate with codified and stereotypical masculine and feminine roles. Montefoschi comes close here to violating Lonzi's dictum to separate the creation of subjectivity along gender lines; however, she is using Jung's analysis of masculine and feminine characteristics to prove that, although everything in the past has been gender-determined, we need to uncover the cultural manipulations of these attitudes which have caused concrete problems. In such a procedure, the positing of the possibility of the existence of general human attitudes is a necessary step.

In answering the question of what to do with the mother, Montefoschi's response is to silence her by refusing the institution itself. Yet, in Montefoschi's system, women are assigned enormous power. They are nothing less than the mediators of a relational model of need and interdependency upon which entire social systems are built. Therefore, they must learn not to give in to the falsely created needs of others for, in so doing, they repress the self-reflexive and critical side of the human subject.

For Italian feminists in the 1980s, the greatest challenge was how to redefine this power and use it constructively. In the eighties, women's groups, no longer united by clearly defined political goals or the premise of their equality based in oppression, started to voice their fears and uncertainties about giving up traditional gender roles. In the transition from "organization" to "movement," feminism was starting to suffer from the discontinuity and fragmentation that is the "inevitable fate of non-hierarchical movements."[42] Many cooperatives that did not dissolve naturally dismantled themselves for fear or under accusation of becoming as hierarchical, authoritarian, and stifling as those institutions the movement had condemned. The lack of a common myth to unite women made difference the most important and most crippling aspect of feminism.

Luisa Muraro explains this particular crisis in feminism as yet another instance where fighting among women is caused by their efforts to sustain patriarchal definitions of them.[43] It is men, states Muraro, not women, who have decreed that all women are equal and alike in their ahistorical essence. Women's fear of difference manifests itself through jealousy (*invidia*), a sentiment that prevents women from recognizing each other as sources of power and knowledge. Reiterating Lonzi's theories, she explains that women do not know how to deal with power and competition because we continue to believe these are not feminine qualities. We cannot redefine ourselves, however, unless we establish a way for women to relate to other women. And this is to be accomplished through the practice of *affidamento* (entrustment).

Both Marianne Hirsch and Jane Gallop have noted that although contemporary theories of the maternal posit the mother as a privileged dissident, when she becomes a real figure she loses her status as powerful goddess and repeats her traditional vulnerability.[44] *Affidamento* redefines the mother-daughter relationship as a symbolic one: the "symbolic mother," usually but not necessarily an older woman, functions to sustain and recognize the gendered nature of the thought, knowledge and experience of another, less experienced woman who has entrusted herself to her. The mentor-guide relationship between two different women facilitates the "vertical" (Muraro avoids the word "hierarchical") transmission of knowledge and authority from woman to woman and the recognition of individual difference. The practice of this social contract provides a structure that permits women to perceive female development in terms other than a form of separation from the stereotypical overly nurturing or hostile, self-effacing maternal background. The resulting empowerment of both women would enable them to tell their stories on paradigms other than those which, as Hirsch points out, reenact Antigone's repression of the mother or Electra's matricide.[45] Speaking of her novel *Demetra* to the Milan feminist research cooperative Melusine, Tiziana Villani claims that her research into the Demeter myth is not meant to rediscover women's subjectivity in the past but is rather part of the process of empowering herself in the present. Her rewriting of the myth distances her from the experience of her own historical mother in order to place herself in a position to accept the mythical mother.[46]

Muraro's point about the inability of women to recognize and empower one another has had more specific literary applications. As part of the establishment of a female genealogy through which knowledge can be transmitted, the Milan group Melusine sponsored readings of various women's writings. These readings were, in part, a strategy to counteract disinterest and downright hostility toward other women writers, reactions Muraro interprets as another manifestation of the negation of the mother and an acceptance of male deprecatory views of women's works. The critical method employed at the group readings was modeled on the practice of *affidamento*: the female reader first identified with the text and critiqued it according to her own personal experiences and associations. According to de Lauretis, the goal of these readings was not only to erase boundaries between literature and life but also to force women to deal with authority and disparity, since some interpretations were more authoritative and well-informed than others. Thus these readings were also lessons in how to learn from other women.[47]

The approach exercised by Melusine and others is similar to "gynetic" types of reading proposed by Jeannette Laillou-Savona.[48] She argues that because contemporary women's writing is still blatantly personal and experimental it can only be read by a kind of corporeal identification with the text that would allow the new themes and meanings to emerge:

This pleasure/desire of the other can be found in a second type of theoretical or critical reading of women's avant-garde literature that I will discuss now. The readings that I will call "gynetic" refuse the discursive academic practice (introduction-development-conclusion) and the demonstrative logic of official discourse. On the other hand, these readings establish a rapport of *identification* between the woman who is writing, the woman (or women) in the text, and the women reading the text. This rapport is so loving and intimate that it will take on erotic connotations. These readings are necessarily both poetic texts and theoretical ones because they express feminist knowledge and convictions. Conscious of their linguistic experimentation, these gynetic readings echo the intense joy of women recognizing other women. This type of reading is practiced by women writers such as Luce Irigaray, Hélène Cixous, Nicole Broussard and Madeleine Gagnon. (233)[49]

This type of reading is certainly the opposite of any generic or formal approach that would risk categorizing women's fictional works according to a scale that hides patriarchal values. Although the approach claims to validate female subjectivity, however, some Italian writers and critics insist that this methodology is contrary to both the goals of feminism and the nature of writing. Frabotta challenges the ability of feminist theory, no matter how it emphasizes difference among women, to deal with "the solitary act of creativity that constitutes writing."[50] Cutrufelli's recommendation to analyze how, in her terms, the flesh becomes word, also reflects an uneasiness with the method described by Laillou-Savona. Cutrufelli, one of the main organizers of readings of women's literature at the Circolo della Rosa in Rome and editor of *Tuttestorie*, a journal for women's creative writings, is most supportive of women's writings. She argues that the patrimony of older women writers is less easily transferred because their works have always been studied according to nonliterary criteria, including that of finding their feminine qualities which are idiosyncratically defined and rarely in relationship to one another. Thus she recommends a genealogy of structures and forms that would show how women have expressed their political, sexual, and personal concerns and how their writings differ from those of men. A genealogy constructed in this manner would be communicable, transmittable, and, above all, literary.[51]

In speaking to the Melusine group on March 19, 1990, Francesca Sanvitale expressed some of the same apprehensions and made similar recommendations. Speaking of her novel *Madre e figlia* (1980), Sanvitale rejected readings that confuse literature with life on the grounds that they further marginalize women's writings from the mainstream by helping to classify them as feminist and thus nonliterary.[52] Moreover, Sanvitale recalled that when she first started to write, the epithet "writing like a man" was the only one that allowed women "access to literature." Although she, unlike Banti, can now proudly maintain that she writes as a woman, she insists that writing like a woman means to come to terms with literary structures. This inability to hold things at a distance ("una presa di distanza"), she remarks, may be one of the reasons that women live without a proper consciousness of themselves (10).

The debate over whether separatism in literature devalorizes women's writings—and, if so, how to construct interpretative categories for these writings that would explicate rather than stifle them—is not without similarity to the general feminist literary debates outlined in the previous chapter. However, although theories on how and when to produce and emphasize difference in the Italian feminist political community are creating differences of opinions concerning how to read and promote women's literature, they are also producing similarities in methods due to beliefs and goals Italian feminists still hold in common.

Disagreement in Difference

If privileging the mother is to allow for the emergence of differences among women, it is doing so through a series of disagreements and schisms as the myth of a united feminist front further crumbles. One major victim was the Centro Culturale Virginia Woolf, which split into two sections in 1988. Group A continues the research into all subjects related to the woman question, whereas Group B allows only those courses dedicated to the study of the theory and practice of sexual difference as defined by Muraro and Cavarero's Milan and Verona groups. At a conference at the center from May 26 to 28, 1989, various opponents of the split accused the followers of the Libreria di Milano of bringing separatism inside the organization instead of having it function as a unifying political and critical strategy. Opponents of the schism criticized Muraro's followers for mistaking valorization of the female for idealization, and for turning the "practice of disparity" into a mystical experience where the symbolic mother guarantees not difference but religious transcendence and salvation.[53] Recognition of differences necessarily leads to division. Feminists from Group A, however, accused their colleagues of stifling rather than encouraging debate among women. Molfino goes so far as to suggest that this attraction to a "strong theory" hides a fear of difference which, this time, is rooted in a fear of dispersion rather than the inability to relate to the mother or the insistence of the patriarchy to define woman as an identical essence (18–21).

To be sure, one problem with the theory of sexual difference is that, in its formulation, the definition of differences among women (that are to emerge) continues to be secondary to general definitions of the differences between the sexes. Since these definitions are based on a negation of previous terminologies and definitions (*contenuti*) more than on methods (*forme*), as Elena Gagliasso points out, certain words have simply become outmoded while we claim to rediscover others and invest them with entirely new connotations: "Justice, equal opportunity, solidarity, commitment and the experience of collective transformation are like worn out clothes, whereas individual initiative, competition, personal supremacy are 'new' discoveries."[54] Competition and the desire to win are important words for proponents of theories of sexual difference and members of Group B at the Centro Culturale

Virginia Woolf, who refuse to talk of the *miseria* of women or who have omitted the word *estraneità* from their vocabulary because it implies a lack of responsibility.[55] Montefoschi had pointed out in her article that it would be difficult for women to assume responsibility for themselves and others because their longstanding social exclusion had at least afforded them the luxury of seeming blameless. The most significant point in Gagliasso's argument, however, is that by analyzing the drawbacks of such cooperatives that have always been part of Italian feminism, she comes to the conclusion that their theoretical weak points derive from the fact that certain differences are not attributable to gender. If we understood this, writes Gagliasso, we would not be so surprised to see "delicate" women, so long excluded from competition in politics and society, playing the competitive and vindictive roles previously reserved for men: "Not everything that is a 'human trait' must be obsessively read as being homologous to the masculine" (53).

Critics of *affidamento* also propose that, in striving to create something specifically feminine, the theory not only reproposes old structures and schemata but avoids dealing with women's inherited problems. One critic argues that although the practice of *affidamento* claims to empower the mother, it is done at the expense of stifling the daughter.[56] The figure of the older mentor woman who replaces the Omnipotent Goddess that feminists deconstructed also reiterates the standard good mother (me) versus bad mother (them) categories. Therefore, certain roles that feminists have stigmatized and rejected as gender-determined need to be reexamined: "To show oneself in certain moments to be fragile and child-like or to assume the [maternal] role does not necessarily mean to flee all responsibility: at times it may even be necessary and indispensable."[57]

Criticisms of the philosophy of sexual difference from both "insiders" and "outsiders" derive from the shared uneasiness among Italian feminists when theory starts to separate from practice, that is, the interpretive act. Nadia Fusini argues against Cavarero's reduction of difference to an absolute singular that cannot be questioned ("quel assoluto singolare che è la differenza") since difference so defined without mediation also prohibits critical thought.[58] Thinking, she continues, cannot take place without mediation and mediation means separation and abstraction, not specular images and identification which are only poor attempts at masking the rival. The transmission of knowledge proceeds through jealousy, competition, even violence. Thus mediation is necessary, but we cannot identify with the mediator without repeating "the same transcendental, ontological oppression that is at the origin of the violence of phallo-logo-centrism" (258). Fusini agrees that feminists need to redefine the category of difference, a category they themselves destroyed in the sixties and seventies when they were fighting for equality and justice for all (251). Like Rosmarin, however, she stresses the interpretive side of the critical act. Quoting Derrida, Fusini argues that difference is not a theory but an act ("la differenza è opera") that militates against identification for its movement by working to defer the triumph of the same ("differire il trionfo dello stesso," 257).

Thus despite the premise that ideas must be valorized by tracing them back to other women, matricides continue to take place. In her 1988 paper delivered at the Centro Culturale Virginia Woolf, "Il concetto di genealogia femminile," Muraro takes Rossanda to task for the ignorance of Irigaray's theories she had demonstrated in her lectures the previous year.[59] Rossanda defines her essay as a mediation on why Antigone, an obviously "premodern" persona who identified with *ate* (death as destiny), reappears in so many male theories. She argues that critical fascination with Antigone derives from the principles of autonomy and disobedience she represents. Traditionally, men have used these basic assumptions to dismantle the pretense to universality of their own laws (30–36). This, however, does not mean that males defined Antigone correctly or did not use her to negate sexual difference. Rossanda argues that Sophocles himself ignores Antigone's sexual difference; in his play, she is not a figure of a "woman" but someone representing unlimited desire as opposed to reason, an interpretation that surfaces again in Lacan, who sees her as the "incarnation of the pure criminal desire of the mother through which man can contemplate the ways of solitude" (15). The denial of sexual difference later made Antigone the figure that enabled man to ponder what separated him from society. Hegel saw her as emblematic of the resistance of the family to the progress of the spirit. Friedrich Hölderlin interpreted her as a vital, immediate "oriental" emotion opposed to Western rationalism. Modern theories place her in a dissident role against institutions, as demonstrated by depictions of her as a terrorist protesting the perverse authority of the State.[60]

Rossanda's interpretation, though markedly feminist, differs from that of Muraro and Irigaray not only because she examines portraits of women by men and cites males in her text. At the end of her argument that Antigone is a constant reminder of the limits of (male) government, she concludes that Antigone's gender is important, despite the false and harmful depictions of her, because she has always occupied the only role in which men have assigned power to women, that is the role of criticizing his yearnings for the infinite. This thematic interpretation, as we have demonstrated, is rejected by the generations of feminists after Rossanda who now interpret their confinement to the role of man's conscience or his savior as part of their reduction to subservience and inequality.[61] When Rossanda declares openly her quarrel with proponents of the theory of sexual difference, however, some striking points of contact are revealed between her and recent feminist critics involved in the construction of the theory of sexual difference. Like Gagliasso, Rossanda refuses to reduce everything to gender principles and speaks of the necessity of positing the existence of general human attitudes in comparison to which we create difference. Rossanda, however, argues that gender difference, though significant on a social level, may have less importance on the level of consciousness and ethics, whereas Gagliasso proposes an ethics truly based in feminine difference.

Rossanda's points concerning Antigone's premodern character bear some similarity to the language used in the charges of mysticism leveled against the emphasis on identification in the theory and practice of entrustment. Moreover, her observations concerning the roles of destiny, history, and the limits of government are also appearing in the discussions of feminists formed by the theory of sexual difference. In Rossanda's interpretation, Antigone is a figure whose idea of destiny and origins is archaic and self-destructive for the *polis*. Whereas Muraro, Cavarero, and Dominijanni argue that positing the principle of sexual difference as a necessary founding thought does not imply any predetermined destiny for the thought itself, which evolves from practice, feminist philosopher Francesca Izzo maintains the contrary.[62] In her review of Luisa Muraro's Italian translation of Irigaray's *Sexes et parentés*, Izzo states that destiny is indeed an integral part of Irigaray's recurring mysticism since Irigaray derives the concept of destiny not from a symbolic mother but from Martin Heidegger, for whom history follows a catastrophic pattern terminating in a world dominated by technology. Irigaray places the defeat of the matriarchy and the loss of women's power over procreation on the path that leads us to technological destruction. Therefore, followers of her theory inevitably fall back on irrational images of women as premodern or as man's savior because, in Irigaray's theory, women return to their origins only to extricate themselves from the technological modern world and to save some initial purity and goodness.[63] More significantly, Izzo claims this contradiction and Irigaray's mysticism are obvious to Italian feminists because, in Italy, practice always corrects theory. Irigaray's method cannot be put into practice because Italian feminist practice takes place in a different social and political context with specific goals. Izzo defines them as "the acquisition of *equality* and a *neuter* personal liberty for women, which means the historical process of exhausting the idea of sexual differences."[64]

Despite the common usage of terminology such as equality, neutrality, and limits of gender in the discourses of Izzo and Gagliasso, Mafai, and Rossanda, there are differences in interpretation stemming from their various backgrounds. Mafai and Rossanda argue for the right of women to assert their difference in front of a justice that remains as neutral as possible. Izzo and Gagliasso consistently make a case for the creation of a neutral justice and equality in a separatist space and mode. Izzo does contend that, in practice, even discussions among women should show how limiting gender can be and how one can eventually learn to overcome it. She is careful to couch such a procedure in "positive" terms. The recognition of gender limits should make women recognize that the partiality of their vision is not something to negate but part of their individual affirmation of self.[65]

Likewise, in the Carta, the word "limits" designates the necessarily partial nature of the feminist political vision and its refusal to generalize and universalize its vision to spheres outside of its own knowledge and experience. When the chair of the women's caucus, Livia Turco, argued for the "limits" of politics, since the extension of politics into all spheres could threaten personal private rights, Dominijanni strongly objected to this usage of the word "limits," reminding Turco that feminists have proven time and time again that the denial of the political nature of all things is a disadvantage to women.[66] These drawbacks, which have been summarized recently in a collection of essays entitled *Feminism as Critique*, are: the mystification of the gender-power relations that constitute the subtext of the modern economy and the State; the repression of women's difference and their exclusion from the public sphere; the trivialization of women's moral aspirations and perspectives; and the double bind between home and work in which women find themselves.[67]

Despite arguments from Dominijanni, Boccia, Muraro, and others who claimed that sexual difference must be realized in the political-public sphere, the Carta was removed from the Communist platform in February 1991. In a subsequent newspaper interview, a delighted Mafai asked Turco in an interview if this did not indicate an acceptance of Mafai's views, a return to the practice of politics instead of philosophical theorizing, and an end to feminist separatism.[68] Turco denied that the decision to withdraw legislation on sexual difference can be interpreted as a defeat, although she said that much of the obscure philosophical vocabulary involved in the redefinition of terms was dividing women and hiding what they had in common. She reminded Mafai, however, that as feminist politics returns to more concrete goals, it does so within a Party where women who hold 35 percent of the positions can make a difference. Philosopher Claudia Mancina interprets the entire episode as the final defeat of the myth of one unified subject ("un soggetto unitario"). Feminist theories and practices of difference assisted in this demise and empowered women to enter a new phase of producing new political categories and individual initiatives.[69]

If "obscure" philosophical vocabulary is hiding similarities, it is reinforcing some as well. In this "new phase" spoken of by Mancina, Italian feminists seemingly divided by ideological traditions, generations, and backgrounds both refuse to reduce everything to gender and continue to explore the possibilities and meanings for gender identification. Ideological and terminological divisions also mask similarities in methods of criticism. Although gender difference is assumed and not hidden, it is formulated in contrast to general and supposedly neutral categories. Italian feminists use the term "limits" to argue for their own right to a partial vision, their right to interpret based on possible theoretical error but truth of experience. This partiality cannot be theoretically posited in such a way as to hide the error, however, because the partiality is itself constructed by comparison to those concepts, attitudes, and structures considered to be general and universal in nature. The writers discussed in the next chapters follow the same trajectory as they test their own vision, derived from many of the theories discussed here, against the assumed neutrality of form.

Notes

1. Donald Meyer, *Sex and Power: The Rise of Women in America, Russia, Sweden and Italy* (Middletown, CT: Wesleyan University Press, 1987), 631ff.
2. This chapter owes much to the more detailed histories of Italian feminism, such as Lucia Chiavola Birnbaum's *Liberazione della donna: Feminism in Italy* (Middletown, CT: Wesleyan University Press, 1986) and Judith Hellman's *Journeys Among Women: Feminism in Five Italian Cities* (New York: Oxford University Press, 1987), although both authors end their discussions at the early 1980s. Given my primary focus, it would also be impossible here to concentrate entirely on explicating and analyzing in detail the theory of sexual difference, which has been the subject of a few recent articles in English. See three articles by Renate Holub: "Weak Thought and Strong Ethics," *Annali d'italianistica* 9 (1991): 124–143; "For the Record: The Non-Language of Italian Feminist Philosophy," *Romance Languages Annual* 1 (1990): 133–140; "The Politics of Diotima," *Differentia* 5 (1991): 161–173. See also Teresa de Lauretis, "The Practice of Sexual Difference and Feminist Thought in Italy: An Introductory Essay"; this essay introduces the English translation by de Lauretis and Patricia Cicogna of *Non credere di avere dei diritti* (*Don't Think You Have Any Rights*), in *Sexual Difference: A Theory of Social-Symbolic Practice*, ed. de Lauretis and Cicogna (Bloomington: Indiana University Press, 1990), the cooperatively written history of the Libreria di Milano feminist group, headed by feminist historian and theoretician Luisa Muraro. Muraro is the author of several works, including

Guglielmo e Maifreda (Milan: La Tartaruga, 1985), a historical, philosophical inquiry into the medieval heresy case of two nuns who defined God as female. See also Rosi Braidotti, *Patterns of Dissonance: A Study of Women in Contemporary Philosophy*, trans. Elizabeth Guild (Oxford: Polity, 1991).

3. Anna Banti, *Un grido lacerante* (Milan: Rizzoli, 1982).

4. Anna Nozzoli, "La donna e il romanzo negli anni Ottanta," proceedings of the conference "La donna nella letteratura italiana del 900," ed. Sergio Gensini (Empoli: Rivista di cittadina, 1983), 54–55.

5. Sandra Petrignani, *Le signore della scrittura* (Milan: La Tartaruga, 1984), 8.

6. Natalia Costa-Zalessow, *Scrittrici italiane dal XIII al XX secolo* (Ravenna: Longo Editore, 1982); Giuliana Morandini, *La voce che è in lei: Antologia della narrativa femminile italiana tra '800 e '900* (Milan: Bompiani, 1980). For a brief outline of the lack of attention paid to women writers in literary anthologies until recently, see Santo Arico's introduction to *Contemporary Women Writers in Italy: A Modern Renaissance* (Amherst: University of Massachusetts Press, 1990), 308.

7. Sergio Pacifici, *The Modern Italian Novel: From Capuana to Tozzi* (Carbondale: Southern Illinois University Press, 1973), and *The Modern Italian Novel: From Pea to Moravia* (Carbondale: Southern Illinois Press, 1979).

8. See, for example, Ian Watt, *The Rise of the Novel* (Berkeley: University of California Press, 1957), and, more recently, Michael McKeon, *The Origins of the English Novel 1600–1740* (Baltimore, MD: Johns Hopkins Press, 1987). By novel, Pacifici means the nineteenth-century realist novel and he does not mention the long prose adventure stories and romances that preceded the realist novel and continued to be written in Italy until late in the century. On this subject, see Folco Portinari, *Le parabole del reale: Romanzi italiani dell'Ottocento* (Turin: Einaudi, 1986). For a study on the relationship of Manzoni's *I promessi sposi* to the romance tradition in general, see Carol Lazzaro-Weis, "The Providential Trap: Some Remarks on Fictional Strategies in *I promessi sposi*," *Stanford Italian Review* 4, 1 (1984): 93–106.

9. Geno Pampaloni, "Introduzione," *I giovani hanno riletto per voi: 40 anni di narrative italiana (1940–1954)* (Rome: Mondadori, 1991), viii.

10. Pampaloni, "Introduzione," viii. The quote is from an unidentified page in one of Maria Bellonci's personal diaries. "I libri sono nostri, di tutti, appartenendo al grande sforzo umano di farsi capire e far capire. Vorremmo che si fosse tutti uniti per salvare i libri dall'indifferenza."

11. Nozzoli, "La donna e il romanzo negli anni Ottanta," 46.

12. Anna Maria Crispino, "Autrici? Visto, si stampi," *NoiDonne: Legendaria*, (May 1990): 10–11.

13. To date, there are twenty-three women's studies centers (*centri di documentazione*) that work together to collect documents on all aspects of the women's movement in Italy. Some are defined according to topics (the center in Bologna focuses on *il materno*; the center located in the Rome Buon Pastore complex along with the Centro Culturale Virginia Woolf focuses primarily on political aspects of the movement; and the DonneWomenFemmes center on the other side of the Tiber River includes more documents pertaining to literature. These centers are working together to form a national network that is effective despite funding problems and are collaborating with similar networks in Europe and abroad. Their efforts are the subject of two publications in which plans, problems, and progress are reported: *Le donne al centro: Politica e cultura dei centri delle donne negli anni '80*, proceedings of the First National

Conference of Women's Centers, held in Siena 1986 (Rome: Utopia, 1988); and *Perleparole: Initiative a favore dell'informazione e della documentazione delle donne europee*, ed. Adriana Perrotta-Rabissi and Maria Beatrice Perucci (Rome: Utopia, 1989).

14. At a conference in Rome in November 1990, Muraro denied that the placing of the debate in a male-run press would cause the *pensiero della differenza sessuale* to lose its marginal, illegitimate, and thus radical status. This conference is reviewed by Paola Bono, who agrees with Muraro, in "Una sfida contro la moderazione: La quasi collana sulla differenza sessuale degli editori Riuniti," *Reti* 6 (1990): 24–26. See also Ida Dominijanni, "Una quasi-collana che sa la differenza," *Il manifesto*, November 9, 1990, 8.

15. "Le filosofe si organizzano e gridano Platone," *La repubblica*, November 10, 1990, 21: "Le filosofe italiane di oggi, di questo fine millennio, non teorizzano la separazione totale dell'altro sesso. Non si considerano militanti a tempo pieno. Non credono, come proclamava la filosofa Carla Lonzi nel suo pamphlet *Sputiamo su Hegel* che femminismo sia eguale a esistenzialismo. Non si tormentano sul rapporto con la madre (anche se lo ritengono un punto fondamentale) né sul linguaggio affettivo (anche se, dicono, è importante). Non si riempiono la bocca della parola 'corpo' e soprattutto non gridano 'io sona mia.'"

16. Miriam Mafai, "Le vedove di Lenin e la deriva femminista," *MicroMega* 4 (1990): 7–15. Mafai describes supporters of the legislation as "Lenin's widows" since Lenin, like they, renounced the illusory nature of equality in democracy. Some angry responses include those of the head of the women's caucus in the Communist Party, Livia Turco ("Noi donne ancora deboli . . ."), and Mariella Gramaglia ("Sesso e democrazia"), both published in *La repubblica*, October 9, 1990, 8.

17. Maria Rosa Cutrufelli, "Sordità tra noi donne: Ecco che cosa può renderci più deboli," *L'unità*, October 30, 1990, 37.

18. *A prova di donna: Interviste sulla svolta del PCI*, ed. Roberta Tatafiore (Rome: Cooperativa Libera Stampa, 1990): "Femminismo/comunismo è l'incontro escatologico all'ennesima potenza di due totalitarismi che si abbracciano anche se fanno finta di scontrarsi" (13).

19. Hellman, *Journeys Among Women*, esp. chapter 1, and Birnbaum, *Liberazione delle donne*, 71ff.

20. Liberation theology was condemned by Pope Paul VI. The debate in Italy has been revived again by the publication of the Italian translation in 1990 of Elaine Pagels's feminist rereading of Augustine and Pelagius in *Adam, Eve and the Serpent* (New York: Random House, 1988). Pagels argues that Augustine's theory of original sin, which concomitantly cast woman in the role of man's eternal temptress, was part of a strategy to redefine the Church's changing relationship to power and government and rationalize some of its own corruption. Although it would have been more logical for Christians to accept Pelagius's ideas about humans' free will and unmediated relationship to God, they opted for Augustine's description that humans were basically corrupt and in need of tradition, authority, dogma, and government, however corrupt, to guide them. The February 1991 edition of the English and Italian version of the Catholic magazine *Trenta Giorni* (*Thirty Days*) covers the contemporary Church debate over free will versus dogma and reviews why Pelagius, condemned as a heretic, is again attracting Catholic followers.

21. Ida Dominijanni, "Il femminismo degli anni Ottanta: Un nodo: Uguag-

lianza e differenza," in *Esperienza storica femminile nell'età moderna e contemporanea*, vol. 2, ed. Anna Maria Crispino (Rome: La Goccia, 1989), 119–127.

22. Luce Irigaray, *Sexes et parentés* (Paris: Minuit, 1987; trans. Luisa Muraro, *Sessi e genealogie* [Milan: La Tartaruga, 1989]). Besides the recent cooperative effort by the Milan Group published in English *Non credere di avere dei diritti*, Adriana Cavarero, Muraro, and other feminists from the Verona Diotima group develop the philosophical implications of the theory in *Diotima: Il pensiero della differenza sessuale*, (Milan: La Tartaruga, 1987). A shorter article by Cavarero summarizes the major points: "L'elaborazione filosofica della differenza sessuale," in *La ricerca delle donne: Studi femministi in Italia*," ed. Maria Cristina Marcuzzo and Anna Rossi-Doria (Turin: Rosenberg and Sellier, 1987), 173–187.

23. Dominijanni, "Il femminismo degli anni Ottanta," 123.

24. Hellman, *Journeys Among Women*, 31.

25. Birnbaum, *Liberazione della donna*, 66–68, 79–80.

26. Hellman, *Journeys Among Women*, 48.

27. Birnbaum, *Liberazione delle donne*, 155. Several 1978 radio interviews, moderated by Rossana Rossanda, are published in *Le altre: Conversazioni sulle parole della politica* (1979; repr. Milan: Feltrinelli, 1989).

28. Birnbaum, *Liberazione della donna*, 180. See also Rasy, *Le donne e la letteratura*, 75–80. Elaine Marx's description of the fundamental dissimilarity between American and French feminism in the seventies is, to an extent, valid for the difference between French and Italian feminism, although the latter two share certain Marxist and psychoanalytical orientations. According to Marx, French feminism emphasized the repression of the unrepresentable "feminine" in language, which led to studies of how the radical feminine could be uncovered in discourse, whereas interrogations into the nature of oppression, common in American feminism, are more linked to a desire to raise women's consciousness. Elaine Marks, "Women and Literature in France," *Signs* 3, 4 (1978): 832–842.

29. For example, Marina D'Amelia, "Fare storia, non politica: Il successo de *La storia delle donne* apre interrogativi tra le storiche," *Reti* 6 (1990): 19–23.

30. Dacia Maraini, "Quale cultura per la donna," in *Donna, cultura e tradizione*, ed. Pia Bruzzichelli and Maria Luisa Algini (Milan: Mazzotta, 1976), 64–65.

31. Maria Luisa Boccia, "Le matrici culturali del neofemminismo: Appunti di lettura sulla presenza di riferimenti al marxismo nel pensiero femminista degli anni Settanta," in *Esperienza storica femminile nell'età moderna e contemporanea*, vol. 2, ed. Crispino, 39–61. See also, by the same author, "Percorsi della mente femminile e forme del sapere," in *Con voce di donna: Pensiero, linguaggio, communicazione* (Siena: Edizioni Centro Culturale delle donne Mara Meoni, 1989), 37–64. Boccia has also written a critical biography on Carla Lonzi, *L'io in rivolta: Vissuto e pensiero di Carla Lonzi* (Milan: La Tartaruga, 1990).

32. Carla Lonzi, *Sputiamo su Hegel: La donna clitoridea e la donna vaginale, e altri scritti* (Milan: Rivolta femminile, 1974). This essay has been republished several times. Excerpts from the essay are included in Bono and Kemp, eds. *Italian Feminist Thought*, 37–59.

33. Although she is less interested in tracing a history of the reception of Irigaray's theories, Holub agrees that such an approach "would surely reveal an almost obsessive Hegelian propensity of these Italian theorists in their understanding of Irigaray." Holub, "For The Record: The Non-Language of Italian Feminist Philosophy," 133.

34. Hélène Cixous, "Le sexe ou la tête," *Cahiers du Grif*, 13 (1976): 5–15; translated by Annette Kuhn as "Castration or Decapitation," *Signs*, 7, 1 (1981): 36–55. This idea had appeared in Cixous's writings before 1976 as well.

35. Luce Irigaray, *Ce sexe qui n'en est pas un* (Paris: Minuit, 1977). The Italian translation *Questo sesso che non è un sesso* (Milan: Feltrinelli, 1978) was done by Luisa Muraro.

36. Cixous, "Castration or Decapitation," 46–50.

37. Besides authoring several fictional works, Rosa Rossi has written a theoretical treatise on the relationship of women to language: *Le parole delle donne* (Rome: Riuniti, 1978).

38. Francesca Molfino, "Psicoanalisi e femminismo: Le radici culturali del neofemminismo," in *Esperienza storica femminile nell'età moderna e contemporanea*, vol. 2, ed. Crispino, 63–75.

39. Silvia Montefoschi, "Il ruolo materno e l'identità personale: Riflessioni sul movimento femminista e la psicoanalisi," *Nuova DWF* 6–7 (1978): 143–173. My translation of this article appears in *The Lonely Mirror: Italian Perspectives on Feminist Theory*, ed. Paola Bono and Sandra Kemp (London: Routledge, 1991). The parenthetical page references are to the Italian version.

40. In *Una donna* (Turin: Sten, 1906; repr. Milan: Feltrinelli, 1978), Sibilla Aleramo raises the question of why mothers who continued to raise their sons to be cruel toward the weak and unfaithful to women were satisfied by exercising an almost tyrannical love over these same sons.

41. Feminist theoreticians have shown that Latin mothers are not alone in exercising this "tyrannical" control over their sons, who, in turn, theorized this behavior as being part of woman's essential and essentially nonimprovable nature. See Sarah Kofman's critique of Freud in "Supplément rhapsodique," *L'enigme de la femme* (Paris: Galilée, 1980), 253–272. An English translation can be found in *Discourse* 4 (1982): 37–52.

42. Hellman, *Journeys Among Women*, 96–201. In radio debates and elsewhere, the practice of a *femminismo diffuso*—that is, the practice of feminism outside of any women's group, since the possibilities of group change had been exhausted—clashed with the continuing claim that organized separatism was a necessary procedure to avoid being repaternalized.

43. Muraro is the main translator of Irigaray's works into Italian. The arguments summarized here come from a workshop given at the Centro Culturale Virginia Woolf in Rome on March 19–20, 1988, titled "Il concetto della genealogia femminile," (Rome: Edizioni Centro Culturale Virginia Woolf, 1988).

44. Marianne Hirsch, *The Mother-Daughter Plot: Narrative, Psychoanalysis, Feminism* (Bloomington: Indiana University Press, 1987), 172; Jane Gallop, *The Daughter's Seduction: Feminism and Psychoanalysis* (Ithaca: Cornell University Press, 1982), 122ff.

45. Hirsch, *The Mother-Daughter Plot*, 197. Muraro underlines the need for women to create their own ethics by reviewing Irigaray's changing interpretations of the Antigone myth. Irigaray first speaks of Antigone as a figure emblematic of female alienation and estrangement; then she argues that Antigone represents a female value system of loyalty and fidelity. Muraro, however, emphasizes Irigaray's more recent interpretation of Antigone's failed revolt as a result of her unconscious complicity with the patriarchal law of the family. This view buttresses Muraro's arguments that women need to create their own ethics and laws in order to avoid complicity and victimization.

46. Tiziana Villani, "Demetra," in *Vivere e pensare la relazione madre-figlia*, proceedings of a seminar held in Milan, February 26, 1990 (Milan: Edizioni Associazione Culturale Melusine, 1990), 2–4. The novel *Demetra* was published by Mimesi in 1989.

47. De Lauretis, "The Practice of Sexual Difference and Feminist Thought in Italy," 8.

48. Jeannette Laillou-Savona, "Dé-lire et délit/ces: Stratégies des lectures féministes (Coward, de Lauretis, Moi, Cixous, Broussard, etc.)," *Canadian Review of Comparative Literature* 15, 2 (1988): 220–253.

49. "Ce plaisir/désir autre, on le trouve peut-être déjà dans un deuxième type de lectures théoriques ou critiques calqué sur cette littérature féminine d'avant-garde et c'est de ce deuxième mode de lecture bien distinct que je voudrais parler en dernier lieu. Ces lectures que j'appellerai 'gynétiques' refusent la pratique discursive de la tradition universitaire (introduction-développment-conclusion) et la logique démonstrative linéaire des discours officiels. D'autre part, elles établissent un rapport d'*identification* entre la femme qui écrit, celle(s) dont il est question dans leur texte et celles qui liront leurs textes. Ce rapport se fait souvent si aimant et si intime qu'il prend des accents érotiques. Ces lectures sont des textes poétiques qui se veulent et sont aussi théoriques car elles expriment des connaissances et des conviction [*sic*] féministes. Très conscientes de leur expérimentation linguistique, les lectures gynétiques se font l'écho d'une joie intense qui est celle de la reconnaissance des femmes par les femmes. Cette lecture est pratiquée par des écrivaines telles que Luce Irigaray, Hélène Cixous, Nicole Broussard et Madeleine Gagnon" (emphasis added; my trans.).

50. Biancamaria Frabotta, "L'identità dell'opera e l'io femminile," in *Donne e scrittura*, ed. Daniela Corona (Palermo: La Luna, 1990), 147.

51. Maria Rosa Cutrufelli, "Scritture, scrittrici. L'esperienza italiana," in *Donne e scrittura* ed. Corona, 242–245.

52. Francesca Sanvitale, "Madre e figlia," in *Vivere e pensare la relazione madre-figlia*, proceedings of a seminar held in Milan, March 19, 1990 (Milan: Edizioni Associazione Culturale Melusine, 1990), 7.

53. See Francesca Molfino, "Fideltà a se stesse e testimonianza reciproca," in *L'apprendimento dell'incertezza: I centri culturali delle donne*, ed. Carla Cotti and Francesca Molfino (Rome: Edizioni Centro Culturale Virginia Woolf, 1989), 16–17. Molfino cites the constant use of the metaphor of entering "la porta stretta" (the narrow gate) for women learning how to practice disparity as an example of the fundamentalist base of these theories. In the same collection see also Manuela Fraire, "Una pratica per una politica," 126–136, for another good documentation of the split. See Renate Holub, "Weak Thought and Strong Ethics," 139–140, for a brief discussion of this aspect and its connection to the "notion of political action as contemplation." Holub emphasizes the practical side of Diotima's mysticism: "What seems to propel the latest research of Diotima is not a facile celebration of the mystical, as it might seem on the surface, but an investigation of how a woman's body, at this point in history, can provide form to fluidity, can capture the real in its presence as well as its absence."

54. Elena Gagliasso, "Articoli di fede? No grazie," *Reti* 3–4 (1989): 52–56: "Giustizia, eguaglianza di possibilità di vita, solidarietà, impegno ed esperienze di trasformazioni collettive sono come abiti lisi, mentre iniziativa individuale, competizione, supremazia personale sono riscoperti 'nuovi.' "

55. Giovanna Borrello, "Il fondamento del pensiero della differenza ses-

suale," Workshop, June 11–12, 1988, Group B (Rome: Edizioni Centro Culturali Virginia Woolf, 1988), 12.

56. Laura Grasso, "Madri e figlie," in *Il filo di Arianna: Letture della differenza
sessuale* ed. Franca Bimbi, Laura Grasso, Marina Zancan (Rome: Utopia, 1987):
39–52.

57. Laura Grasso, "Madri e figlie": "Mostrarsi in certi momenti fragili e
bambine non significa fuggire dalla responsibilità e dall'assunzione del ruolo,
assunzione in certi momenti necessaria e anche indispensabile" (51).

58. Nadia Fusini, "Commento alla relazione di Silvia Vegetti-Finzi," in *La
ricerca delle donne: Studi femministi in Italia*, ed. Maria Cristina Marcuzzo and
Anna Rossi-Doria (Turin: Rosenberg and Sellier, 1988), 249–261.

59. Rossanda's course notes are now published as part of her lengthy introduction to a new translation of Sophocles' *Antigone*, trans. Luisa Biondetti
(Milan: Feltrinelli, 1987), 7–60.

60. Rossanda acknowledges a great debt to George Steiner's *Antigones* published in 1984. The Italian translation of this work was published by Garzanti
in February 1991.

61. See Borrello, "Il fondamento del pensiero della differenza sessuale," who
argues that the liberation of woman from this image is the beginning of her
realization of her own liberty from assuming the illusory responsibility for
patriarchal institutions like the family (11).

62. Ida Dominijanni, "Le origini di fronte," *Il manifesto*, January 10, 1991, 3;
Francesca Izzo, "Il materno tra origine e storia," *Reti* 2 (1989): 23–26.

63. Although Izzo disagrees with Muraro and Cavarero's interpretation of
Antigone, she does sympathize with the political goal of their interpretation of
Irigaray's separation of reproduction from technology because of its feminist
purpose. Cavarero and Muraro argue that this separation is positive since it
moves us away from definitions of reproduction as automatic and is part of the
process of restoring the power of regeneration to the mother.

64. "La conquista della *uguaglianza*, della libertà personale (*neutra*) delle
donne-il che vuol dire processo storico di esaurimento delle differenziazioni
sessuali" (24, emphasis added).

65. Francesca Izzo, "Immagini del soggetto moderno: Etica e soggettività,"
Reti 3–4 (1989): 304.

66. Ida Dominijanni, "Politica sotto processo: Rifondazione comunista, democrazia, soggetti del cambiamento. Un seminario," *Il manifesto*, December 20,
1990, 10.

67. Seyla Benhabib and Drucilla Cornell, "Introduction: Beyond the Politics
of Gender," in *Feminism as Critique*, ed. Seyla Benhabib and Drucilla Cornell
(Minneapolis: University of Minnesota Press, 1988), 9. The points listed are
examined in depth by the following scholars in their respective essays: Nancy
Fraser, "What's Critical About Critical Theory: The Case of Habermas and
Gender," 31–55; Iris Marion Young, "Impartiality and the Civic Public: Some
Implications of Feminist Critiques of Moral and Political Theory," 56–76;
Seyla Benhabib, "The Generalized and the Concrete Other: The Kohlberg-
Gilligan Controversy," 77–95; and Maria Markus, "Women, Success and Civil
Society: Submission to, or Subversion of, the Achievement Principle," 96–109.

68. Miriam Mafai, "Compagne, l'ideologia adesso non basta più," *La repubblica*, February 20, 1991, 15.

69. Claudia Mancina, "Perché non si può imporre per statuto la politica della
differenza," *L'Unità*, February 17, 1991, 2.

Chapter 3
From Confession to Romance

When speaking of Italian feminist novels of the 1970s, Anna Nozzoli emphasizes their radical content and assumes a neutrality of form.[1] In contrast to the self-contained structures of verbal play that characterized much Italian avant-garde prose of the sixties, feminist writings that aspired to represent and disseminate truthful information concerning women's lives appeared more "traditional," at least on a formal level. Their language was purposely straightforward and nonliterary; Nozzoli terms it a kind of "degré zero stilistico."[2] Their nemesis, as Nozzoli describes it, was the "privatizzazione" of the feminine role that Carla Lonzi, among others, had begun to theorize (152). Despite the many political and juridical victories of the feminist movement, women were still viewed as the affective center of the household when affective values were undergoing constant devaluation in a capitalist economy. The popular slogan of neofeminists, "the personal is political," stressed the inseparability of the political and personal realms: the exclusion of women from public to private domains that society considered unproductive was a political action, the roots and ramifications of which feminist writers strove to define, examine, and expose.

The most popular literary form among Italian feminist writers, as in other countries, was the autobiographical confession. The confessional form appeared to offer to many Italian women writers an intimate yet unrestricted space in which to perform their political, psychoanalytical, and social analyses. This choice, however, also reflects women's problematic relationship to literature and their own literary past. The confessional genre has long dominated women's writing, although it has rarely, if ever, depicted the successful liberation of the female writer.[3] Elisabetta Rasy attributes women's preference for confessional and other private genres to tradition: women's active appearance on the literary scene was linked, as in her example, Madame de Lafayette's *Princesse de Clèves*, to the promise to give the real story behind the scenes, the truth about the mysterious and silent feminine domain.[4] Romanticism's emphasis on nostalgia and subjectivism helped keep women writers in private genres such as the diary and the memoir.

Women's personal narratives, including their autobiographies, have been criticized for certain formal deviations from male confessions and autobiographies such as their disconnected, fragmentary, and cyclical nature, their concentration on personal and marginal details, and their failure to develop the writer's relationship to establishment history.[5] Despite such deviations, however, these writings are still characterized by the same search for self-understanding and self-possession found in male autobiographies. Janet Gunn, in her phenomenological approach to autobiography, argues convincingly that the self as an absolute and ineffable essence outside of and apart from society is itself a generic construct of classical autobiographical theory, a construct based on the self's privileged position in the Cartesian cogito.[6]

Gunn's analysis demonstrates only how male autobiographical writings challenge rigid, fallacious generic restraints. Women's confessional writings, however, have been tainted with the ignominy of failure that critics seek to explain in a larger context. For Claudine Hermann, this search for a private, autonomous self is the lot to which women have been confined historically for lack of any self-acquired, social identity.[7] In her discussion of feminist confessions in England, America, and Germany, Rita Felski relates the search for a pure female self to the ideology of essentialist feminists. The inevitable failure of this philosophy expresses itself through constant guilt feelings, self-accusations, and contradictory, utopistic statements.[8] Despite these drawbacks, Felski reads feminist confessions as part of a general critique, similar to that of Christopher Lasch's views of the narcissism of the bourgeois class which results from its preoccupation with the self, autonomy, and privacy (Felski, 107).[9] Felski points out that the more feminist writers concentrated on their own personal subjectivity, the more amorphous and less expressive the self became.[10] Other feminist critics, such as Sigrid Wiegel, blame the failure of these confessions more directly on their formlessness which, she claims, prevented the writer from depicting a coherent, critical self and confirmed prejudices that women's literature was naive and self-indulgent.[11]

Despite these problems, it is undeniable that these confessions, at the time of their publication, responded to women's need to see that their personal problems were communal, social, and political in nature. This was certainly the case for most Italian feminist confessions written and published in the 1970s. These texts helped to clarify the many insidious ways women's personal domain and inner freedom were defined and delimited by cultural and religious myths of gender, specifically those concerning women's sexual nature. The function the confessions did not fulfill, however, is as important as the one they did. If confessions written by men and women challenge fallacious generic restraints, especially the myth of the autonomous self, women's attempts to do the same primarily revealed the extent to which women continued to conform to patriarchal standards.

In this chapter, we will show how the categories of the confession, picaresque, and romance reflect the movement of Italian women writers from a critique of an all-oppressive patriarchy to an analysis of their own myths of wholeness and integrity. In all three genres, formal constraints function to show the limits of gender, no matter who defines it. Although the confession did not permit writers and critics to perform a self-analysis without acknowledging and reaffirming male dominion, it was often structured around two strong mythical and religious female stereotypes in Italian culture, the Virgin and the Whore.[12] These figures appear in many forms in all the genres to be discussed. The limitations of particular generic conventions, however, not only shape the arguments therein but also help them gain in expression. In Armanda Guiducci's *Due donne da buttare: Una donna di buona famiglia e una exprostituta confessano il fallimento della loro famiglia* (1976), both narrators, by conforming to generic restraints, unveil many of the seductive and destructive elements of these myths. Dacia Maraini's *Memorie di una ladra* (1972) relies on themes and conventions coming from the picaresque tradition to depict the same ultimate helplessness of women in the face of social and literary stereotyping.[13] Although, as Felski writes, feminist confessions rejected the romance plot of love and marriage and helped formulate the feminist cultural critique of the oppressive implications of these institutions for women, the romance form provides the main structuring principle in Maraini's *Donna in guerra* (1975), Maria Schiavo's *Discorso eretico alla fatalità* (1990), Francesca Sanvitale's *Madre e figlia* (1980), and Biancamaria Frabotta's *Velocità di fuga* (1989). In these narratives, romance elements of fantasy and illusion, the quest plot, and other conventions are exploited to represent women's aspirations and failures in a more creative light and in ways not permitted by the other forms.

Feminism and Fiction in the 1970s

Both confessions included in Guiducci's *Due donne da buttare* flaunt the circular, repetitive, detailed nature traditionally criticized in women's personal narratives. Guiducci's frustrated housewife immerses the reader in descriptions of her endless and repetitive duties as house-keeper, wife, and mother to which society assigns no productive value. The housewife's remarks about the incapacity of the household machines (*elettrodomestici*) to save time reflect topical protests of feminists against a powerful consumerism that reinforces the role of traditional housewife and that of superior male provider.[14] These and other criticisms of society judiciously reinforce the narrator's generically determined goal to present an intelligent and lucid self that has somehow remained intact despite banal adversity. The housewife is careful to separate herself from her more obsessive acquaintances, who frantically swallow hormones to defeat the aging process or who have allowed the tedium of their lives to drive them into insane asylums. Women, she explains, are innately rational beings endowed with a *senso pratico*, as opposed to men, who think in theoretical and abstract terms. Her much-vaunted common sense, however, leads her to isolate herself from feminist groups such as the Comitato delle arrabbiate, which she denounces as being too unrealistic in their demands. Thus her personal and generic need to effect a rational presentation of self creates a paradox characteristic of many women's confessions: having confronted the seemingly inescapable difficulties of her (female) situation, the narrator adopts survival mechanisms such as withdrawal, isolation, and establishment of personal boundaries instead of directly contesting these difficulties.[15]

The force of the housewife's criticisms and her search for self-understanding are most seriously undercut, however, by the need to prove her innocence. To fulfill this generic prerequisite, the housewife must frame much of her social criticism in the context of her cooperation. In so doing, she reverts to portraying herself as a stereotypical, passive, obedient, self-sacrificing housewife. The housewife is not a rebel, nor is her confession a plea for the reevaluation of her activities; she agrees as well on their trivial and useless nature. Her only crime to which she pleads innocent is that she conformed. As a child she had believed the dictums of her father and schoolteachers: "Whoever does not have a house is a pathetic misfit" ("Chi non ha casa è una poveretta, una spostata"); "A woman without a home is like a snail without a shell" ("Una donna senza casa è una lumaca senza chiocciola") (11). She had dutifully and proudly given birth to the required male offspring (*figli maschi*), and had successfully fulfilled her less than heroic tasks of fighting dust and finding bread on Sunday mornings all her married life. Cooperation with the patriarchy is inevitable and always doomed as her example of how even the preparation of food, the fundamental function of the housewife and mother, has been reduced to a macabre encounter with pollution and death:

Then they tell you to protect yourself from cancer: Sure. The meat is covered with food coloring and there's poisonous smog found in the cow's milk. A woman knocks herself out for twenty years in the kitchen to come up with poisoned meals. Eating to kill oneself makes no sense. (33)[16]

Public cooperation and revolt in isolation are bound to fail, and the housewife's rational self dissolves in the reservoir of male prejudices that she herself retains. Her increasingly intense fear of aging confirms her inability to formulate an identity independent of male judgment. Overwhelmed by helplessness and fear, she capitulates to an apocalyptic vision of the uncontrollable and hostile environment: generic constraints of rationality and innocence conspire to create the image of a crazed stereotypical housewife who is helpless to effect social change:

Oh I see an immense black cloud the sewers will all explode black columns of smoke all the grease in the world boiling over all the dust we chased away will return from the depths of the ocean and will destroy the earth. (66)[17]

The final image of the stereotypical crazed housewife, a necessary part of the demonstration of Guiducci's point concerning the inseparability of the personal from the political, also brings to the fore the main contradiction between women's confessions and the form itself. If, in a successful confession, a pure autonomous and complete self must rise above society, the female narrator cannot be pure outside of society's definitions of purity for her. In her study of the figure of the Virgin, Marina Warner shows how the successive array of images that accrued to Mary from virgin, to queen to divine goddess, was rooted in man's desire to define himself as a superior, independent, and most important, whole being. This desire is also reflected in the many images of virgin goddesses in pagan antiquity whom Mary resembles since she, like many other Church figures, partially derives from these sources. As Mary became the mediator through which man could glimpse the possibility of sinless reproduction and perfection, each permutation further denigrated real women as the Mother Goddess became an effective instrument of asceticism and female subjection (49). In *Due donne*, the housewife is caught between an unattainable image of the untainted, selfless nourisher and the degraded real image of woman she tries to rise above. And, although the housewife proudly asserts she is not ready to give up, her constant negations of any responsibility for her fate ensure the ultimate futility of her ritualized and trivial battles.

A similar pattern, despite differences, is presented in the prostitute Stella's confession of her experiences as a professional call girl before she met Gèc, who forced her to go straight and get a job as a salesgirl in a department store. Stella's belief in the myth of the strong, independent self is evident in her rational and humanist view of the individual in society and her refusal to be considered a victim:

A victim of society. That's a neat little thought and it makes one feel so noble and compassionate. But it never occurs to these people that we are society. Instead, men—all of them: judges in their underwear, those nervewracking students—just pass the buck. People are always looking to place the blame in the corner of society they aren't standing in. (102)[18]

Stella's narrated self-image, like the housewife's, is not an independent one, but rather the result of an attempt to appropriate patriarchal values and language. Stella attributes her rise from a simple street-walker to a better-paid call girl to her ability to suppress weak, feminine characteristics: she flaunts frigidity as a safeguard against becoming dependent on men for sexual gratification, as is the case with other, weaker prostitutes who have become dependent on drugs as well. Stella views feminine power in capitalist terms: if women are commodities in society then the only logical thing to do is to raise one's price.

Because Stella rejects, on the surface, patriarchal images of women and blames individuals instead of society, she can, like the housewife, point out many contradictions and injustices in society. In the end Stella admits, however, that all things considered, the prostitute has even less power than the housewife: "If women are powerless, prostitutes are worse-off, they can do less than nothing" (115). The female trickster must inevitably be tricked by the society she, like the housewife, has cooperated with. Feelings of alienation, anonymity, and guilt cause Stella to reenter society in which she claims, as Gèc's girlfriend, she is again an "individual." Yet just as Stella cooperates with patriarchal values to leave society, so must she cooperate with them to return. The figure of the penitent whore incarnated in the Magdalene figure provides the formula for her to redeem herself. As Warner's title for her study makes clear, however, both the Virgin and the Whore are alone among their sex. Not surprisingly, as a social "individual" Stella experiences even more profound feelings of marginality and lack of solidarity with other women: "I don't trust anyone now, especially women" ("Non ho più confidenza con la gente, specie le donne," 110). Dirt, the symbol of the lost battle with the patriarchy that defines both the housewife and the prostitute as worthless and guilty, becomes an obsession for Stella as well. Her last words reflect pathetic hopes that her new bath lotion will absolve all guilt and make her feel clean again: "Spero tanto nel mio nuovo dopobagno" (124).

*   *   *

Whereas *Due donne* depicts two females who marginalize themselves by cooperating with formal and social imperatives, in Maraini's *Memorie di una ladra* the picaresque form provides the framework for the depiction of a willful outsider. The seemingly indestructible narrator, Teresa, survives innumerable beatings, bombings, inhumane prisons and insane asylums, and family persecution, to mention only a few of the adventures in this action-packed, linear plot.[19] The picaresque genre derives from criminal confessions, causing Claudio Guillen to identify it as the "confessions of a liar."[20] Although the confessional pieces of Guiducci display the aporia of the belief that the personal self can be kept separate from the social, the picaresque tradition has always reaffirmed that there is no material survival outside of society. Like the traditional *picaro*, Teresa prefers estrangement and roguery to any traditionally prescribed female role. She always somehow adjusts to social demands, however defined, that are imposed on her. Once again revolt will reveal itself as cooperation.

Memorie di una ladra is the result of extensive research by Maraini in the late sixties on the deplorable conditions in women's prisons. In an interview that serves as an introduction to the book's second edition, she speaks of how reeducation in women's prisons suppresses all individuality and creativity since its goal is to produce model housewives (v). But in the episodic, action-packed narrative itself, such ideological points are given short shrift by the practical, down-to-earth Teresa who moves from one adventure to another, never improving except to learn from experience how to become a better thief. Like the traditional picaresque orphan, Teresa is thrown unprepared into a harsh society whose values she has to learn anew. Society, its hardships, inequalities, and oppressions, becomes the natural foe of the *picaro* (or *picara*) who, in his or her judgments, displays a strong sense of moral rectitude. Typically Teresa rails incessantly against the cowards, many of them male, who betray her both in sex and in burglaries, and thus have "forced" her to go to jail. Her sense of honor is based on the rigid standards of *omertà*, the underworld's code of solidarity, which is based on remaining loyal and silent while taking the rap alone.

Generally, the *picaro*'s actions betray his desire not to challenge but rather to conform to and enjoy the system. Maraini identifies with Teresa's rather concrete relationship to food and admires what she terms her total estrangement from the values of a consumer society. Teresa's obsession with food, however, and the many descriptions of meals bought with stolen money, "soldi spesi bene" (215), are generic traits which betray that she is not totally indifferent to improving her material existence. If Teresa does not marry and settle down like many of her female cohorts in crime and in tradition, she is most happy when she finds a "good job," such as the one passing on stolen American travelers' checks. The hours and money are good, the work load light; most important, she feels a sense of fulfillment since the job allows her to display her native intelligence and her acquired shrewdness:

I got a good job The work load is light I enjoy myself without working too hard. But you need some brains here, you bet you need to be intelligent schrewd, a fast talker and know when it's time to clear out. (213)[21]

Such burlesquing of society's values reveals a spirit of cooperation that is as hypocritical as the society the narrative criticizes so well. Thus the form defines both possibilities and limits. Although Teresa may appear freer than Guiducci's narrators to refuse involuntary involvement with the traditional feminine role, her success, however much it reflects the economic changes in postwar Italian society, depends on her limited ability to manipulate the patriarchal institution. Cooperation with the picaresque form does not, however, invite self-deprecation: in contrast to Guiducci's insecure and more pathetic narrators, the picaresque form allows for the depiction of an unrepentant female who can unmask society's hypocrisy without embarrassment, but only because she is society's model student.

Although Guiducci's narrators expose strategies of oppression in society, their cooperation with generic restraints, especially the need to prove innocence, prevents them from challenging stereotypical images and assuming responsibility for their lives. Likewise, because her identity is constructed according to the rules of the picaresque, Teresa typically blames others or the force of destiny for her actions, thus begging the question of whether she experiences true autonomy or any sense of personal responsibility. The inability of these literary forms to deal with the questions that were becoming important in Italian feminist theory could explain why the picaresque is avoided by their feminist writers in general, although some picaresque texts are now reappearing. Dacia Maraini presents the autobiography of self-assured prostitute Carla Corsi, in *Ritratto a tinte forti* (1991), as another picaresque-type narrative that needs to be part of feminism's self-reevaluation.[22] Nonetheless, though feminism empowers Corsi to write, she does so to voice her opposition to all those (feminists included) who oppose and downgrade what she believes in, the social value of the institution of prostitution.

*   *   *

In *Donna in guerra* (1975), Maraini confronts the theme of accepting
responsibility for one's life in her depiction of the transformation of a
withdrawn, dependent female who hides behind her traditional subservient wife role into a woman ready to accept the risks involved in
taking charge of one's self.[23] Narrator-protagonist Vannina is a meek
and mild elementary schoolteacher of Sicilian origin married to a
Neapolitan mechanic named Giacinto, who, despite many good characteristics, is hopelessly paternalistic. Giacinto's paternalism is not consciously malicious but instinctive and natural, or so he believes. He
blatantly disregards his wife's intellectual and sexual needs, relying on
her to cook, wash, clean, and accompany him to the cafe for an evening
ice cream, in short, to represent the feminine which he defines as a
natural, biological state: "*By nature*, you are good-hearted, calm, affec-
tionate, patient, submissive" ("Tu, *di natura*, sei buona, calma, affet-
tuosa, paziente, remissiva," 145, emphasis added). Therefore, any action by Vannina that contradicts this restrictive definition of the female
is wrong because it is "against nature" (141). Patriarchal theories of
gender difference rooted in ontology or biology govern the behavior
and self-image of the women as well as the men. Vannina complies with
Giacinto's requests because she believes in his superiority. When Suna,
one of the catalyst figures in Vannina's transformation, tries to point
out the obvious self-serving nature of Giacinto's attitudes on sex and
his behavior toward her, Vannina thinks to herself:

I didn't know how to respond. I take what Giacinto says and make it my own. I
never even think of contradicting him. I think he is better than me, that he's
right, that what he says is good enough for both of us. (91)[24]

For the most part, however, the narrative does not dwell on Vannina's
internal thoughts but focuses on her social and political encounters.
Vannina participates in political meetings and witnesses political terrorism exercised by her new acquaintances, who kidnap a corrupt prison
warden and force a confession from him at gunpoint. Along with Suna,
she interviews exploited poor and uneducated women in Naples involved in *lavoro nero*, piecework done at home for meager wages.
Throughout these and many other adventures, Vannina's narrative
stance remains descriptive and objective. Augustus Pallotta emphasizes
this objectivity when he argues that the text is not a novel, or "the psychological treatment of individual rapport with reality," but a "utilitar-
ian didactic approach . . . capable of demonstrating lucidly the intellectual tenets of feminism and the social problems affecting women."[25]

If the representation of socio-political problems takes precedence over that of psychological development, the narrative is still not a documentary but a fictional representation of political, psychological, and feminist theories that both unmask and comply with the romance genre. From the beginning of the romance tradition in Greek and Roman literature, through its many displacements until the present time, the actions of romance's stereotypical characters have been justified with philosophical, psychological, and even proverbial theories or truisms. The characters, who could be extremely realistic and even radical at times due to the inclusion of many topical theories and attitudes, had no need to learn and develop. Ruled by chance, fortune, or God, and immersed in adventures which took place in hostile environments peopled with individuals motivated by self-interest or uncontrollable passions, romance characters needed only to survive their adventures and reach a certain tranquility. Human dependency on higher powers for survival was implied by the unchanging nature of the characters and the interpolated narratives or digressions which, as they still do in *Donna in guerra*, demonstrate the difficulties encountered by those seeking independence, and the general chaos resulting from individual searches for self-satisfaction.[26]

The modern romance, as Kenneth Bruffee tells us, instead of preaching human beings' dependency upon the higher powers, explores the difficulties encountered in freeing oneself from long-standing social structures, traditional human relationships, and the dependent mentalities they foster and maintain.[27] Describing the male elegiac romance in this century, Bruffee lists several characteristics of the genre which also apply to *Donna in guerra*. In elegiac romance, the traditionally passive protagonist confronts his or her own complexly rooted resistance to change in a cultural, social, and political milieu undergoing profound and irresistible transformations. Due to its adventure plot, romance does not try to render mental processes directly, as is the case in some modern novels and the *Bildungsroman*; rather, it creates a thematic relationship between the outside world, the hostile social environment, and the narrator's quest. The quest is most often unknown at the beginning, and the recalcitrant narrator learns late that he or she must create something new: a self that is responsive to new needs and that can survive without heroes and nostalgic illusions (59–72).

Donna in guerra reverses the archetypal romance quest of adventures and separations that lead to the marriage of two essentially passive protagonists. Instead, a married woman, after a series of adventures and a brief separation from her husband, decides to divorce and, in her own words, start all over again. The symbolic nature of the adventures is announced clearly by the abrupt arrival of Vannina's menstrual period, "a trickle of beneficent blood" ("un rivolo di sangue benefico"), which arrives on the first day of the couple's vacation in a poor southern fishing village; here the liveliest moment is in the early evening when the bored wives of rich German *industriali* leave their villas and come to the piazza to find bed partners among the willing, adaptable village youth. This obvious symbol, however, as well as others in the narrative, is isolated by the mundane events that immediately follow. Giacinto leaves early every morning to fish, and Vannina fills the day by shopping, cleaning, washing, and ironing—banal activities she describes in the same matter-of-fact, nonjudgmental way that she narrates the story. This banality is underlined in Vannina's oft-repeated mock chant of the archetypal housewife—"I washed the dishes, scoured the saucepans, rinsed the glasses" ("Ho lavato i piatti, ho sgrassato le pentole. Ho sciacquato i bicchieri")—which first appears on page 4 and is varied only slightly during the narrative. Often this litany is repeated in place of a reaction or judgment from Vannina to some controversy she is reporting, thus making any progressive change in her more difficult to gauge.

Initially, Vannina's only unusual excursions are trips to the laundry of Toto and Giottina, two strong, lively Sicilian types who, in mock allegorical fashion, tell of magical transformations and wild sexual acts which supposedly take place in the villas of the rich at night:

—At the Villa Trionfo lovemaking has turned into whoring—Whoring has turned into sperm—Sperm turns into poison—The maid becomes the mistress—She carries golden coins sewed into her dress—And walks like the devil, on tiptoe—Did you see them when they came down for a stroll?—The mistress in front like a queen, her husband three steps behind, and the maid last with her tinkling bangles—She wore bangles round her ankles like a Muslim slave—A slave who eats up her masters. (12–13)[28]

Yet none of these women, who chant in witchlike fashion, eat pastries, iron, and recount these "unsettling imaginative games" ("inquietanti giochi dell'immaginazione," 14) to a passive and slightly nauseated Vannina, preach revolt. Instead, they offer consolation and relieve boredom in this private and isolated feminine world.[29]

Typically, Vannina is not anxious to effect change and is suspicious of those who advocate it. Therefore, her passiveness, more than her "reasoning and reflection" as Pallotta suggests, makes her a less stereotypical and a stronger character. She copes with the noisy Neapolitan family upstairs, who throw their garbage on her or in her courtyard, by following Giacinto's advice to grin and bear it: "It's better just to ignore those people; if you react it just makes things worse" (60).[30] To complicate matters further, this philosophy seems justified by narrative events. A brief outburst of rage results in a door being slammed in her face, and when she is convinced by Suna to file a complaint, the family successfully accuses her of attacking the grandmother in public. Likewise, among Vannina's acquaintances, those who revolt end up causing more trouble for themselves. Furthermore, since most of the characters' actions are motivated by known philosophical, psychological, and political theories, their actions become more predictable and they themselves become more stereotypical as the narrative progresses. Even Suna, a beautiful and relatively well-off paralytic, through whom and with whom Vannina participates in the adventures and who preaches female emancipation, independence, and sexual liberation, falls into the easily recognizable trap of using sexual promiscuity to compensate for her handicap. Despite her fervent rhetoric against male domination, she develops a traditional dependence on her fickle lover, Santino. She dies from a fall brought on by her depression when Santino is arrested and she loses him as a lover.

Suna's final characterization as the pathetic abandoned woman has disturbed critics hoping to find in her a new feminist and/or female figure.[31] Romance weaves its story around stereotypes, however, and Suna is not the only character who reverts to traditional patterns. Vittorio, the Leftist terrorist, despite his radical political views still perceives women as objects who in revolution should remain as subservient as before. His marriage to a submissive and rich Swiss virgin is a critically parodic, but typical and predictable ending for such a macho-terrorist type. Vannina herself, in a rare moment of introspection, defines her love for Giacinto as a need to depend on a strong male figure although she recognizes his faults. When Giacinto tells her he knows her love for him derives from her dependency on him, she thinks:

It's true. When he talks like this he is like an old man who has consciously renounced all desire for possessions. But there is a terrible strength in those blond arms of his and with that strength he keeps our marriage together. I'm in love with those arms. (145)[32]

Such commonplaces that have always served in romance to enhance the verisimilitude of the characters' emotions and actions here emphasize the difficulty of freeing oneself from the archaic patterns of behavior and meaning which continue to inform judgments and perceptions.

Suna has a significant function in this romance. True to romance form, the narrative ends on an epiphanic note: Suna appears in a dream to Vannina to offer her crutches to the now-crippled Vannina who, after attempting to fly, crashed to earth and lost both legs. Bruffee writes that in the male elegiac romance the narrator's liberation is often announced when he ceases his admiration for another deceased male (15, 27–28). Patricia Merivale points out that in the female variant the bond between the narrator and the person she reports on is only of faint interest since female solidarity, in contrast to its male counterpart, is slowly and unexpectedly revealed.[33] These recognition scenes, receiving impetus from theories that focus on relationships among women, will continue to be prominent in women's romances in the 1980s. Vannina's relationship to Suna is indeed cool at the beginning, and Suna is never a role-model for her.[34] Her crutches, however, give Vannina the strength to decide to abort Giacinto's baby, which resulted from a surprise sexual attack, and to strike out on her own.

In contrast to the confession and the picaresque forms in which cooperation with generic constraints isolates the narrators, *Donna in guerra* ends with a call for solidarity in the fight against one's limits. As is also typical of romance, the call for commitment to change includes no specific advice on how to implement such transformations. Romance characters receive no magic wand; if Suna's crutches appear to be a dubious aid, it is partly because in modern romance all who depend on archaic myths, theories, philosophies, and truisms, which reappear in displaced and disguised forms, are crippled in some way. To begin again, Vannina must abandon her passive nature and become involved, despite her vulnerability to those fundamental structures of meaning that shape her understanding.

With literary conventions as crutches and guides, Guiducci and Maraini revealed similarities in strategies of oppression and unmasked the illusion that political fact could be separated from private life.[35] With these works, literary feminism began the difficult task of displacing the literature of the past according to the perceptions of women as a historical group, a movement described by Monique Wittig as unavoidable if women writers are ever to move on to revised representations and new terminologies.[36]

Romancing the (M)Other

The strict relationship between the personal and the political implied at times by the gender/genre relationship in the foregoing narratives appeared too mechanical for feminist critics in the 1980s who argued for a different rapport between the personal and the political.[37] Italian feminist critics and writers, proceeding under the banner of "difference within" and inalienable gender bonds, focused their attention on repositioning and reinterpreting prominent female figures in history, a shift reflected in the course offerings of the Centro Culturale Virginia

Woolf.[38] Thus in Rossana Ombres's *Serenata* (*The Call*, 1980), the renunciation of women's oppressed past after a series of romance adventures takes on a more allegorical tone. Ombres, whose poetry collection
(*Ipotesi di Agar*, 1968) had received much acclaim, published her first
novel, *Principessa Giacinta*, in the mainstream press Rizzoli in 1970.
This novel, like Alice Ceresa's *La figlia prodiga* (1967) and Silvia Castelli's *Pitonessa* (1978), although feminist in nature, is consistent with
the type of experimental writing fashionable at the time. The female
protagonist, enclosed in a room to escape corruption and pollution,
only communicates by telephone to the newspaper for which she
works. As the plot progresses, however, a possible love and abandonment plot is implied to explain the neurotic actions and prose of the
protagonist, who identifies periodically with Martin Luther's wife,
Catherine, while waiting for a manuscript that may have been lost or
stolen in conjunction with a previous matrimony. *Serenata* is a more
straightforward, chronological refusal of the traditional love story.
Sara, a consultant for a publishing house, is sent on a trip to southern
Italy to interview an author who claims to have finished another masterpiece. The manuscript, announced by the author's mother, is a
hoax. During her stay, however, Sara meets a man and is struck by the
conventional *coup de foudre* in a scene she compares with the angel's
Visitation of the Virgin Mary. Several chapters later, Sara returns north
and rejects the call (*la serenata*) in realistic parodic style when she
refuses to accept Giacinto's phone call.

Despite their many differences, *Serenata* and *Donna in guerra* are
replete with stereotypical images of women as goddesses, virgins,
witches, and whores who represent the rich yet contradictory feminine
past women writers could draw from. As Lucia Birnbaum points out,
Italian feminists, taking male perceptions into account, viewed their
past as a mixed legacy.[39] In the works that women writers produced,
descriptions of ancient goddesses, like Sekmeth in a short story by
Dacia Maraini, or the many fictional representations or analyses of the
Demeter-Kore myth, depicted these female figures as symbols of destruction, infertility, and revenge and not only dignity, wholeness, and
autonomy.[40]

Maternal power and influence are the subject of two recent theoretical works: Adriana Cavarero's long essay on Demeter in *Nonostante
Platone* and Silvia Vegetti-Finzi's latest book, *Il bambino della notte*.[41] Cavarero reviews the Demeter myth as an allegory of the appropriation of
woman's sexuality and her right to choose to procreate or not. In *Il bambino della notte*, Vegetti-Finzi treats this appropriation through the case
history of a young child, Anna, whose neurosis is caused by her refusal
to accept a socially imposed stereotypical feminine identity. Despite

their different frameworks and emphases, both works seek a definition of women's creativity that is not based in biology and production. Vegetti-Finzi defines her political goals in terms akin to those of Cavarero: she wants to investigate how women can channel their natural (and originally genderless) feelings of liberty, spontaneity, and autonomy into a more positive, productive ethical model and, at the same time, find a way to transmit that model to subsequent female generations.

Vegetti-Finzi's conclusion even more closely resembles Nadia Fusini's detailed reading of the confessions of the powerfully tragic woman figure in antiquity, Phaedra, in *La luminosa: Genealogia di Fedra*.[42] Both authors reject the autonomous, all-powerful mother myth. Vegetti-Finzi locates the conception of this myth in the egocentric and egotistical human unconscious ready to believe in its omnipotence and to act regardless of the results of its actions. In *Il bambino della notte*, Vegetti-Finzi views the resistance of her eight-year-old client Anna to her socially defined femininity as part of the child's desire to achieve maturity defined as completeness. Thus the maternal images the overly dependent Anna draws for Vegetti-Finzi already resist the social institution of maternity and can never be pure manifestations of any preexisting maternal power that needs to be rediscovered.

In *La luminosa*, Fusini uses the Phaedra myth to outline another paradigm of reclaiming and/or refusing the mother, which also defines the proper place of women's sorrows as one inevitably linked with the mother and silence. If men openly lament their earthly fate, women's sorrows are always linked to some silent, prehistoric maternal source that she needs to possess and deny in order to recover the wholeness Eros had broken apart. The return to the maternal is problematic initially because Phaedra, daughter of Pasiphaë and a bull, inherits guilt and sexuality through the maternal line (68). In addition, Pasiphaë herself was never autonomous because her sexual act was decreed by a higher power who turned her into a metaphor for female receptivity. Both son and daughter want to possess "the maternal thing" ("la cosa materna") that represents permanent desire and completeness through the recovery of one's origin: "The person born is the realization of the desire of the mother, being born one wants only the mother, to repossess her in order to possess one's beginning and desire, that is one's own origin."[43]

Phaedra's attempt to repossess her origins while fleeing guilt leads her back to what Fusini calls the "irreparable internal duality of feminine nature," represented by Phaedra and Hippolytus, themselves permutations of the splitting of the Goddess Mother into Aphrodite and Artemide (150). These contradictions are disclosed progressively to Phaedra through a series of revealed similarities to the mother.

Phaedra then oscillates between fleeing from the mother or offering her the renunciation of her own desire in sacrifice, a renunciation Fusini describes as a perversion of any true love for the mother. Nonetheless, Phaedra follows the latter course in Euripides' play and the contradictions are ultimately resolved in death and silence.

Traditionally in romance Eros is the main motivator of the characters. If Eros separates the characters and causes many adventures, it also brings them together at the end with the promise of everlasting happiness and completeness. Female romances in the 1980s tell tales of women's adventures with love personified in a series of female mediators: the mother (Sanvitale), the female lover (Schiavo), or the femme fatale (Frabotta). Although feminist theories of identification with other women are present, female mediators are as contradictory and incomplete as all romance mentors who sometimes aid, sometimes harm those they are supposed to protect. In the confession, the generic need to prove innocence forced the narrator to cooperate with fallacious myths. In these romances, however, the difficulties encountered in cooperating with the mediator indicate the possibilities and dangers involved in returning to the mythical "cosa materna."

Several years ago René Girard distinguished between novelistic and romance literary inspiration on the basis of mediation: whereas in the novel the mediator of desire is openly defined, in romance he or she is hidden and only intermittently revealed.[44] Mediators are hidden because the characters, who believe they have freely chosen the model they imitate, deny the spontaneous nature of desire by placing it in an object. The all-powerful nature of romance's Eros is ideal for such self-deception. In Francesca Sanvitale's *Madre e figlia*, the narrator as daughter announces her desire as one of making her mother *luminosa*, that is, whole and able to speak.[45] In Fusini's work, the title *Luminosa* again refers to Phaedra's ill-fated project to speak together with the mother clearly and unambiguously about her origins and desires.

*   *   *

In *Madre e figlia*, the mother, Marianna, does speak in direct dialogues and dream sequences but never clearly or without contradiction. The daughter's attempt to reclaim her mother and thus her own origins, like Phaedra's, establishes a trajectory of the desired and feared fusion with the mother. Images of fusion and confusion abound in the narrative. At one point the narrator—who speaks in the name of Sonia, the mother Marianna, and the author's alter ego—looks into the mirror and can no longer differentiate herself from Sonia or the mother (86). The lack of distance between mediator and the subject, writes

Girard, produces a destructive rivalry as the subject more aggressively affirms her desire or right to possession and becomes less capable than ever of renouncing the inaccessible object of desire (13), which is precisely what happens in Sanvitale's romance.

Another function of these fusions is to reveal the myths of purity, redemption, and wholeness that motivate Sonia's romancing of the mother. Like Phaedra, both mother and daughter try to reclaim their origins by expiating the sins that mark their own contradictory heritage. In the beginning account of the mother's origins, Marianna recapitulates her mother's tragic involvement with a man called Fritz, the only man she ever loved. Fritz was involved with a married woman before his engagement to Marianna's mother. When he announced the engagement to his married lover, the woman committed suicide and Fritz called off his marriage out of guilt. Determined to vindicate her mother's frustration, Marianna runs away with a handsome, married soldier, although this compensatory act fails and dooms her to a life of misery, poverty, and loneliness. Marianna becomes pregnant, and with the birth of the illegitimate Sonia, her love adventures come to a halt. Her remaining travels are now motivated by the need to hide her daughter from the soldier's hysterical wife who wants to kill Sonia. It is later revealed, however, that this revenge story was invented by the Colonel to keep Marianna away so that he could raise the son of another woman for whom he had abandoned his wife.

The Colonel's romanesque orchestration is only one of the many fictitious plots that structure the lives and transformations of these women while keeping them in stereotypical molds. The narrative is divided into four parts although digressions, lamentations, and predictions typical of romance's circular structure hinder the obvious forward chronological movement of the plot describing two women aging in time. Sonia's development is not represented through change in behavior but rather as a series of fated metamorphoses. Part 1 and Sonia's childhood come to an end when she is "transformed into the heroine of a novel" (56). In a religious school play, Sonia plays the "heroic" role of an unmarried woman who offers to be executed in the place of another woman sentenced to death. This exchange is motivated by the fact that the sentenced female has children to raise, whereas Sonia's childless personage is essentially superfluous. Thus Sonia's first transformation in a literary plot that mirrors life prepares her to accept her fate to sacrifice herself to redeem her mother.

Sonia's religious education teaches her the same message of helplessness and acceptance of destiny that the romance recounts even in antiquity due to its system of external causality. Romance characters are usually virtuous, as their actions show. Although their goodness and purity may appease the higher powers who eventually reward them, these characteristics derive from the higher powers themselves. Modern Catholicism reinforces this paradigm: Sonia is a model child but "all she knew was that she needed to be aware that (this goodness) came from God and not from her" ("Tutto ciò che sapeva era, doveva tenere presente che [questa bravura] veniva dal cielo e non da lei," 56).

Part 2 and Sonia's adolescence end with the revolt against her father. Sonia believes herself free enough to eclipse the father and reclaim the mother in whose name she executes the sacrifice of her own desire by entering into a loveless marriage so that she can financially support her mother. On a realistic level, however, her new "father" role brings with it a partially critical distance from her mother. She now sees how much of the squalor of their tormented lives was less determined by fatality than by her mother, who locked herself into the role of the helpless, abandoned woman. Even when relatively well-off, her mother over-spends and is incapable of asserting any independence. Recognition of her mother's faults still produces no change in Sonia's behavior, which continues to be patterned on myths that will enable her to purify and redeem her mother. Significantly, the narrator describes Sonia's assumption of financial responsibility for her mother not as a sign of her developing autonomy but rather as one that Sonia has moved from imitating literary plots to more powerful and covert mythical ones (116). Thus, in the third section, the tripartite narrator seeks to explain the motivations for Sonia's behavior by reconstructing "disconnected analogies, sentiments that are unknown to her and constantly changing" (158). Sonia, now over forty, undergoes an abortion because the child she insisted on having against her husband's will has been diagnosed with Down's syndrome. Sonia's decision to revolt against her husband's authority by becoming pregnant is, again, not a result of a conscious affirmation of self but rather, the narrator explains, it was based on yet another confused interpretation of redemption myths. Sonia wanted abstract salvation for her (first) child, and since salvation comes from creating new life ("Per lui Sonia desiderava astratta salvezza e la salvezza veniva dal procreare altra vita"), Sonia became pregnant to fulfill her ritualistic role (158).

Since Sonia is unaware of the models she is imitating, these images reveal themselves without enabling her to learn from them. Paola Blelloch suggests that the final depiction of the mother as a "venerable old queen" who comes to the narrator in a dream, "reintegrates the elderly Marianna in her rightful position and transforms her into a queen returning to an ancient palace."[46] In this image, however, the mediated model Sonia has been striving for is fully revealed and with it the negative results of the quest to repossess *la cosa materna* (the maternal thing). According to Girard, in romance, the placement of the mediated image as an idealized spirit provides the distance necessary for the subject to develop on his own. If this is true for male romances (and seems possible in Maraini's romance since Vannina never totally identifies with Suna), in *Madre e figlia*, the return of this symbol functions to predict that the romance plot, which in theory could repeat itself forever, will probably do so in this case. Sanvitale herself has argued against interpretations of the final vision as one that represents either Sonia's liberation or her ability to rid herself of the *bagaglio gravoso* (oppressive baggage) she has taken on herself as a result of the experience.[47] Because Sonia never recognizes the impossibility of her quest, she can only continue to pursue the impossible fusion through more predetermined metamorphoses that deny difference between the two women. These endless permutations into sameness, emphasizes Sanvitale, impede women's entry into real history. *Madre e figlia* is sometimes called a novel of manners because it includes constant references to the main historical events of the century. But these events, while providing some believable motivations for another flight or the reappearance of a long-lost relative, make no real imprint on the lives of these women who are in search of wholeness.

*   *   *

Madre e figlia includes many stylized, framed panoramas, frescos, or photos that serve, in Blelloch's terms, as "starting points for a reconstruction of the past and a premonition of future occurrences."[48] This rhetorical convention, known as *ecphrasis*, has long been part of romance where, besides its entertaining and informative function, it primarily reinforces the idea of underlying permanence despite superficial variations. In *Madre e figlia*, ecphrasis functions to foreground those dangerous repetitive situations that impede the development of a critical distance on the part of Sonia or Marianna. Representational forms have the same function in Maria Schiavo's *Discorso eretico alla fatalità*, the story of a failed lesbian relationship between an aging actress and a sensitive narrator cast in the form of a tragic romance. All the characters in the narrative act out stereotypical roles and hide behind traditional texts to explain or excuse their actions. Here, however, the critical and liberating function of form is brought out in the narrator's contemplations on the technique of *chiaroscuro* in a Caravaggio painting. Form (*la tecnica*) allows one to isolate a certain point, to bring light to a certain aspect of a subject. However, the contrasting darkness that surrounds the illuminated point reminds the narrator of the impossibility of total explanations (55–56).

The totalizing discourse under examination is here again determined by a mysterious omnipotent feminine presence who, in this text, is overtly designated as the fatal Eros of romance. The fact that Eros is female does not help the narrator, who directly addresses and accuses "Fatalità" of trying to make of her another paradigmatic form of failure. The narrator describes her story as an exploration of the archaic models of love behind which "Fatalità" hides the quest for the impossible and thus turns every love affair into a parodic repetition of the love for the mother (14–15, 25) At the end of the story, the narrator claims to realize that her responsibility for the failed love affair, which had indeed followed recognizable and absurdly repetitive patterns, is attributable not only to the inability of the actress to accept openly her homosexual tendencies demonstrated by her insistence on playing false and superficial roles. In addition, she and the lady were seeking the illusory spoils of romance's fated quest, that is, to protect themselves through love from the defeats life brings. The narrator's desire to restore wholeness in herself by possessing and thus rehabilitating the lady, who had become a semi-recluse, caused her own complicity in the repetitious plot she had just recounted:

I realized perfectly well that it was a contradiction in terms to speak of *one* experience as if it would always be the same experience. However, that was how I had experienced it; as if multiplicity were the deceptive wrapping of the collapse of unity. . . . I could not stand variation and in multiplicity I saw only the image of *one*. (190–191)[49]

Romance characters develop in accordance with the type they represent. In *Discorso eretico*, all characters bear only generalizing names which indicate how they will react. The narrator designates herself as "il Poeta": her lover, who is first presented as "La gran Dama Decaduta," later becomes "La Dama Triste" and, at times, simply "l'attrice." The narrative is divided into two main parts. The first section deals with the attraction of the narrator to the sensitive, artistic nature of the former actress who now leads a very secluded life. The actress's best friend, the "Guardian Angel" ("l'angelo custode"), functions, as could be expected, to protect the lady from admitting her lesbian tendencies to herself and to others. The narrator also pursues an image the "Dama" is mediating for her, however, the ideal of love as a perfect fusion and comprehension between two adults, that "improvvisamente identico" capable of providing her with joy (85). The relationship loses all promise when the young poet reads aloud some mocking verse to the hypocritical Guardian Angel and, in so doing, makes her intentions for the actress clear. The embarrassed actress spurns her and, in part 2, the dejected narrator undertakes a series of trips back to maternal sources for an explanation. However, her search for the *madre omnipotente*, which takes her to the island of Mozia and her mother's grave, reveals nothing. (In *Madre e figlia*, Sonia had also taken her son to this supposed ancient matriarchal site to look for some explanation of her destiny.) A second trip to Greece ends in a revelation, but it arises from a realistic, chance event rather than the mythical, fated ones the narrator had been attempting to recreate. Aggravated at witnessing the refusal of a tourist to give up his seat on a bus to a tired and dirty gypsy woman, the narrator offers the woman her seat. In a gesture of female solidarity, she then rejects the place the same man gallantly offers her. The narrator claims that this appearance of the omnipotent mother in the figure of a poor gypsy woman enables her to recognize her own misguided beliefs.

This unexpectedly revealed similarity, reminiscent of Suna's empowering appearance to Vannina in *Donna in guerra*, enables the narrator to act in a specific situation. Both before and after this epiphanic moment, however, similarities function, as in all the female romances, to call attention to repetitive, stereotypical behavioral patterns. After the narrator's "liberating" experience in Greece, the actress visits her once again in her home and the narrator-poet finds herself again playing the same false roles that reveal more similarities than differences between her and the "gran Dama" she had so criticized. The narrator ends, however, by expressing gratitude to the woman she claims had "mediated" the recognition of her own inequities and difference. The narrator-poet's praise of the lady assigns a more positive role on a thematic level to the practice of female bonding. Still, on the structural plane, the story recounts an impossible and failed identification based on the reappearance of the same myths and structures of mediation found in *Madre e figlia*. Moreover, Schiavo questions her own findings by recalling, at the end of the story, the standard romance topos of the insuperable power of love. Although the poet claims the revelation of the Mother Goddess figure in the gypsy cured her of her search for maternal completeness in the "Dama," she finishes her address to the omnipotent love figure with the acknowledgment that this lesson will last "at least until the next time you strike" ("Almeno fino al tuo prossimo colpo," 193). Philosophical revelations of difference do not translate into action and achieve the immediate, albeit limited, results that certain unexpectedly revealed similarities do. Both experiences, however, as the narrator states, structure the story of the confrontation with the powerful goddess myth that the narrator-poet has just told (193).

*   *   *

Schiavo's style in *Discorso eretico*, like that of Sanvitale, oscillates between mythical poetic tones and realistic scenes and dialogues that mirror the disconnection between illusion and reality depicted therein. Biancamaria Frabotta's *Velocità di fuga* also moves among these two contrasting stylistic registers. Alberto Moravia describes the text as a biography of a violent and egotistical generation; indeed the frank treatment of themes of sex and violence have motivated some to describe the work as "moraviana."[50] Walter Pedullà, however, discounts descriptions of the work as solely a feminist or postfeminist critical documentary. According to Pedullà, Frabotta's consistent use of literary language and themes combine to narrate a general story of a naive and generous adolescence from which the participants (including Frabotta) now need to distance themselves to establish their moral and intellectual maturity.[51] For Rossana Rossanda, the achieved maturity represents a specifically female initiation that can proceed only by constant negation of the Other.[52] Maria Luisa Boccia agrees that this work portrays an initiation into a distinctly female, solitary identity.[53] Frabotta's narrator cannot identify with men, but has not yet learned a way to enjoy her similarities with other women. Therefore, the narrator's discovery of her *unicità* reveals that female "difference" is synonymous with the solitude that all women experience (24–25). Boccia is disappointed that this solitude prevents Frabotta from depicting a regenerative and positive female figure.

Indeed, *Velocità di fuga* includes all of the foregoing themes and characteristics. Yet it is also a romance structured around a search for identity and wholeness through the reclaiming of an archetypal female figure, here named Dirce.[54] The young, naive, narrating "I" desires to liberate herself from any traditional female image and has ambitions to be a writer. She has the typical, possessive mother who tries in vain to discourage these ambitions as well as her daughter's involvement with Eugenio, a radical student and aspiring writer. Eugenio is the narrator's recognized *maestro di vita e di stile*. He is inextricably linked to his male mediator, Beniamino, a forty-year-old, divorced political science instructor who imbues Eugenio and his other loyal student, a drug addict, with Marcusian theories on society and the family. As intellectuals, all of the characters believe in the power of ideas to assure some control over events and protection for themselves. Eugenio argues that he is the strategy behind Beniamino's thoughts and can thus use the professor as he pleases to fulfill his own goals. The narrator espouses most contemporary feminist theories such as the one that informs her first quest: to lose her virginity before marriage in an act of revolt against bourgeois society and its regulation of female sexuality. In *Velocità di fuga* as in any romance, however, ideas still primarily function to depict the characters in general terms, since the outcomes of their quests are usually determined by factors that show them to be less in control than they would like to believe.

Although Eugenio is the narrator's master in real life, to accomplish her second goal, that of becoming a writer, the narrator communicates every evening with female writers and literary personages such as Katherine Mansfield, Djuna Barnes, Virginia Woolf, Karen Blixen, Simone de Beauvoir, and the Princesse de Clèves. These nocturnal missives are imitative *esercizi di stile* in and through which the narrator progressively differentiates herself from each one of her narratees. These theoretical initiatory passages that are repeated every evening are as inconclusive as the narrator's more mundane quest to lose her virginity. Eugenio, who persists in demanding that she play for him the role of consecrated purity, refuses to consummate their relationship. However, Eugenio's ideological reticence causes the narrator to formulate her third and final quest: she will find out the identity and significance of the mysterious female Dirce, whose name both embarrasses and provokes Eugenio. In *Velocità di fuga*, the narrator pursues the female romance adventure plot as a result of a contradiction that has characterized romance from the beginning of the tradition: the inability of the characters to put their own ideas into action, especially when these ideas contradict their fated destiny.

Frabotta herself describes the figure of Dirce as the "eternal feminine" that feminism of the seventies failed to explicate and replace.[55] The search for Dirce results in the uncovering of several versions of the search for the *cosa materna*. The poet-narrator turned detective first uncovers Beniamino's estranged wife, Olga, a feminist artist figure whose frustration over the irrelevancy of her husband's ideas caused her to burn his books. She is now a proponent of feminist ontologies that stress the body as the primary locus of creativity and knowledge. Olga leads the narrator to Dirce, whom she first sees at a feminist manifestation in Rome. The mysterious femme fatale, dressed pathetically in clashing clothes and colors, is urinating behind the pines of the Porta Pinciana. Olga proudly points out that the stream that arrived at the street and hit a passing cyclist is proof of Dirce's magical powers to "pisciare più lontano di tutti" (139), although another passerby immediately contradicts Olga's declaration that Dirce is the source of the stream. Dirce herself seems unaware or uninterested in Olga's maternal preoccupations with her and she frustrates the narrator's attempt to define her by refusing to answer any questions.

Dirce has no need to define herself, however. The narrator's search uncovers three different yet not totally contradictory stories on her identity, all of which derive from the image of the female as regenerate sexuality or from the female desire to reclaim one's origins by reclaiming the feminine for oneself, here displaced to very basic levels. Beniamino's story, revealed shortly before he ingloriously takes away the narrator's virginity in the shelter of a Roman doorway, is that he found the mysterious, uneducated vagabond on vacation in Ginostra. After Beniamino generously shared her with Eugenio, Dirce became pregnant and Eugenio forced him to bring her back to Rome where Olga could arrange an abortion. Olga, however, is interested as well in establishing herself as the creator and discoverer of Dirce who, she says, is a fugitive from the police. According to Olga, both males abused her sexually, although it was Beniamino who insisted on the abortion since he could not tolerate the possibility that Eugenio may have fathered the child. The final version is given to the narrator by Amanda, the down-to-earth wife of a fellow student, who had initiated the narrator's search by informing her of Olga's whereabouts. Amanda announces proudly that she is the sole discoverer of Dirce, a somewhat mentally deficient waif with a nice body. Amanda had tried to help by getting her a job modeling undergarments. When Dirce failed, Olga and Beniamino used her in their orgies until Dirce got pregnant and Olga left Beniamino.

Amanda concludes the third and most prosaic claiming of origins for Dirce by reprimanding the narrator for her dreamy nature and total lack of common sense. To these qualities Amanda ascribes the inability of the narrator and Eugenio to get rid of the narrator's now lost virginity.[56] As a result of her adventures, the narrator claims to understand more fully how her role as seductress and muse helped to perpetrate Eugenio's treatment of her; however, like Schiavo's poet, she admits that she is still humanly, or more precisely femininely, fallible due to the reappearance of the same recurring myths and structures. In her final letter to Eugenio, she accuses him of the same inability to function without crippling myths (202). When speaking to Amanda, the aspiring writer, like Schiavo's narrator, defends the irreality of ideas and myths since they are what inspire and structure writing.

Paola Redaelli suggests that *Velocità di fuga* be read as a modern parable of how women gain access to writing by speaking to the impossible at night and to real readers during the day.[57] All the romances discussed in this chapter, despite their differences, utilize romance's characteristic underlying disjunction between the characters' ideas and their actions to analyze their resistance to change, however mediated. The romance convention of hidden mediators forces the protagonists to deal with questions of how to contend with differences among women, although none of the texts presents a coherent attack or defense of Italian theories on sexual difference or *affidamento*. Difference cannot be avoided because each text represents the problems women have in dealing with each other as well as in overthrowing traditional feminine roles.

Romance's generically determined disjunction also mandates a separation in each text between the realms of literature and life, the former being a place for unrealizable ideas, the latter a place in which specific, limited actions occur through unexpectedly revealed similarities. This is not a reiteration on the part of these women writers of their traditional antagonistic relationship to writing. If the search for original wholeness tends to bring characters out of history and real life, as is the case to varying degrees for all of the characters in the narratives discussed here, it also leads these writers to exploit the literary myths and structures necessary to write their stories. In her review of *Il bambino della notte*, Lidia Campanaro writes that the attempt to define woman as other than the statue or the vase is, paradoxically, both the beginning of her adventures in society and the beginning of her problems.[58] In the final chapter, Lidia Ravera and Sandra Petrignani will be presented exploiting romance structures to examine the images of women that feminism has produced. In the works discussed in this chapter, though, the romance form, whether interpreted in realistic, allegorical, or ironic modes, provides the means through which several different Italian women writers have begun to define those specific adventures that determine their difference.

Notes

1. Anna Nozzoli, *Tabù e coscienza* (Florence: La Nuova Italia, 1978), 147–170. For a good discussion of Italian cultural or neofeminism, see Lucia Birnbaum, *La liberazione della donna: Feminism in Italy* (Middletown, CT: Wesleyan University Press, 1986), 79–103. Another more personal but very informative account of Italian neofeminism can be found in Susan Bassnett's *Feminist Experiences: The Women's Movement in Four Cultures* (London: Allen and Unwin, 1986), chap. 3.

2. Nozzoli, *Tabù e coscienza*, 167–169. Nozzoli explains that many feminist writers, especially Armanda Guiducci and Dacia Maraini, purposely used vulgar language and faulty grammar and punctuation, as well as dialectical expressions, to attack the artifice of literary language and demonstrate how language perpetuates the divisions between oppressed and oppressor. Many of the quotations in Italian included in the first part of this chapter provide examples of this tendency.

3. Carolyn Heilbrun, *Reinventing Womanhood* (New York: Norton, 1979), 71ff.

4. Elisabetta Rasy, *Le donne e la letteratura* (Rome: Riuniti, 1984), 37–40.

5. See Estelle Jelinek's introduction to *Women's Autobiography* (Bloomington: Indiana University Press, 1980), 10–20.

6. Janet Gunn, *Autobiography: Towards a Poetics of Experience* (Philadelphia: University of Pennsylvania Press, 1982), 6–7. Although Gunn is not a generic critic, she agrees with other reader-centered approaches to genre: "Genre is an instrument of reading . . . [that] enables the reader to locate himself or herself before the text" (21).

7. Claudine Hermann, *La voleuse des langues* (Paris: Editions des femmes, 1976), 77.

8. Rita Felski, *Beyond Feminist Aesthetics* (Cambridge, MA: Harvard University Press, 1989), 114.

9. Christopher Lasch, *The Culture of Narcissism: American Life in an Age of Diminishing Expectations* (New York: Norton, 1978).

10. Felski borrows this point from Richard Sennett, *The Fall of the Public Man* (New York: Knopf, 1977).

11. Sigrid Wiegel, "Woman Begins Relating to Herself: Contemporary German Women's Literature: Part One," *New German Critique* 31 (1984): 82.

12. Marina Warner's comments in her monumental study *Alone of All Her Sex: The Myth and the Cult of the Virgin Mary* (New York: Knopf, 1976) are especially pertinent for Italian society and its women writers. Warner writes that the Virgin and the Magdalene form a diptych of Christian patriarchy's idea of women, leaving no place for a single woman who is neither a virgin nor a whore. The Church venerates two ideals of the feminine—consecrated chastity and regenerate sexuality—and thus "cannot conceive of a single female saint independently of her relations (or lack of relations) with men" (235).

13. Augustus Pallotta, in "Dacia Maraini: From Alienation to Feminism," *World Literature Today* 58 (1984), describes the text as a "remarkable, latter-day picaresque novel" (n. 362).

14. See Bassnett, *Feminist Experiences*, 116: "However in the marketing of the 'new life' through advanced technology (. . . Italian coined a new word *elettrodomestico*, an indication of the extent of the reorganization of the running of the home), care was taken to stress the continuation of old values." Bassnett quotes Italian feminist writer Adriana Seroni, who writes: "Enormous riches . . . have all been sacrificed on the altar of chaotic development of twisted private consumerism. In the wake of all this, woman, her image, and her beauty have been degraded to serve a political vision. . . . She has been shut out for the most part from production, and has been exalted as a symbol and instrument of twisted consumerism" (117).

15. Elissa Gelfand, *Imagination in Confinement: Women's Writings from French Prisons* (Ithaca, NY: Cornell University Press, 1984), 126.

16. "Poi si dice il cancro sfido io! Anche il manzo lo imbrattano di genuino non c'è neppure l'aria nel latte delle vacche c'è smog veleno. Una donna si sbatte venti anni in cucina per preparare veleni e pranzi funebri mangiare per morire non ha senso."

17. "Ah già vedo un immenso polverone si spaccheranno le fogne tutte d'un colpo si alzeranno colonne nere di smog tutto l'unticcio del mondo in gran bollore tutta la polvere scacciata tornerà dal profondo del mare offuscherà la terra."

18. "Una vittima della società. E un bel pensierino e fa sentire tanto nobili, compassionevoli. Ma nessuno di questi sfiori il cervello neanche una volta che la società è ognuno di noi. Invece gli uomini . . . tutti: gli onorevoli in mutande,

gli studenti tiraseghe—giocano a scaricabarile. . . . Voltano sempre la testa a cercare la società nell'angolo dove loro non stanno."

19. Like Guiducci's *Due donne*, *Memorie di una ladra* is based on a real-life account. Maraini admits to making many changes in the presentation of the story, however. For example, she comments that Teresa lacked any chronological conception of time; therefore, for purposes of clarity, in the rewriting of the text, which Maraini claims to have done three times, she adheres to a strict, chronological order (*Memorie*, vi–ix). *Memorie di una ladra* was reprinted by Bompiani in 1984; all further parenthetical references are to this later edition.

20. Claudio Guillen, *Literature as System: Essays Toward the Theory of Literary History* (Princeton, NJ: Princeton University Press, 1971), 120.

21. "Ho trovato un bel mestiere il lavoro è leggero mi diverto pure e guadagno senza fatica. Toccava aver un po' di cervello, questo si, toccava essere intelligenti e furbi e sapere parlare, sapersi disimpegnare quando tirava un brutto vento."

22. Carla Corsi, *Ritratto a tinte forti*, (Florence: Astrea, 1991).

23. Dacia Maraini, *Donna in guerra* (Turin: Einaudi, 1975), trans. Mara Benetti and Elspeth Spottiswood (New York: Italica Press, 1988); all translations come from this edition. Although Giovanni Cecchetti, in his introduction to Bruce Merry's *Women in Modern Italian Literature: Four Studies Based on the Work of Grazia Deledda, Alba de Céspedes, Natalia Ginzburg and Dacia Maraini* (Townsville: James Cook University of North Queensland Press, 1990), claims Maraini's radicalism in her texts provides an example "of how extreme feminism can weaken its very cause," two other male critics have supported Maraini's feminist viewpoint. Anthony Tamburri, in "Dacia Maraini's *Donna in guerra: Victory or Defeat?*" (in *Contemporary Women Writers in Italy: A Modern Renaissance*, ed. Santo Arico [Amherst: University of Massachusetts Press, 1990]), writes that Maraini is speaking here to men and saying that "solutions to the plight of women require the cooperation of both the male and the female" (149). Merry himself claims Maraini's novels provide an update of the classic account of women's issues in Sibilla Aleramo's *Una donna* (Turin: Sten, 1906) (Merry, 196).

24. "Non sapevo che rispondere. Quello che dice Giacinto lo faccio mio. Non mi è mai venuto in mente di contraddirlo. Penso che è migliore di me, che ha ragione, che lo amo, che quello che dice ha valore per tutti e due."

25. Pallotta, "Dacia Maraini: From Alienation to Feminism," 362.

26. For an excellent, in-depth discussion of the early Greek and Roman romances, see Arthur Heiserman, *The Novel Before the Novel: Essays and Discussions about the Beginnings of Prose Fiction in the West* (Chicago: University of Chicago Press, 1977). A recent discussion on the relationship between women and love in these romances is given by P. L. Furiani, "Di donna in donna: Elementi femministi nel romanzo greco d'amore," in *Piccolo mondo antico: Le donne, gli amori, i costumi, il mondo reale nel romanzo antico*, ed. P. L. Furiani and A. M. Scarcella (Perugia: Edizioni Scientifiche Italiane, 1989), 43–106.

27. Kenneth Bruffee, *Elegiac Romance: Cultural Change and the Loss of the Hero in Modern Fiction* (Ithaca, NY: Cornell University Press, 1983), esp. chap. 2, "Elegiac Romance: A Modern Tradition."

28. —Alla Villa Trionfo l'amore si fa sputazza.
    —La sputazza si fa semenza.
    —La semenza si fa veleno.
    —La serva si fa padrona.

—Portasse le monete d'oro cucite nel vestito.
—Camminasse come il diavolo, sui piedi in punta.
—Li vedesse quando scendono per la passeggiata.
—La padrona innanze, come una regina, il marito dietro a tre passi e la serva in fondo, con i bracciali che fanno tirintin, tin tin.
—I bracciali li tiene alle caviglie, come una schiava musulmanna.
—Una schiava che si mangiò i padroni.

29. These scenes, both in style and function, are reminiscent of the visits of Vittorini's narrator, Silvestro, to Ezechiele's cave in *Conversazione in Sicilia* (1941; in *Opere di Elio Vittorini*, ed. Maria Corti [Milan: Mondadori, 1974]). Joy Potter, in "The Ideological Substructure in *Conversazione in Sicilia*," *Italica* 52, 1 (1975): 50–69, defines Ezechiele's humanist criticisms of the *mondo offeso* as impotent and useless since they represent an intellectualist position of isolation and withdrawal from the world of experience and thus restrict culture to the function of consolation.

30. "Quella gente lí bisogna fare finta che non c'è, se reagisci è peggio."

31. Tamburri, in "Dacia Maraini's *Donna in guerra*," 141 and in n. 12, calls Suna a catalyst for change "despite her sometimes contradictory behavior." Tamburri also notes that Suna herself is involved with a self-absorbed male, Santino, who openly exploits her physically and financially.

32. "E vero. Quando parla cosí sembra un vecchio che ha rinunciato coscientamente ad ogni volontà di possesso. Ma ha una forza terribile in quelle sue braccia bionde e con questa forza tiene in piedi il nostro matrimonio. Io sono innamorata di quelle braccia."

33. Patricia Merivale, "Through Greene-Land in Drag: Joan Didion's *A Book of Common Prayer*," *Pacific Coast Philology* 15 (1980): 139–152.

34. Vannina first describes Suna as "una che fa teatro . . . improvvisamente l'ho trovata ridicola e antipatica" (59). Even when she follows Suna to Naples to aid Suna's investigations of exploited female workers, Vannina admits that she is primarily going to see Orio again. Vannina had a brief affair with Orio who is now dying of a stomach tumor.

35. In their next novels, both Maraini (*Il treno per Helsinki*, 1984) and Guiducci (*A testa in giù*, 1984) examine again many of the myths and social conventions that were revealed by the generic experiments of the seventies. In *Il treno per Helsinki*, Maraini uses the Don Juan theme to structure her story of the female protagonist's discovery of the patriarchal underpinnings of Communist ideology. See Carol Lazzaro-Weis, "The Experience of Don Juan in Italian Feminist Fictions," *Annali d'italianistica* 7 (1989): 382–394.

36. See Ann Rosalind Jones, "Inscribing Femininity: French Theories of the Feminine," in *Making a Difference: Feminist Literary Criticism*, ed. Gayle Green and Coppélia Kahn (London: Methuen, 1985), 91.

37. Teresa de Lauretis, in *Feminist Studies, Critical Studies* (Bloomington: Indiana University Press, 1986), calls for "a recasting of the notion that the personal is political which does not simply equate and collapse the two . . . but maintains the tension between them precisely through the understanding of identity as multiple and even self-contradictory" (9).

38. Birnbaum, *Liberazione della donna*, 173–174. Seminars concentrated on motherhood, images of mothers in the past, lives of female saints, and the legacy of pagan and Christian goddesses.

39. Birnbaum, *Liberazione della donna*, 174.

40. Dacia Maraini, "Sekmeth," in *Racconta*, ed. Rosaria Guacci and Bruna Morelli (Milan: La Tartaruga, 1989), 109–120.

41. Silvia Vegetti-Finzi, *Il bambino della notte: Divenire donna, divenire madre* (Milan: Mondadori, 1990). Vegetti-Finzi, a clinical psychologist and psychology professor at the University of Pavia, has also written the two-volume *Storia della psicoanalisi* (Milan: Mondadori, 1986) and various essays on feminine subjectivity. Cavarero and Vegetti-Finzi are reviewed together by Bia Sarrasini, "Sulla soglia, la madre," *NoiDonne* (December 1990): 64–66.

42. Nadia Fusini, *La Luminosa: Genealogia di Fedra* (Milan: Feltrinelli, 1990).

43. Fusini, *La Luminosa*, 148: "Chi nasce è desiderio di madre che si realizza, e nascendo non vuole altro che la madre, ripossederla per posseder così il proprio inizio, e desiderio. La propria origine."

44. René Girard, *Deceit, Desire and the Novel: Self and Other in Literary Structure* (Baltimore, MD: Johns Hopkins University Press, 1976). The French version, *Mensonge romantique, vérité romanesque* appeared first in 1961. The first English translation was published in 1965.

45. Francesca Sanvitale, *Madre e figlia* (Turin: Einaudi, 1980), 4.

46. Paola Blelloch, "Francesca Sanvitale's *Madre e figlia*: From Reflection to Self-Invention," *Contemporary Women Writers in Italy: A Modern Renaissance*, ed. Santo Arico (Amherst: University of Massachusetts Press, 1990), 124–137. See this essay for an excellent discussion of Sanvitale's stylistic experimentations.

47. Francesca Sanvitale, "Madre e figlia," in *Vivere e pensare la relazione madre-figlia*, proceedings of seminar held in Milan, March 19, 1990 (Milan: Edizioni Associazione Culturale Melusine, 1990), 16.

48. Blelloch, "Francesca Sanvitale's *Madre e figlia*," 130.

49. Maria Schiavo, *Discorso eretico alla fatalità* (Florence: Giunti, 1991): "Mi rendevo perfettamente conto che era una contraddizione in termini parlare di *una* esperienza come se si trattasse sempre della stessa. Eppure, come tale io la vivevadentro di me: come se la molteplicità fosse solo l'involucro ingannevole di una unità fallimentare . . . Non sopportavo la variazione, e nella molteplicità vedevo l'immagine dell'*uno*."

50. Alberto Moravia, "Paura del benessere," *Corriere della sera*, September 2, 1989.

51. Walter Pedullà, "Scrittori d'oggi: Un promettente esordio," *Avanti*, May 23, 1989.

52. Rossana Rossanda, "Riconoscersi per negazione: Storia di un apprendistato femminile," *Il manifesto*, September 2, 1989.

53. Maria Luisa Boccia, "Solitudine di un io femminile," *Reti* 3–4 (1989): 22–25.

54. Paola Redaelli, "Se la notte viene alla luce," *Lapis* 5 (1989): 65, also describes *Velocità di fuga* as a "long voyage through feminine figures . . . in search of an identity."

55. Interview with Silvia Neonato, "D'amore (forse) si muore: Due generazioni sullo sfondo del femminismo," *Secolo XIX*, February 18, 1989.

56. Frabotta, *Velocità di fuga*, 188: "Everybody knows that you are still a virgin. It's not surprising; considering that absolute lack of a sense of reality that characterizes both of you!" ("Lo sanno tutti che sei ancora vergine. Non c'è da stupirsi: con quella assoluta mancanza di senso della realtà che vi contraddistingue!").

57. Paola Redaelli, "Se la notte viene alla luce," 66.

58. Lidia Campanaro, "La potenza generativa delle donne in un vuoto di immagini e di parole," *Il manifesto*, December 7, 1990, 5.

Chapter 4
The Female *Bildungsroman*

Despite the general disapproval of generic criticism among feminist critics, the rubric *Bildungsroman* and all its variants have managed to gain some theoretical currency among feminist critics, at least on this side of the Atlantic.[1] As the review in Chapter 1 shows, this category is most often used to analyze the ways in which nineteenth- and early twentieth-century women novelists represented the suppression and defeat of female creativity, autonomy, and maturity. In theory, the *Bildungsroman* plot, with its emphasis on the reintegration of the whole individual into society, is easily distinguishable from that of the romance, where reintegration is primarily effected through love and marriage. Since women's "development" was so often synonymous with finding a marriage partner, however, the female *Bildungsroman* retained affinities with romance, and Annis Pratt defines the form as one in which "social realism is apt to become mixed with elements of romance."[2] Pratt differentiates between the more authentic *Bildungsroman* quest, "the search for self in which the protagonist begins in alienation and seeks integration into the human community where he or she can develop more fully," and a related, more spiritual quest, "the self's journey in relation to cosmic power or powers." The spiritual quest is found in works she classifies as female novels of rebirth and transformation which also end with the rejection of love and marriage (136–138). Felski also identifies a female subcategory of the *Bildungsroman*, the "novel of self-discovery," where growth is depicted as a voyage inward toward a more mystical resolution of women's alienation (128–138). In both categories, however, alienation is depicted as a result of oppressive gender norms.

Pratt notes similarities in the fictional conventions found in both the romance and the *Bildungsroman*. Characters in the *Bildungsroman*, like those of romance, are types described by normative and generalizing theories. In the *Bildungsroman*, the typicality of the characters is still pronounced because they are supposed to be learning to desire generally accepted, socially mediated goals. This technique, of course, serves to help women writers and their readers criticize and reject hypocritical gender norms in various ways. According to Pratt, in the "realistic" narratives of Jane Austen, Fanny Burney, and Maria Edgeworth, the independence of the protagonists is portrayed when they distance themselves from those people, male or female, who are exaggeratedly stereotypical. In many other female *Bildungsromane*, the female protagonists retreat to nature, renounce love, and voice outrage or disappointment over their failure to achieve any recognizable autonomy.

Like the confession, the *Bildungsroman* form has also been invoked to classify and describe radical autobiographical feminist works of the 1970s that originally claimed no relationship to any literary tradition. Both Sandra Friedan, in her study of women's autobiographical writings in the seventies in Germany, and Rita Felski argue that feminist writers use the form to reject its archetypal message of accommodation to society after they reveal the processes of social conditioning in their lives, and recognize their repression by society and their own participation in that repression.[3] To be sure, in much of this literature, as in the early generic experiments discussed in the previous chapter, the existence of an authentic female identity that needed to be liberated from patriarchal tyranny was implied. In Italy in the seventies, the generic rubric was never used. Yet, narratives such as Giuliana Ferri's *Un quarto di donna*, Gabriella Magrini's *Una lunga giovinezza*, and Carla Cerati's *Un matrimonio perfetto* are three among many feminist novels that could fit into this category.[4]

The *Bildungsroman*, then, owes its unique position as the only consistently acknowledged generic category in feminist criticism to the fact that it, like the confession, was generally perceived to be less formally restrictive and thus more capable of effecting radical social criticism. Its stubborn reappearance in feminist criticism is also due to its relationship to the debates among feminist critics concerning concepts of representation and experience. Many critics use the term "female *Bildungsroman*" to defend the representation of women's experience in writing as a necessary means to fulfill the goal of finding a new female identity. Despite her differences with the editors of *The Voyage In*, Joanne Frye still defends the *Bildungsroman* as a blatantly representational form that has a "decided place for the experiential base of feminist criticism . . . and clear relevance to the urgency of female self-definition."[5] Bonnie Hoover Braendlin defines the form in similar terms when she states that the *Bildungsroman*, viewed theoretically, reflects "an author's desire to universalize personal experience in order to valorize personal identity."[6]

Frye, Braendlin, and Felski deny that feminist theories in the eighties that see female identity as multiple or self-contradictory or are skeptical of the critical power of naked subjectivity in women's _Bildungsromane_ invalidate the category's usefulness.[7] Felski uses the _Bildungsroman_ to justify again the need for personal histories in women's writing and extends its critical potential to contradictory trends in feminism: even if the utopian longings for wholeness and authenticity through reunification with nature found in these works undercut the possibility of female development the form should portray, these works participate in the ongoing feminist critique of its own theoretical shortcomings, as feminism continues to "negate the cultural authority of one version of women's experience in order to put alternative visions in its place" (151). Felski rejects the Marxist theory that personal histories are essentially conservative because they posit a false resolution of fundamental economic and social contradictions on a psychological and subjective level. The new plots and themes in these narratives further the production of a new feminine subjectivity even if, in these less experimental representations of women's resistance and survival, the issue of the fictionality of literary representation is not of concern (151–153).

Nonetheless, the problems inherent in using the _Bildungsroman_ as a useful critical tool for writers and critics go even deeper than feminist debates over concepts of the self, experience, and representation, although they are not unrelated to each other. The term itself derives from German philosophy, and its application to fictional narratives has had such a troubled history that Jeffrey Sammons argues that the whole idea of the _Bildungsroman_, at least in the nineteenth century, is more a critical myth than a reality.[8] In his review of those novels commonly classified as _Bildungsromane_, Sammons has little difficulty showing how far these authors were from depicting how the self develops through positive relationships to society.[9] Depictions of alienated, failed types predominate, and the form rapidly became less concerned with the depiction of social problems than with the problems involved in self-knowledge. More often than not, even this process is left incomplete as the protagonists retreat from society into isolation or self-destruction through union with nature. Sammons's article is partly a response to the comments of Martin Swales in his book _The German Bildungsroman from Wieland to Hesse_.[10] Rather than questioning the generic rubric as Sammons does, Swales maintains that to solve the dilemma of the _Bildungsroman_, as critics like to do, is to destroy the form. For the term to be valid, the central problematic of the _Bildungs-_

roman could only be irresolution and alienation. What is integral to the *Bildungsroman*, he correctly observes, is its questioning of the narrator's and ultimately the reader's capacity for reflexivity, and its concern to articulate the values and assumptions upon which human experience rests.[11]

Consequently, the "male" *Bildungsroman*, at least in its German manifestation, is not so dissimilar in its goals and results to its "female" equivalent, which also typically substitutes inner concentration and withdrawal for active accommodation and rebellion. Alienated social outcasts with the potential to self-destruct due to overwhelmingly crippling relationships to nature and religion are characteristics shared by many female protagonists of the form.[12] To be sure, the originators of the *Bildungsroman* were interested in problems of representation, the relationship of the individual to the group, and questions of subjectivity, which they saw in aesthetic as well as social terms. Thus women writers, like their male counterparts, have traditionally turned to the *Bildungsroman* not to subvert its structures, but rather to flaunt the contradictions in the form, which critical theory often tries to explain away. All writers of *Bildungsromane* call for the right to describe experience in epistemological rather than teleological terms. It is no surprise that, in the seventies, the form was used to defend the right of feminist and women authors to describe their own reality and to legitimize these experiences in their difference from those of men.

In order to explain the *Bildungsroman*'s stubborn inability to depict a character's suitable social adjustment, critics other than Swales have isolated a series of unresolvable dualities in the form. Pratt speaks of a double bind resulting from the form's "tone of protest" that tends to associate everything "demonic" or "regressive" with society and everything revolutionary or progressive with "the individual hero or heroine who has a vision of liberation."[13] In *The Dialectics of Representation*, Susan Wells discusses how the *Bildungsroman* tradition has always been shaped by debates concerning the representation of subjectivity and identity.[14] For Wells, the dialectic of representation in any text centers on the interplay between those aspects of the text that connect it with the lived world, which she places under the rubric "typical," and those aspects that resist interpretation, here called "indeterminate." On the one hand, the typical register represents relations between individuals and groups, locates the text in history, and assumes intersubjectivity as an interpretative ground.[15] Usually the main themes of the *Bildungsroman* belong to the typical register, whose stated function is to present the text as a transparent and natural reality that indicates the individual's relationship to the universal. The indeterminate, on the other hand, refers to how the work represents itself as a text: it is in the realm of the indeterminate that the illusion that the text is representing a world outside itself is dissolved. The indeterminate register emphasizes the basic paradox in all representation, which is that "representations are not objects . . . but enter into their full existence when their material being as marks on a page has been swallowed up and forgotten, and they have become thoughts in the mind of the reader" (50).

Significantly, in the *Bildungsroman* the most "typical" of all questions, the relation between individuals and groups, provokes one of two answers from the indeterminate register: "socially critical answers, in which the individual attempts to transform or transcend social relations, and utopian answers, in which social relations are beneficently arranged to foster the growth of the protagonist" (141). Critical and utopian impulses which proceed by negation and abstraction belong to the indeterminate register. The relevancy of the *Bildungsroman* to current feminist critical debates and writing lies precisely in the fact that the form has always exposed the tensions, contradictions, and difficulties involved in linking the representation of subjectivity to the criticism of social and political structures, even if the form itself is based in an unresolved dialectic between its intent to represent experience and its negative critique of social and political structures.

The *Bildungsroman* also serves as a good example of the difficulty of representing philosophical ideas in a literary text. Wells observes that in the philosophy said to inform the *Bildungsroman*, the dichotomy between the self as subject and the self as object is somehow erased.[16] In the literary form itself, however, this is not the case. In the *Bildungsroman*, indeterminacy is part of the genre's theme and purpose, which is the representation of a conscious human self-formation. In creating himself or herself as an object, the protagonist must undergo a process of alienation in order to achieve self-consciousness. The total alienation of many nineteenth-century *Bildungsroman* protagonists indicated the victory of the indeterminate register over the typical and a breakdown of the dialectic. It is in the interaction between the two that the reader sees relations being formed in their historical and discursive context.

In his reading of the *Bildungsroman* in nineteenth- century European culture, Franco Moretti rephrases the dialectic between typicality and indeterminacy in historical and thematic terms. For Moretti, the *Bildungsroman* is the symbolic form of a modernity that depended on a new concept of youth and sought its meaning in the future rather than the past, as did precapitalist culture.[17] Youth, he continues, is modernity's essence and its image in modern literature is conveyed by the attributes of mobility and inner restlessness, the main qualities of male and female *Bildungsroman* protagonists.[18] For Moretti, the myth of modernity with its overvaluation of youth and progress clashes with the static teleological vision of happiness and reconciliation found in the endings of both Jane Austen's *Pride and Prejudice* and Goethe's *Wilhelm Meister*. The classical *Bildungsroman* strove to make both men and women feel at home with their prejudices, which defeat change but produce happiness. As Moretti points out, for Schiller and Goethe, happiness signified the end of becoming (24). The genre's basic paradox is that capitalistic rationality, purely quantitative in nature and dependent on constant growth, cannot generate the *Bildung* that the genre presents as its ideal. Attempts to return to the "precapitalist" world, where maturity is theoretically possible and defined as the "definitive stabilization of the individual with his world" (27), produce nostalgic calls for what has been lost. The impossibility of reaching the goal of maturity, transcendence, stability, and identity in the *Bildungsroman* traditionally causes the characters to set up limits, to redefine boundaries in order to preserve the besieged "self."

Moretti's critique, besides outlining a few themes that will have special relevance to the works we are about to examine, implies that the form's oft-noted conservative tendencies do not necessarily derive from the female psyche or any specific feminist theory. The historical and discursive contexts of women's narratives of development are certainly open to the influence of feminist concerns that have evolved from exposing patriarchal oppression and to an examination of the mother-daughter theme in the context of the emotional, economic, and symbolic structures of family and society. The notion of home and the desire for stable identities and truthful origins are still appealing concepts despite their conservative implications that have been reinforced by the political atmosphere of the 1980s. In representing and deconstructing these societal structures, the depictions of "growing up female" in Italy to be examined here retain distinct affinities with the thematic and formal materials of the *Bildungsroman* tradition. In the parodic narratives of Ginevra Bompiani (*Mondanità*), Laura Lilli (*Zeta o le zie*), and Marisa Di Maggio (*C'era una volta un re . . .*), it is the exaggerated typical register that flaunts the fictional nature of the text. These *Bildungsromane* allow recognizable feminist ideas and motifs (the indeterminate) the creative and critical power to deny momentarily the repressive structures represented in the typical register and overcome the reality of women's problems, although, in the end, the protagonists must disappear.

Dacia Martelli's *Chi perde la sua vita* and Fabrizia Ramondino's *Althénopis* privilege the typical register of the dialectic behind which the protagonists again disappear. The emphasis on different sides of the dialectic allows for variations in the shared themes: how women are educated to despise themselves and other women, how the patriarchy refuses to recognize them as individuals, and how women learn not only to accept subjugation by males but to aid in maintaining their own subservient status. In representing these themes, the authors exploit the genre's opposition between happiness and freedom, identity and becoming. Alice Ceresa's *Bambine* exaggerates both registers, and in so doing, calls into question both the ability of the typical register to represent reality and the indeterminate to criticize and understand the causes of sexual difference.

*   *   *

The motifs of loss, youth, home, and community mingle with topical feminist ideas and theories in Bompiani's *Mondanità*, published by the feminist press *La Tartaruga* in 1980.[19] The stereotypical characters in *Mondanità* and the string of adventures in which they participate appear to derive more from the *conte philosophique* than from the *Bildungsroman*, which is usually associated with realistic genres. Although Marianne Hirsch declares the *Bildungsroman* to be "one of the major fictional types of European realism," it was precisely its type of realism that excluded it for so long from the novelistic canon of Western literature.[20] The Anglo-Saxon critical tradition since Ian Watt has defined narrative realism as the portrayal of the protagonist's development through time in a specific historical setting.[21] As correct as this definition may be for certain narratives, it excluded the *Bildungsroman*, whose adventures originally derived from the romance and whose characters developed only in the mental *Nebeneinander* (contiguous space) since they, like romance characters, experienced great difficulty putting any newly acquired knowledge into practice.[22] Moretti argues for a definition of realism in the *Bildungsroman* fashioned on the theories of Mikhail Bakhtin and Yuri Lotman, who define narrative realism as the presence of many viewpoints operating simultaneously. The representation of discontinuity and the denial of a final interpretation locate "realism" in the reader's ability to master "the intersection of various subjective positions," none of which the text totally validates. Realism in the *Bildungsroman* for Lotman and Moretti lies in its "language of restlessness and change" (94–96).

In *Mondanità*'s plot, replete with long voyages, unexpected reappearances, magical happenings, and transformations, ideas offer a preferable alternative to women's "real" destiny. The theoretical goal of the *Bildungsroman*, to portray the protagonist's coming to consciousness, is here linked to a specific feminist idea: Sophie must accept Simone de Beauvoir and Carla Lonzi's well-known challenge to women that they become the bearers of life's existential meaninglessness and refuse the many myths man has created concerning women to assure himself of meaning.[23] Sophie, who had been abandoned by her husband in a mosque in Istanbul during a family vacation at the beginning of the narrative, receives, toward the middle of the text, an explanatory letter from her husband, Niki. He justifies his abandonment of his wife by accusing her of refusing these roles: "Because you are the women who offers to death the sacrifice of presence. . . . I want to find my death, not my life" (82).[24] At the end of the story, Sophie travels to Paris to meet her husband and son. The encounter never takes place, however, because Sophie mysteriously disappears after an epiphanic moment in which she realizes she must accept her new feminist role of representing the nothingness her husband so fears. In her place, the two men find a yawning black cat with whom her son, Hannibal, immediately falls in love and takes home for a playmate. Sophie's cousin remarks that the cat, who will play the game in a different manner, will teach Niki the "mystery of presence" (109).

After Sophie is abandoned, she, like many *Bildungsroman* protagonists, retreats to a secluded place to contemplate her past and find herself. In *Mondanità*, this place is a run-down French chateau inherited by Sophie's cousin Isadore, an effeminate snob who, like his dusty chateau, never quite made it to the desired social register. The chateau is inhabited by a cast of exaggerated, comical female types through whom Bompiani introduces the critique of myths of neutrality and universality in writing and society. Madame de Miral, a depressed aging beauty who had always respected social conventions, resides in the chateau with her daughter Virginie, who is writing her dissertation on a tyrannical older English woman writer, Hermie Nicholson. Hermie quotes Jane Austen to prove women should suppress the expression of the passions in their writings in order to write correctly: "She would maintain, quoting Jane Austen, that anguish and torment are not necessary to an artist who desires perfection" (59).[25] Virginie's structural analysis of Hermie's books reveals that they are all the same, and that her characters, not unlike the inhabitants of the chateau, are superficial types whose behavior is predictable and repetitive: Hermie's characters are akin to "masks who recite their parts and then disappear: One plays the young man, the other the woman, the third, the old man. Like certain people" (63).[26]

Sophie's sojourn in the chateau leads to a description of life in isolated women's communities, a topos found in all Italian female *Bildungsromane* in the 1980s. The "reign of the mothers" (*il regno delle madri*) is a mythical, magical place full of constantly talking *streghe* (witches) who Hannibal's father believes are holding his son captive.

Although Sophie is saddened by her son's departure, she herself recognizes the limitations of this feminine world that obliges her against her will to participate in the archaic struggle to keep her son with her. The female types she observes here, hopelessly entangled in petty power struggles, cannot provide her the means to become different or to adjust to her new social situation.[27] Thus she acquiesces to Hannibal's departure, asking only that, in his travels, he seek love rather than death.

In the same chapter a recapitulation of Sophie's past reveals that she was always a wanderer in spirit. Raised in Greece by a Hungarian mother and French father, Sophie wanted to know and experience all cultures. Still, however, she spoke Greek in defiance of her parents in a gesture meant to display her desire to have a homeland. When she leaves her home, as a result of her marriage to Niki, an older man, it is not to learn about herself, which is the reason the typical male protagonist gives for his journeys. Rather Sophie states she wants to be _recognized_: "I don't believe I need to know myself. . . . I would prefer to be recognized" (51).[28] The inability of women to be recognized as anything other than a type is a main complaint among theoreticians of sexual difference; however, the expression of this theme that is found in all female _Bildungsromane_ is shaped by the parameters of the form. Although the genre criticizes the prosaic typicality of its characters, the protagonists themselves, like Sophie, can only interact socially as types. In the _Bildungsroman_, as Wells and others point out, the criticism of typicality does not result in the formation of a new subjectivity but rather in the representation of an amorphous, vaguely defined self always involved in negation and flight.

Predictably, Sophie's review of her youth unleashes overwhelming feelings of nostalgia and prompts a return voyage home to a blind mother who can no longer see how her husband ignores her and to a father who has never forgiven her for leaving. Her mother, an aristocrat married to a bourgeois, had waged a private war against her father by insisting on the observance of useless protocol. These actions had caused the child Sophie to sympathize with her father, who appeared to be a victim inside the home. Her mother's strategies now seem similar to the self-destructive quarrels among women at Isadore's chateau. The main lesson Sophie realizes she had learned from her mother is also one reminiscent of Hermie Nicholson's recommendations for writing: her mother's oft-repeated dictum to suppress her feminine instincts, passions, and desires, to become "indifferent," that is, "less like a woman" ("meno donna") in order to acquire some power in a man's world. Sophie is called a "disertore" and a loser since she has ignored the rules to make women, like her mother, a "vincitrice" (33).

Sophie's confrontation with her mother and aunt, neither of whom has ever traveled, gives rise to other conversations in which the standard unresolved conflict in the *Bildungsroman* between happiness and the compromises it entails and the goal of freedom reappears. Sophie's aunt Myrto, a more worldly type who had been always described with "masculine" adjectives, had motivated Sophie as a child to break with the images and tactics proffered by her mother. Sophie is now more critical of her aunt, whom she accuses of complicity with the patriarchy by agreeing to manipulate the rules rather than trying to change them: "You have accepted the game, with all its rules, including that of treason" (96).[29] Sophie accuses Myrto of settling for happiness as Goethe would have defined it: to learn how to win by playing the game according to previously determined rules. Her aunts retorts: "I believe happiness is being invited to play the game" (97).[30]

Sophie leaves with these words ringing in her ears. Playing the game, or games in general, was never her strong point. In fact, Sophie's Hannibal had strongly criticized her and the women in Isadore's chateau for forsaking play in order to engage in irrelevant chatter (72). Sophie's final metamorphosis symbolizes her reentry into the active playing field with a new identity. Indeterminate themes such as women as presence, as acceptors and promulgators of the philosophy and meaninglessness of life enter the realm of the real and concrete when Sophie becomes a cat, who throughout the narrative is a symbol of presence. Sophie's metamorphosis indicates the triumph of an imaginary utopia that resolves momentarily the *Bildungsroman* conflicts by reordering society, here to feminist desires. The indeterminate, by representing the triumph of the imaginary in this text, becomes real. Still, entry into the real means to take on an identity with circumscribed limits. The liberty of Sophie as a cat, like that of Günter Grass's dwarf in *Blechtrommel*, does not necessarily ensure she can change the rules of the game or that she will not need to change identities again in the future.

Sophie's escape effected through a temporary triumph of the indeterminate over the real is more successful than the flight of Laura Lilli's protagonist Zeta. *Zeta o le zie* is another feminist experiment in breaking down reality by exaggerating the typical.[31] Scenes describing Zeta as a child learning to dance in step with her many aunts, one indistinguishable from the other, in a cemetery are comical representations of feminist theories denouncing masculine denials of women's difference and definitions of her as death. In *Zeta o le zie*, Lilli uses her background in philosophy several times when she deploys the axiomatic method to unmask the logic of masculine superiority and feminine oppression.[32] Her ideas also seem to move the plot, however, such as when Zeta mathematically derives the formula to justify her flight. In the next chapter, she disproves the same idea, as is typical in this form which challenges the social efficacy of any idea.

Zeta, married to the chauvinist Ypsilon, who refuses to sleep with her since she was not a virgin at the time of their marriage, eventually does follow the call of the siren to end up rather prosaically keeping house for a whale, an improvement she admits to be somewhat modest after such a monumental escape effort. In *Zeta o le zie*, feminist logic seems more reasonable and thus more "real" than the convoluted social structures and philosophies formed by patriarchy's exaggerated rationalism. At its publication in 1980 and again at the time of republication, however, feminist writers and readers, still a long way from linking their theories to a workable practice, used the form to gauge practical gains. The work ends on an upbeat note because Zeta is satisfied, at least temporarily, with her modest "real" gains, which consist of getting paid and thus recognized for her housework.

Marisa Di Maggio's *C'era una volta un re . . .* is another fantastic, satirical rendition of growing up female.[33] The atmosphere of *C'era una volta* is more akin to the magic realism of García Márquez; fantastic events and learned mythical and literary allusions alternate with references to an impoverished postwar Sicily not much changed since Giovanni Verga's time. In the first chapter, from the picture that adorns her "altar grave," the recently deceased Mamma Lucia observes herself being replaced, but not forgotten, since it is only in death that a degraded woman recuperates her reputation as a saintly person. While growing up in a small Sicilian village, the child protagonist Marianna and Mamma Lucia both witness a series of stock events: the myth of prosperity in America breaking up homes, forced marriages, a love affair between a young priest and a cousin that results in his transfer and subsequent death from a broken heart, religious recitals, and so on. Change penetrates every aspect of this town, whose inhabitants struggle to reinterpret all vicissitudes according to various pagan and Christian myths. Thus, for the residents, the priest's ill-fated love for the young girl could be another version of either the Galatea myth or the story of Adam and Eve. Di Maggio's modern version of the Demeter-Kore myth relates Mamma Lucia's replacement, Cosima, searching for her daughter, who spends the night with her supervisor. The rules learned during childhood are meant to keep in place "the surreptitious and soporific status quo maintained in effect by truths as moldy as stale bread, by apocryphal gospels, eternal maxims and glorious mysteries" (49).[34]

As the narrators in the more realistic *Althénopis* and *Chi perde la sua vita* will do, Marianna eventually leaves the town to attend university and "continue her life" in a less mythical setting where she can grow and develop. Real life, where these structures continue under a different guise, provokes a similar crisis in Marianna to the one that forced her to leave her home and makes her want to return:

eating clouds to satisfy one's hunger . . . to be pursued by the island . . . to flee the island while speaking about it, to recreate it through memory from afar, to love it while pretending to hate it. . . . She left to return. (123)[35]

Predictably, Marianna's return arouses overwhelming feelings of nostalgia for the sense of security and meaning of life that those who had never questioned dominant social and symbolic norms appear to possess. Since the novel had already comically unmasked these structures, the protagonist cannot turn back, although she begs Donna Giulia to give her an infusion to "chase away the melancholy" and relieve her of the onus of mundane life in time, typicality, and meaninglessness. Donna Giulia has nothing for Marianna, who, before beginning to roam again in time, comments: "And she helped me die, she who cannot die" (129). Marianna again disappears "with her heart full of monsters and trifles, and her soul besieged by the fascinating fable of the past" (131).[36]

Despite the critical and imaginative power of ideas and the indeterminate register in the parodic *Bildungsroman*, narrators, unable to find a real place for themselves in society, simply disappear when forced to return to real life. In Di Maggio's narrative this disappearance is explained as indicative of the loss of contact with the maternal, timeless realm to which she can no longer return and the lack of a viable alternative space. The difficulties of returning to the *regno delle madri*, indicated in these parodic narratives, are given more detailed analysis in two more "realistic" *Bildungsromane*, Dacia Martelli's *Chi perde la sua vita* and Fabrizia Ramondino's *Althénopis*. In *Chi perde la sua vita*, both males and females are forced to alienate themselves from the creative power their past harbors due to gender prejudices. A recipient of the literary prize Noi Donne in 1983, *Chi perde la sua vita* is an interrogation into childhood in central Italy in a *piccolo borghese* environment before 1968. It is also the story of the revenge of two degraded, alienated mothers. Martelli's narrator originally believes it possible to avoid degradation by receiving an education and imitating the patriarchal values that taught her to suppress and detest characteristics of the weak, despicable *femmina*. Since this image is itself a construction of the patriarchy, in refuting it she still becomes a reflection of her mother's asexuality and inability to relate to life. The same is true for Lucio, the artistic type who introduces her to both life and literature and with whom she falls in love, only to find out later he is a homosexual. His mother, while inculcating in him a nostalgia for the traditions and folklore of the countryside from which she came, had also made him incapable of dealing with the adult social order. Her possessive love, which had made him totally dependent on her, prepared him not for eternal, maternal life, but death.

The narrator, an industrious and successful student, is sent to Castelfranco, a small village north of Padua, to teach after completing her studies in mathematics. Upon arriving in Castelfranco she meets Lucio, an actor and artist whose open life-style and interest in friendship, literature, and the arts reacquaints the narrator with those aspects of herself she had so long suppressed. She describes her encounter with Lucio as an "initiation into loving life" (95), a gift she claims his mother had given him. This discovery inspires her to delve into her past to examine her own relationship with her mother and her environment to explain her suppression of her now-awakened sexuality.

The growing-up-grotesque archetype discerned by Annis Pratt as a common structuring motif in *Bildungsromane* written by women dominates the narrator's examination of her childhood.[37] The narrator confronts women's degraded status at play, in church, and in the home. Curse words mocking the female body spoken by children in the courtyards and commandments such as "Thou shalt not envy thy neighbor's wife," which indicate to the narrator the status of women as objects, help her formulate her goal to escape her biological destiny through education. She begins to sense, however, that many of her actions have compensatory goals: for example, originally her good marks in school and desire for an education were offerings to the father to redeem the mother's failure to provide him with a male offspring.

In the sphere of formal education, the young protagonist, like Virginia Woolf's Mary in *A Room of One's Own*, faces a myriad of negative pronouncements on women. Examples cited include Pythagoras: "There is a good principle that created order, light and man and an evil one responsible for the creation of chaos, darkness and women"; Saint Augustine: "Woman is a chance and defective abomination"; and Goethe: "A woman must learn at a very early age to play the role of the servant to which she is destined" (118).[38] To learn culture from an anthropomorphic point of view does not, as Judith Fetterley has pointed out, increase women's power but rather doubles her oppression. She suffers

not simply the powerlessness which derives from not seeing one's experience articulated, clarified and legitimized in art, but more significantly, the powerlessness which results from the endless division of self against self, the consequence of the invocation to identify as male while being reminded that to be male—to be universal . . . is to be *not female*.[39]

Thus, at the end of part 2, the narrator successfully arrives at the status her mother, so well-versed in misogyny by patriarchal culture, wanted for her: a "serious, official and neuter teacher" (147).

Lucio originally functions as the typical "green-world archetype," that is, the male personage found in many female *Bildungsromane* whose sexual relationship with the protagonist prefigures her own regeneration and rebirth.[40] On a trip with Lucio to the village where he was raised and from which his mother came, the narrator is seduced by the beauty of nature and its domestic and cordial character. Traditionally, contact with nature channels female protests into fantasy; while viewing various drawings on ancient ceramic artifacts, the narrator is inspired to envisage what she believes to be a different type of love relationship between men and women since it is not based on degradation and exploitation: "But now, it seemed to me that sex could be viewed as a gift of pleasure men offer to women, and I felt that if offered this way peacefully and simply, a woman could accept it" (89).[41] Watching and listening to the old villagers, the narrator dismisses progress as a myth of modernity, and expresses her desire to return to this primeval, timeless world.

The destructive effects of this idealized world, however, clearly render a return to any previously defined natural identity or state both impossible and undesirable. The narrator concludes that life in this small village in Padua and his mother's possessive love left Lucio unprepared for and unable to cope with life and women. Part of this conclusion could be attributed to the feelings of indignation and rejection she experiences when, after witnessing Lucio make passes at a fellow she dates in a naive attempt to make him jealous, she can no longer ignore his homosexuality. The correctness of her final judgment is reinforced by the news of Lucio's suicide, at which point the story concludes. The narrator receives the news after stating that she joyfully witnessed the rise of feminism whose theories concur with and validate her own evaluations. If *Chi perde la sua vita* recounts the disappearance of the narrator behind a series of typical, misogynistic definitions of her, she now finds, in theory, a collective and enabling identity in feminism.

Ramondino's *Althénopis*, published in 1981 and recently translated into English, is another story of a disappearance, that of a young girl behind the object sign *woman*.[42] The form is a chronological, sometimes poetic, but mostly realistic rendering of a childhood in a Neapolitan petit bourgeois family. *Althénopis* begins during World War II, when the narrator's family is forced to take refuge in the grandmother's residence in Santa Maria del Mare to escape the bombings, and continues into the late 1970s. The viewpoint of the narrating child is not simply a technique to reveal the corruption of the adult world. The narrator speaks as a reflective adult who now wants to unearth those structures that led to her final metamorphosis. Although Ramondino is not a declared feminist writer, her inquiry into how this estranged and creative narrating consciousness is formed is traversed with feminist themes that direct her critical rejection of the typical register.

Althénopis is divided into three parts that correspond to childhood, adolescence, and adulthood. Physically, the narrator describes herself in typifying terms: as a darker-skinned Italian, she is not capable of commanding any special consideration in a culture that idolizes blonds. In the first chapter, the narrator deconstructs the mythical image of her grandmother, *la nonna*. For the young child, this energetic woman who was always dressed in black and seemed to emanate light although she wore no jewelry, was a person of epic proportions. It is no coincidence that the narrative begins with an analysis of the primeval mother, the model in critical contrast to whom the other women in the family define themselves. The grandmother does indeed belong to the timeless, prehistoric maternal realm separate from that of the men who are occupied with more transitory events (6). The grandmother is endowed with magical powers such as her ability to cook many sugary delights for the children despite wartime rationing.

The grandmother's predilection for exaggeration, which endears the woman to her grandchildren, instead provokes cries of outrage and disgust from her own children. They decry her grandmother's unscientific way of cooking, her irrational religiosity, her insistence on writing songs and poems in her uneducated dialect, and her romantic and seemingly incestuous love for one of the male grandchildren because, in their view, these are the typical characteristics of a woman who, through mismanagement and hasty deals, lost the family fortune. These faults are excused by the narrator, for whom the grandmother and the house full of incense altars and religious paraphernalia represent a refuge from her mother's asceticism and intellectualism: "our mother . . . did not have a body, she had gestures, above all she had 'thoughts,' she had headaches" (8).[43] The chapter ends with a discussion of the relationship between older people and children as observed during visits of the narrator and her friends to a nearby retirement home. The children make fun of the elderly, who strike back with their own mean practical jokes, causing the narrator to comment that the derisive relationship between the two widely separated generations was really their way of playing with one another. She observes, however, that this activity itself is conditioned by the similar marginalized status of the children and the elderly.

These and other reflections provide a more socio-cultural backdrop to the grandmother and are typical in this narrative where purely psychological explanations are usually avoided. From the grandmother, the narrating voice proceeds to the outside world, the piazza where basic social relationships are established early in life. The majority of the chapter titles in part 1 (for example, "The Piazza," "The House," "The Paths," "The Villas," "The Sidewalks") emphasize the extent to which geography, architecture, and demography play an active role in the construction of the narrating voice. The economic structure of the town is mirrored in the position of the houses on the piazza: only the rich can directly face the center. How other children are handled by their parents, for example, if they are made to work at home or if they are beaten, is a subject of obvious interest to the child-narrator. Their treatment, which, of course, is a reflection of their socio-economic level, appears to the narrator to be determined by the position of their houses. These spatial relationships also spark the beginnings of the narrator's realization of her own differences from the other children, something she initially refuses.

The narrator's horizon widens as the children explore the "paths" ("I sentieri") which take them to the country, where they can observe the family and play rituals of peasants. From there, she goes to the villas of the rich where, through the grandmother, the narrator's family can still gain occasional entry. The narrator is constantly making generalizations concerning the people she meets. Despite the seeming superficiality of these theorizations, such as the observation that poor children play more spontaneously than rich children, whose play is always structured and more conscious, they serve to demarcate the historical and social position of the narrator, that of a petit bourgeois child in wartime Italy. Furthermore, the narrator uses these partial theories to elucidate relationships she had already begun to discuss. For example, the observation that the rich relatives serve very little food in contrast to the peasant belief that abundant food reflects wealth is a cause for more reflection upon the adversarial relationship between the mother and grandmother on that subject. Here this relationship is analyzed in terms of their identifications (or attempted identifications) with the contradictory ideologies of different classes. In addition, although these generalizations place the characters in typifying and understandable categories, at the same time they expose the various ideologies as being humanly created myths and not eternally representable truths.

Nostalgia for the mythical stability provided by the family and the childhood community informs the narrating voice throughout. The longest chapter in part 1, entitled "Zio Alceste" (Uncle Alceste), provides the most detailed, critical depiction of this supposedly stable female community, where many patriarchal values are internalized and transmitted, of all the *Bildungsromane* discussed in this chapter. Zio Alceste, who still lives with his mother, occasions much jealousy on the part of the other aunts who measure their worth according to how long they can keep their children, especially their sons, at home. In essence, the matriarchy mimics male expectations of women and, in so doing, perpetuates its subservient status. The female community admits only married women: unmarried ones have no identity. Educated women arouse even less interest. The family story that the grandmother's sister was one of five women in the last century to achieve a university degree is greeted with remarks that her pretentiousness probably explains why her daughters could not find husbands.

Like the narrator's mother, most of the aunts have suffered from some undefined and incapacitating type of illness during their reproductive years, which passed only when they achieved the status of grandmother. The realm of the matriarchy is indeed akin to Moretti's preindustrial world. The need of these women to establish strong identities motivates their acceptance of patriarchal limits in exchange for freedom and, more important, their refusal to develop. Indeed, as the narrator notes, in the matriarchy, it is impossible to *become* anything; the highest possible honor is to be born into it. Men are excluded as well from this inverted or perverted power structure, unless they have failed in some way and thus pay for entry into the oppressed. For example, the devastated husband of one of the aunts who had run away with another man receives as much sympathy as the wayward aunt receives criticism.

As the family prepares to return to Naples at the end of part 1, signs of imminent growth and development abound. Watching her girlfriends being removed from school to do housework or get married, the narrator is relieved to be escaping what she recognizes as a stifling female destiny. The family leaves Santa Maria del Mare in September 1948 to "occupy the social position commensurate with their social standing" (61). With the unexpected death of her father, however, independence and development stop, and the narrator and family must go to live with relatives. Accordingly, the narrator finds it more difficult to recount her life in a chronological, developmental way. In part 2, the narrator notices that she is becoming a victim of her own method of describing herself and others solely in terms of functional relationships: no longer having a free and teasingly ("scimmiesca") critical imagination, she is regarded as "a gesture, someone who does something like carry a cup, look for a sandal, lean over and pick up a handkerchief" (180).[44] The narrator's menstruation resuscitates the grandmother in her mother, who now begins to take on the latter's characteristics and functions. In part 2, the psychological and the poetic, that is, the indeterminate, take precedence as the narrator tries to refute this functional identity. Her reluctance to leave adolescence is expressed in several hallucinatory paragraphs. Footnotes, which appear throughout the book to explain language usage, customs, and historical events, become even more prominent and accentuate the growing gap between the two registers, a gap which, in turn, reflects the increasing inability of the narrator to control and understand her main discourse. Toward the end of part 2, an answer comes to the narrator in an epiphanic scene based on the *tolli leggere* (take this and read) motif. Opening a book at random under the shade of a tree in the garden on a hot day, the narrator finds these verses:

> La clef que tu cherches n'est pas là
>   jette-toi dans la vie et tu la trouveras. (220)[45]

Motivated by these words, the narrator leaves for university, feeling, in her own words, invincible.

Although the child narrator had never identified with the matriarchy, its power is revealed in the brief final section where it motivates two very real transformations. In part 3, the narrator returns home as a third-person, omniscient narrator seemingly denied of all subjectivity. The brief third part is entitled "Bestelle Dein Haus." This German citation, identified in the text as coming from one of J. S. Bach's cantatas, is followed by a quotation from Johannes Brahm's *Requiem* announcing the final transformation to take place at the Last Judgment.[46] The narrator witnesses the regression of her mother to a childlike sexuality that she gleefully expresses by giggling and saying "I am a baby" whenever she is reprimanded for touching her genitals. Franco Moretti points out that, in the *Bildungsroman*, the idealization of youth is parodied by equating youth with senility, as Flaubert does to his hero at the end of *L'education sentimentale*. This transformation reinterprets the *Bildungsroman*'s idealization of youth as an example of the patriarchal oppression of female sexuality, a theme that runs throughout *Althénopis*. As a child, the narrator observed that, at country festivals, only children and older, overweight women were allowed to dance openly. Since both groups were either to old or too young to be seen as sexual beings, the narrator concludes that this is an example of the patriarchy's monitoring of female sexuality. Likewise, the illnesses of many bourgeois women during their reproductive years is seen as a result of their inability to express themselves as autonomous sexual beings. The illness was a way for them to rationalize this impotency.

The second metamorphosis, that of the first-person narrating voice to the third-person, is represented by the narrator's retreat behind the sign "Daughter," who now speaks to her "Mother" in terms of signs and not words.[47] The "Mother" belittles the small ephemeral successes of the returning prodigal "Daughter" and demands she play the role that would allow the older woman "to sow together an endless present with its past," reminiscent of the attempt of Di Maggio's protagonist to reconnect after her failure in society (*Althénopis*, 234). The critique of the bourgeois family continues in purely spatial terms now that the indeterminate narrating consciousness has seemingly been eliminated. The bathroom, the dining room, and the living room metonymically subsume and represent the secret motivations in the petit bourgeois family. The realism of Balzac has returned, and the final chapters are presented as a realistic, transparent picture of the southern Italian petite bourgeoisie whose so-called universal values stifle all change in the interest of preserving and perpetuating itself.

The retreat to a third-person narration does not symbolize the destruction of the indeterminate but rather forces its critical and alienating tendencies to take on, like Bompiani's cat, some representable form. Although the narrator seems to be totally subsumed by her socially prescribed role, the poetic and critical indeterminate voice is still operating in the literary quotes that adorn the final chapter. The daughter has not completely divorced her emotions from her review of the deterioration of her mother and the family, as implied by the title of the last chapter, "Die mit Tränen saën, werden mit Freude ernten" ("Those who sow with tears will reap with joy").[48] The deliberate placing of the narrating voice in a typifying and socially prescribed position, that of the Daughter, paradoxically allows the narrator to continue to describe and criticize an archaic environment that, like Mamma Lucia's grave, will also disappear.

The narrator's melancholy fits the traditional pattern of the nostalgia of the *Bildungsroman* protagonist in the female Italian *Bildungsroman* in the 1980s. All the texts examined so far unmask the "real" as being nothing but a series of myths and prejudices, yet still emphasize the undesirability or impossibility of returning to any idealized past history or state of being. The endings in *Mondanità* and *Chi perde la sua vita*, despite their different stylistic modes of presentation, depict protagonists positioned to face a difficult future. Despite differences, the works of Di Maggio and Ramondino share a poetic prose that, while destroying the fictitious past, enacts another type of connection to it. Marianna cannot return to Donna Giulia's world, not only due to her criticism of it but also because that world is disappearing, as references to the concrete effects of the "economic miracle" in the 1960s suggests: even Mamma Lucia's grave and house have been replaced by more modern structures. Likewise, Ramondino's mother's world, despite its solid and permanent appearance, is itself poised for disappearance. Thus although both texts deny the possibility of the representation of a new female identity, something the *Bildungsroman* could never do, links to the past are formed in language, both critical and poetic. Di Maggio's prose, a mixture of tactile descriptions with abstract references and everyday speech with poetic language, is similar to Ramondino's "baroque" style that describes "people, objects, atmospheres, colors, tastes, smells and sensations with intensity and great clarity." [49] Both writers use language to figure the rapprochement of two separate and separated worlds, the literal and the symbolic, the typical and the indeterminate that they are depicting and criticizing.

*   *   *

The *Bildungsroman* dialectic continues to produce similarities in difference in the recent works of Alice Ceresa and Sandra Petrignani, who by pushing the form to its extreme seem to be destroying the form. Ramondino's omniscient observing narrator reappears in Alice Ceresa's *Bambine* with a microscope to review all of the shared themes of the female *Bildungsroman* in search of the detail that could reveal the answer to the many questions these narratives have presented for contemplation. Ceresa, raised in Basel by a German mother and an Italian father, published her first novel, *La figlia prodiga* (*The Prodigal Daughter*), in 1967. This work is a linguistic exercise in the destruction of the traditional realistic notion of character and representation in fiction. Ceresa begins her unpunctuated text by declaring that in a traditional text, character should emerge from the plot and not preexist it (13). The prodigal daughter denies all cultural determination, just as the narrative denies plot formation and strives to be a representation of presence.

In Ceresa's dense prose, feminist themes, such as the denunciation of the reduction of women to their merely reproductive function, the need for a separate female politics, and a way to improve relationships among women, are interspersed with more general theories on the liberating function of experimental literature. In contrast, Ceresa's *Bambine* initially seems to be a more traditionally written narrative. Although Ceresa writes here in properly punctuated sentences, distinct paragraphs, and chapters, the text's "realism" quickly dissipates into hallucination as both registers of the *Bildungsroman* dialectic merge.

Bambine is an "investigation" into the childhood and adolescence of two sisters in a middle-class small town, located everywhere and nowhere. There is no real plot development; the event presented in each chapter is really a pretext to the dissection of reasons for the questions that all the *Bildungsromane* include: what cultural elements produce women's degraded status; how the bourgeois family reinforces this defective formation; and finally, what silences and impedes a fruitful mother-daughter relationship. All characters are pure functions and every peculiarity added to their description reinforces both their typical yet, paradoxically, their ultimately undefinable natures. The spatial description of Santa Maria del Mare given by Ramondino's child narrator in the first part of *Althénopis* is here reduced to a four-page description of the layout of the town where the two girls are raised. Yet despite this excessive clarity or, more precisely, because of it, the town defies any individualizing conceptualization. Likewise, the omniscient narrator's abstract observations of each member of the family, their surroundings, and their few, repetitive actions engender no specific, provable conclusions but instead more descriptions behind which the members disappear. For example, several analytical descriptions of the feared father, "il signore e padrone di questa casa," (13) result only in fixation on his large nose, feet, or bald spots which are all possible loci of his power. The mother, as well, despite attempts to bring her to the foreground by examining her activities, is reduced to images of her matronly dresses and hats.

Bambine includes reminiscences of scenes, themes, and motifs that have become part and parcel of the Italian female *Bildungsroman* in the 1980s. The children's observance of pathetic and ridiculous female stereotypes, school experiences, middle-class narrow-mindedness, and children's freedom from gender prejudices are all themes present in the other texts discussed in this chapter. None of these scenes, however, produces a coherent theory on why one sister is afraid of the dark or likes to play with dolls, whereas the other seems more daring and intellectual, questions the narrator claims to want to answer. Although the reader could offer his or her own conclusion, the scientific narrator refuses to chose one theory over another, claiming that development is more a matter of inscrutable destiny than anything else (83). This return to an externally directed causality—like that of romance and which characterized many nineteenth-century *Bildungsromane*, including its prototype *Wilhelm Meister*—initially appears in contradiction to any positive didactic message the form could disseminate. The situation is further complicated when the two sisters, after adolescence, together review their own past to find out the reasons for their oppression and for their difference. Their varying interpretations and faulty memories paradoxically make their theorizing appear more limited than it sometimes appeared in other texts.

These contradictions, however, are consonant with the form itself: while affording women writers the context in which to disclaim those social structures and conventions through which patriarchal beliefs are expressed and perpetuated, the *Bildungsroman* dialectic continues to undermine representation of any theoretically defined and fixed self. Ceresa's *Bildungsroman* has several affinities with the second novel of a much younger writer, Sandra Petrignani.[50] In *Il catalogo dei giocattoli*, Petrignani reviews her childhood through a series of vignettes describing the toys she played with and how she developed her (gendered) viewpoint by interacting with these neutral objects.[51] Indeed, since in both narratives the domination of the typical register brings all plot and character development to a halt, the authors seem to deny subjectivity through the destruction of the dialectic. Yet in both narratives, as the exaggerated typical register also fails to represent anything, it becomes clear that the texts are highly subjective behind their scientific front. Despite the inability of Ceresa's sisters to find or represent suitable answers to their inquiries into what composes sexual difference, they remain "immobile watching the world with their asymmetrical human look, one eye wide open contemplating what can be contemplated, the other absent and following the transitory nature of human organisms and the uselessness of things in general" (116).[52] Thus rather than destroying the *Bildungsroman*'s dialectic by reducing the form to stasis, *Bambine* ends by both reaffirming its power to dissect the values and assumptions on which human experience rests and positing the existence of some sort of female subjectivity, posing as a universal one, that leads the dissection.

Whereas in the narratives of Bompiani and Di Maggio, feminist ideas became real by mystical transformations, thus crossing into the realm of the typical, for Ceresa the registers remain separate, yet they are connected in a new way. Like the baroque language of Di Maggio and Ramondino that itself figures a different relationship to the concrete, Ceresa's final image shows that the sisters continue to exist in one realm (rather than disappear) and critically contemplate from the other realm new ways of looking at things. At the same time, their one supposedly absent eye, which contemplates those more general, non-gendered, philosophical, and ultimately unanswerable questions, indicates their participation in rather than marginalization from principles of "universal thought." Although attempts to represent subjectivity in the *Bildungsroman* are generically impossible, the girls, Ceresa's narrator, and other women writers will continue in various ways to analyze and create by using their individual and collective *sguardo asimmetrico umano*, the "asymmetrical human (read female) point of view" that is both representing its formation in discourse and ironically denying that very formation, as their *Bildungsreise* (voyage) through form and language continues.

Notes

1. The *Künstlerroman*, in which a woman's growth is documented through her development as an artist, is another popular category among feminist critics. See, among others, Susan Gubar, "The Birth of the Artist as Heroine: (Re)production, the *Künstlerroman* Tradition and the Fiction of Katherine Mansfield," in *The Representation of Women in Fiction*, ed. Carolyn Heilbrun and Margaret Higonnet (Baltimore, MD: Johns Hopkins Press University, 1983), 19–59. A bibliography of the use of the *Bildungsroman* to study English-language texts has been prepared by Laura Sue Fuderer, *The Female Bildungsroman in English: An Annotated Bibliography of Criticism* (New York: MLA Publications, 1990).

2. Annis Pratt, *Archetypal Patterns in Women's Fiction* (Bloomington: Indiana University Press, 1981), 13.

3. Sandra Friedan, *Autobiography: Self into Form: German-Language Autobiographical Writings of the 1970s* (Frankfurt am Main: Peter Lang, 1983), 99–117.

4. Giuliana Ferri, *One-Fourth of a Woman* (Padua: Marsilio, 1973); Gabriella Magrini, *An Extended Childhood* (Milan: Mondadori, 1976); Carla Cerati, *A Perfect Marriage* (Padua: Marsilio, 1976).

5. Joanne Frye, *Living Stories, Telling Lives* (Ann Arbor: University of Michigan Press, 1986), 79.

6. Bonnie Hoover Braendlin, "*Bildung* in Ethnic Women Writers," *Denver Quarterly* 17, 4 (Winter 1983): 77.

7. In her introduction to *Feminist Studies, Critical Studies* (Bloomington: Indiana University Press, 1986), Teresa de Lauretis openly calls into question the feminist dictum of the seventies, "the personal is political," arguing that in practice this slogan had more often than not translated to the "personal *instead* of the political" (9). Several years earlier, Franco Petroni, in "La narrativa della 'contestazione,'" *Belfagor* 33, 5 (1978): 603ff, criticized feminist writings on the same grounds. Although Petroni calls "la riscoperta del privato . . . uno dei meriti del movimento femminista," the feminist use of the *privato* in literature, in his opinion, all too often executes a programmatic and one-sided devaluation of public life.

8. Jeffrey Sammons, "The Mystery of the Missing *Bildungsroman* or What Happened to Wilhelm Meister's Legacy?" *Genre* 14, 2 (1981): 229–246.

9. Sammons considers the following nineteenth-century *Bildungsromane*: Novalis's *Heinrich von Ofterdingen* (1800); Joseph von Eichendorff's *Ahnung und Gegenwart* (1815); Eduard Mörike's *Maler Nolten* (1832); Gustav Freytag's *Soll und Haben* (1855); Adalbert Stifter's *Der Nachsommer* (1857); Wilhelm Raabe's *Der Hungerpastor* (1864); and Gottfried Keller's *Der Grüne Heinrich* (1854/55; revised edition 1879/80).

10. Martin Swales, *The German Bildungsroman from Wieland to Hesse* (Princeton, NJ: Princeton University Press, 1978).

11. Swales, *The German Bildungsroman*, 98–102. In his concluding chapter, Swales mentions that one could argue that the works of many contemporary women writers, such as Doris Lessing, could be called *Bildungsromane* because

of their affinities with the tradition. He believes that the *Bildungsroman* is and should be primarily thought of as a specifically German genre, however, and he claims women should come up with another term. Many of Swales's main ideas are found in his article "The German *Bildungsroman* and the Great Tradition," in *Comparative Criticism*, ed. Elinor Shaffer (Cambridge: Cambridge University Press, 1979), 91–105.

12. For a discussion of this relationship of women to nature in the female *Bildungsroman*, see Pratt, *Archetypal Patterns in Women's Fiction*, 16–24.

13. Pratt, *Archetypal Patterns in Women's Fiction*, 37. Pratt borrows the term "tone of protest" from Northrop Frye, *The Secular Scripture: A Study of the Structure of Romance* (Cambridge, MA: Harvard University Press, 1976), 83.

14. Susan Wells, *The Dialectics of Representation* (Baltimore, MD: Johns Hopkins University Press, 1985).

15. Intersubjectivity is defined by Wells as the communicative and transformative power of language. In Wells's context, language does not operate without the intervention of human subjects: it can only derive from them. Intersubjectivity is a rhetorical concept that "locates the relation of power and discourse within communities of speakers and hearers. It asserts finally the power of speakers to transform the discourse that they enact" (14).

16. Wells points out that the dichotomy between internal and external was seen by German classical theorists as expressing two aspects of the same entity. Much of this theory was explained by asserting that the self as subject and influenced by art could transcend the specialized individuality caused by contemporary culture. See Wells, *Dialectics of Representation*, 139.

17. Franco Moretti, *The Way of the World: The Bildungsroman in European Culture* (Norfolk, VA: Verso, 1987), 4ff.

18. Most of the texts Moretti classifies and discusses as *Bildungsroman* are written by men: Stendhal's *The Red and the Black* and *The Charterhouse of Parma*, Honoré de Balzac's *Lost Illusions*, and Gustave Flaubert's *Sentimental Education*. He does, however, include Jane Austen's *Pride and Prejudice* alongside Goethe's *Wilhelm Meister* as examples of the classical *Bildungsroman*, and concludes his study with George Eliot's *Mill on the Floss*, a text, he claims, that destroyed the genre at the end of the nineteenth century.

19. Ginevra Bompiani, who teaches English literature at the University of Siena, has written several novels, including *Specie del sonno* (Milan: La biblioteca blù, 1975; French trans. 1976), *L'incantato* (Milan: Garzanti, 1987), *L'attesa* (Milan: Feltrinelli, 1988), and *Vecchio Cielo, Nuova Terra* (Milan: Garzanti, 1988). She is also the author of *Spazio narrante* (Milan: La Tartaruga, 1978), a critical study of nineteenth-century British women writers.

20. Marianne Hirsch, "The Novel of Formation as Genre: Between *Great Expectations* and *Lost Illusions*," *Genre* 12 (1979): 300.

21. Ian Watt, *The Rise of the Novel: Studies in Defoe, Richardson and Fielding* (Berkeley: University of California Press, 1957), esp. chapter 1.

22. Both Swales and Sammons speak of the epiphanic moments in many *Bildungsromane* which are never realized in everyday life. A common example is the climactic chapter in Thomas Mann's *The Magic Mountain*, where Hans Castorp has a vision in the snow of the wholeness of humanity. This "knowledge" has no rehabilitative function for Castorp in the chapters that follow.

23. Simone de Beauvoir, *Le deuxième sexe* (Paris: Gallimard, 1949). Most of these ideas are found in part 3, entitled "Les Mythes." This feminist idea was also propagated by Carla Lonzi and Mary Daly. In *Beyond God the Father*,

(Boston: Beacon Press, 1973), Daly writes: "This becoming who we are requires existential courage to confront the experience of nothingness. . . . I am suggesting that, at this point in history, women are in a unique sense called to be the bearers of the existential courage of society" (32).

24. "Perché tu sei la donna che offre alla morte il sacrificio della presenza. . . . Io voglio ritrovare la mia morte, non la mia vita."

25. "Sosteneva, evocando Jane Austen, che angosce e tormenti non sono necessari a chi si contenta della perfezione."

26. "Non sono personaggi, sono maschere che recitano il loro canovaccio e poi svaniscono. Uno fa il giovane, l'altro fa la donna, un terzo il vecchio. Come certe persone."

27. Hermie's niece explains to Sophie that the fight between Hermie and Virginie is like the generational fight symbolized by Hansel and Gretel, the children who want to eat the house and the elderly witch who wants to eat them (68).

28. "Non credo di aver voglia di conoscermi. . . . Preferirei essere riconosciuta." When Niki asks her why she is searching for recognition, Sophie bluntly answers, "Because then I will know that I have arrived home" ("Per sapere che sono arrivata a casa") (51).

29. "Lei ha accettato il gioco, con tutte le sue regole, compresa quella del tradimento."

30. "Io credo che consista (la felicità) piùttosto nell'essere invitati a giocare."

31. First published by the feminist press La Tartaruga, *Zeta o le zie* was republished in 1989 in Bompiani's less expensive paperback series, which indicates the popularity of the text.

32. After graduating in philosophy, Laura Lilli studied American literature at Smith College and at Yale University. She now works as a journalist in Rome. Together with Chiara Valentini she published *Care compagne: Il femminismo nel PCI e nelle organizzazioni di massa* (Rome: Riuniti, 1978). A volume of short stories, *Ortiche e Margherite* (Verona: Essedue Edizioni), appeared in 1987.

33. Published in 1985, *C'era una volta . . .* was awarded the Premio Donna Città di Roma. It was also the recipient of the national and prestigious Premio Viareggio for a significant first work.

34. "Lo status quo surrettizio e soporifero mantenuto in vigore da verità ammuffite come pagnotte rafferme, da vangeli apocrifi, massime eterne e misteri gloriosi."

35. "A mangiare nuvole per saziare la fame . . . a lasciarsi perseguitare dall'isola . . . per fuggire l'isola parlandosi dall'isola, per vederla da lontano e ricordarla tutta, per amarla pretendendo di odiarla. . . . Se ne andò per ritornare."

36. "Il cuore pieno di mostri e carabattole, il cuore pieno e l'anima assediata dall'avvincente favolo del passato."

37. Pratt, *Archetypal Patterns in Women's Fiction*, 29.

38. "C'è un principio buono che ha creato l'ordine, la luce e l'uomo, e un principio cattivo che ha creato il caos, le tenebre e le donne"; "La donna è un essere occasionale, abominevole e difettoso"; "La donna deve imparare fin dalla più tenera età a tenere il ruolo di serva a cui è destinata." The narrator gives examples of being obliged to repeat such negative value judgments such as when, in writing a high school composition, she is requested to include the judgment of nineteenth-century critic Francesco De Sanctis on the art of the 1700s, which he classifies as "corrupt, feminine and vulgar." It was Giuseppe Parini, he continues, who brought "virility" to art in Italy (118–120).

39. Judith Fetterley, *The Resisting Reader: A Feminist Approach to Modern Fiction* (Bloomington: Indiana University Press, 1978), xx.

40. Pratt, *Archetypal Patterns in Women's Fiction*, 19.

41. "Ma ora mi sembrava bello che il sesso poteva essere inteso come un dono di piacere che l'uomo faceva alla donna, e sentivo che come tale, con semplicità, serenamente, la donna poteva accettarlo."

42. Fabrizia Ramondino, *Althénopis* (Turin: Einaudi, 1984). *Althénopis* is Ramondino's first novel; the English translation (Manchester: Carcanet, 1988) is by Michael Sullivan. All the following translations from Italian and German are my own. Ramondino has established a major reputation for her short stories and other writings, mostly centered on her beloved Naples. Together with Andreas Friedrich Müller, she has recently published *Dadapolis: Caleidoscopio napoletano* (Turin: Einaudi, 1989), a collage of portraits of Naples, its history, and its people.

43. "Nostra madre . . . non aveva un corpo, aveva i gesti, ma sopratutto aveva i 'pensieri,' aveva mal di testa."

44. "Un gesto, un fare qualcosa: portare la tazzina, cercare un sandalo, chinarmi a raccogliere un fazzoletto."

45. "The key you are searching for is not here. Go out into life and you will find it."

46. "Bestelle dein Haus: Denn wir haben keine bleibende Statt, sondern die zukünftige suchen wir. Siehe, ich sage euch ein Geheimnis: wir werden nicht alle entschlafen, wir werden alle verwandelt werden und dasselbige plötzlich, in einem Augenblick, zu der Zeit der letzen Posaune": "Prepare your house: Because we do not live in a stable city we will look to the future for one. I have a secret to tell you. Not everyone will die, but everyone will be changed, in an instant, in the flash of an eye, at the sound of the trumpets of the Last Judgment."

47. "Ormai non si parlavono più con le parole, la Figlia et la Madre, ma per segni"; "They no longer spoke with words, the Daughter and the Mother, but through signs" (233). The words "mother" and "daughter" are capitalized in the text so as to emphasize their object status. For an excellent discussion of this section, see Adalgisa Giorgio, "A Feminist Family Romance: Mother, Daughter and Female Genealogy in Fabrizia Ramondino's *Althénopis*," *The Italianist* 11 (1991): 128–149.

48. This quote is also taken from Brahms's *Deutsches Requiem*.

49. Giorgio, "A Feminist Family Romance," 130.

50. Another text that could be examined in this rubric would be Clara Sereni's *Casalinghitudine* (Turin: Einaudi, 1987) in which the narrator's *Bildung* is organized around a series of recipes that allow her to fuse with certain maternal figures while establishing her difference from them.

51. Petrignani's book, published by a small press, was so enthusiastically received that Rizzoli immediately awarded her a contract for her third book, *Come cadono i fulmini*, released in March 1991 (see Chapter 7 herein). Her first book, *Le navigazioni di Circe* (Rome: Theoria, 1987), is a kind of mythical *Bildungsroman* in which Petrignani finds a mythical correlative for her own development as a woman writer. See also Maria Corti's *Il canto delle sirene* (Milan: Bompiani, 1989).

52. "Restano immobili a guardare il mondo con il loro asimmetrico sguardo umano, un occhio grande aperto a contemplare il contemplabile, l'altro assente segue altrove la transitorietà degli organismi viventi e l'inutilità delle cose in genere."

Chapter 5
The Historical Novel: History as Female Subjectivity

The emergence of women writers onto the Italian literary scene, according to Neria de Giovanni, was made possible by the post–World War II neorealist movement which encouraged true-to-life testimonies of personal experiences, in this case the experience of the war.[1] Neorealism's anti-literary, truthful approach to social analysis was brought into question by the avant-garde literary groups of the 1960s and early 1970s. Nonetheless, writes de Giovanni, neorealism encouraged women writers, and its demise could not diminish their productivity. Rather, the crisis in neorealism, especially its faith in the social and collective value of literature, motivated a shift in focus in women's narratives toward historical writings. In opposition to neorealism's faith in the power of literature as an effective instrument to change social consciousness through the collective recounting of experiences, women writers "interiorize" history and use it as a means to know themselves.

De Giovanni correctly notes that the shared goal to use history to explore oneself unites those "first-generation women writers," such as Anna Banti, Fausta Cialente, Maria Bellonci, and Gianna Manzini, to the many contemporary women writers in the eighties who have returned to the historical novel to portray women's private histories and protest their exclusion from official History (105).[2] Shared goals result in shared themes, and many traditional themes in women's writing, such as the depression and weariness of women's subordinated and isolated status, continue to appear in contemporary historical fictions. The historical novel is also mediating bonds between different types of women writers of the same generation. In September 1990, Dacia Maraini was named the third consecutive woman writer to receive the prestigious Campiello literary award for her historical novel *La lunga vita di Marianna Ucrìa* (1990). The previous year, the prize was awarded to Rosetta Loy for her fourth novel, *Le strade di polvere* (1987), a historical saga of the personal trials and tribulations in the life of a peasant family in Piedmont from the end of the French domination through the early years of Italy's unification.[3]

Although both Maraini and Loy are now in their mid-fifties, their previous writings are distinctly different from one another. The novels of Loy, who was born and raised and is still living in Rome, are essentially stylized "generational" narratives ranging from descriptions of childhood during fascism in *La bicicletta* to bourgeois life in the fifties and sixties in *L'estate di Letuché*.[4] Loy, who claims to be unable to recognize herself in any literary tradition, does insist that, in spite of her perceived isolation, feminism's emphasis on the restoration of the equality denied to women ("parità negata") greatly inspired her and her works.[5] In contrast, Maraini's feminist beliefs and activities have always informed her numerous novels, plays, and poetic works which aggressively unmask the androcentric Italian social system.[6]

Significantly, both historical works still differ from one another in that they include autobiographical themes that have always been part of the individual author's previous narratives. As we have demonstrated in previous chapters, the generic classifications of romance and *Bildungsroman* show how the construction of a female voice through forms and fiction in contemporary writings has resulted in a less overtly personalized and autobiographical type of narration. Yet, despite their advantages, both the *Bildungsroman* and romance represent, either realistically or allegorically, those factors that have kept women out of official History. In contrast, historical fiction seems to offer women writers the possibility to reverse their marginalized historical status and become visible. Just as typicality and limits—that is, what makes representation possible in the *Bildungsroman*—interfere with the purported goal of representing a new subjectivity, so will the formal characteristics and traditional difficulties involved in representing change and progress in the historical novel often contradict those meanings critics and writers seek to write into the form. Nonetheless, the experience of women writers with historical fiction is not only uncovering a female genealogy of women writers; it is also bringing these writers in from the margins as their works participate in more public literary and political debates over the significance and direction of historical interpretation.

The increased production of historical narratives written by Italian women is due, in part, to the increased emphasis in the 1980s on women's history. During this time, Italian female historians enthusiastically received the works of Joan Kelley, Joan Scott, and Natalie

Zemon-Davis and their theories that women did indeed have their own distinct history. In recent years, Italian writers and historians have produced their share of women's histories to help fill in the silences patriarchal history had long imposed on women and their activities.[7] Italian women historians, however, are far from agreement as to whether women's history should be pursued from the viewpoint of the family, of socio-economic structures, or from the more politically charged feminist perspective of how women as active protagonists produced strategies of resistance and different definitions of female subjectivity across the ages.[8]

Another problem, as Paola di Cori points out, is how to represent the female subjectivity under observance in any of these methods: is female subjectivity a series of isolated ruptures in patriarchal history, the kind of alienated, momentary revolts that science fiction often portrays in the continuing story of patriarchal superiority; or, she asks, can we speak of a continuing story of a developing consciousness that is transmitted through conflict, interrelationships, and participation in society?[9] In order to pursue the latter approach, di Cori insists, feminists have to modify their separatist approach to women's history. And, although the study of women's history as a separate entity has provided many useful insights into a previously ignored and undervalued domain, the continuation of this approach cannot produce a history of women commensurate with another feminist goal, namely to show that women can continue to grow and develop and to confront themselves (107).

Di Cori's objection to studying women's history as a separate entity is based in the familiar practical fear that this segregation will effectively decrease knowledge of women's real relationships to society and their ability to function in it, as her comparison of history to science fiction shows. Nevertheless, the question of how to demonstrate continuity, growth, and subjectivity is not only an issue in feminism, but also a narratological and representational problem that historical and fictional discourses share. Controversial historians, like Hayden White, who argue that these shared techniques insure the fictitious nature of historical discourse, continue long-standing debates over the boundaries between fiction and history.[10] Linda Hutcheon has coined the term "historiographic metafiction" to describe a plethora of texts appearing in many national literatures in which historical facts continue to blur history's relationship to truth and its opposite, the fictional lie. History's truth can be challenged by invented characters, as is the case in E. L. Doctorow's *Ragtime*; by known characters who are given a fictitious past, as in texts like Jon Banville's *Copernicus* and *Kepler*; or by history's forgotten figures, such as Antonio Salieri in the film *Ama-*

deus.[11] Hutcheon links the revival of historicism in narrative to postmodernism's mandate to think contextually and critically (93). Although many of these works, like postmodernism itself, have been called apolitical, Hutcheon argues that these "elevations of private experience to public consciousness . . . create a new critical and communal awareness of past and present errors of oppression, omission and commission" (93–94).

If, as Hutcheon claims, these fictional refigurings of history have as their goal the reinstatement of reading as an "act of community" (93), Italian feminist and women writers clearly share these "postmodern" goals. Narratives such as Marta Morazzoni's *La ragazza col turbante* (*Girl in a Turban*) and Marisa Volpi's *Il maestro della betulla* (*The Birch Tree Painter*), to which we will return later in this chapter, even qualify as "historiographic metafictions."[12] In his guide to Italian narratives in the 1980s, Sergio Pautasso notes that these two fine narratives are part of a general trend in Italian literature to return to history in the wake of the new Left's demise.[13]

As the debate among women historians shows, however, the method of recuperation of past history is important, because method largely determines the results of the inquiry just as narrative form shapes messages as well as imposes limits. Historian Gianni Pomata responds to Paola di Cori by noting: "Our problem is not simply what to write (changing the content of history), but how to write: experimenting with new forms of historical narrative more adequate to the cognitive aims of women's history."[14] The discussion in this chapter will center around how differing representations of history, destiny, and causality in the historical fictions of several Italian women writers have shaped their narrative responses to the changing Italian literary, philosophical, and social context. Although these works do not always create forms consonant with any specific cognitive aim of women's history, the amorphous historical novel has provided a common ground for women writers from several generations and backgrounds to come together to represent both their personal and their collective "female" histories as they bring many feminist and female themes into the mainstream literary tradition.

History: From Object to Subject

Even if many Italian women are writing historical fictions, their reaction to the classification of their work as a "historical novel" is usually one of negation and dismay. At the end of a presentation of her book *La briganta*, at which most of the discussion centered around why the book was or was not a historical novel, Maria Rosa Cutrufelli bluntly asked the audience what the devil a historical novel was ("Che cavolo è il romanzo storico").[15] In a personal interview Rosetta Loy refuted the rubric as applied to her own work, saying that a historical novel has to present real characters as did Alessandro Manzoni's *I promessi sposi* (*The Betrothed*), although Loy's characters are in fact based on family descriptions of her Piedmont ancestors. Cutrufelli and Maraini reject the status of their works as historical novels on the grounds that they, unlike Manzoni, do not strive to create a factually true picture of the past, yet they admit to careful and detailed historical research in preparation for their narratives. None of these demurrers really serves to distinguish what these women do from anything Manzoni tried or did in *I promessi sposi*. The repeated denials demonstrate, however, that for any Italian writer who essays the historical novel Manzoni's legacy immediately presents a problem.

I promessi sposi, first published in three volumes between 1825 and 1827, is the story of two humble ("umili") peasants separated by corrupt aristocrats symbolic of the decadent remains of the feudal system, foreign invasions, and the Black Death. The happy reunion in the end has been touted at various times in the novel's long critical history as a symbol of the rebirth of a nation and its literature and as the epitome of what is wrong with Italy and its literature.[16] Manzoni himself, in *Del romanzo storico* (1850), criticized his own and other historical novels as "aberrations" that purport to be able to represent a higher truth through the proper mixture of history and invention. Manzoni's adoption and later rejection of the historical novel is symptomatic of the enthusiasm and distrust that has traditionally accompanied the mixing of history and poetry or fiction in the Western tradition. Although Aristotle originally separated history from literature, this separation has been slowly undermined through the centuries. Poetry's superiority was based on its ability to liberate itself from the particular truths to which history was limited and thereby to achieve a more philosophical truth. Following the indications of Cicero and later those of Saint Augustine, who claimed that history could fit into a general providential scheme, Christian theologians and Renaissance theorists, including Petrarch, placed rhetoric in history's domain. Yet historical discourse conceived as an eloquent, thus communicative act must take into account the author's intention and the audience's belief—concepts that naturally challenge the idea that history itself can re-present an independent, referential truth outside of discourse. Even if fifteenth-century debates did not push this problem to its limits, the groundwork for debates over the nature of truth and the possibility of its representation was already laid.[17]

When, in the nineteenth century, history became the common denominator and marker of prestige in the many hybrid literary works that, in Romantic fashion, boasted of breaking down the distinctions between genres rather than reinforcing them, the old debate between history and rhetoric, between invention and truth reared its vexed head. Historians and writers undertook to strengthen rather than merge their lines of demarcation. At approximately the same time that German historian Leopold von Ranke was redefining history to make science the barrier between historical research and imaginative writing, an ever-increasing multitude of writers of fiction, including Manzoni, were also denying the possibility of any successful synthesis of history and prose. The Manzoni of *Del romanzo storico* was primarily concerned with the dangers of contradiction and duplicity in the historical novel. Although he still believed in an ideal truth that the creative imagination could represent, he rejected any synthesis of historical and poetic truth. History found its truth in fact. The poet, and Manzoni, found their truth in God.[18]

The historical novel appeared in the European narratives toward the end of the eighteenth century as a vogue, and a most durable one at that. Narratives of the prolific Walter Scott, the initiator of the genre, appeared to signal a reform of the adventure romances of the preceding century. The historical novel boasted of a more tightly woven plot, a more psychologically and socially based characterization, and a more precisely chronological narration. Since these characteristics were found in the realist novel as well, genre critics Robert Scholes and Robert Kellogg emphasize the link of the historical novel to the rise of realism. For them, the historical novel can be best understood as a subgenre of the realist novel, which can be traced back to the empirical side of primitive, heroic narratives.[19] In *I promessi sposi*, history, no longer a neutral backdrop for hair-raising adventures, represents a tool humans can, in theory, use to understand themselves and their environment. Nonetheless, Manzoni clearly relegates it to a subservient role in relationship to the fictional imagination: history merely supplies the facts, whereas the imagination allows us to grasp the psychological complexity of the passions and emotions that make human beings act.[20]

Critics who wish to speak of the historical novel as a separate genre experience immediate difficulties due to its protean nature. Historical novels tend to be cast in other generic forms, observes writer and critic of historical novels Lion Feuchtwanger.[21] The most commonly borrowed form is that of the popular *feuilleton* with its paternalizing tone and melodramatic effects. Feuchtwanger and other critics who see the true historical novel as a separate genre resolve the problem of how to distinguish between a truly literary historical narrative and a pulp imitation by attributing a metaphysical function to the novel's form. The true historical novel is one that nourishes the cultural life of the reader and represents a higher truth than that of history: it must fill in history's "lamentable hiatuses" and incite the reader to think about society and the individual.[22] The authentic historical novel, then, defeats the efficacy of genre: it must exceed the limits of the form in which it is cast in order to make its humanistic intent and essence obvious to the reader.

In addition to the denial of formal consistency in the novel on the part of some critics, behind the continuing controversy over whether fiction or history better represents the truth lurks the belief that the primary function of both systems of writing is to re-present or make visible some truth that exists outside of the strictly literary sphere. Even Georg Lukacs's Marxist and dialectical approach to the subject is an attempt to validate the historical novel's representational ability.[23] In *Theory of the Novel*, a work Lukacs later dismissed as having been a product of his early allegiance to Hegelian idealism, he presents Hegel's views that all novels originate in the dissolution of the epic, which itself reflected the loss of totality in ancient Greece. The novel's historical components represent the efforts of the text to find its way back to the origin, attempts that only force it to see its own limitations through representations of fragmentation, alienation, and lack.[24] According to David Carroll, in Lukacs's later discussions concerning the historical novel, the theorist replaces the abstract, literary typologies found in the *Theory of the Novel* with a dialectical historical model. History or historicity becomes paradoxically that which makes representation possible; certain historical representations enact the dialectic to ensure the return of humans to their original harmonious state (99–101). This viewpoint, found in *Del romanzo storico*, causes Lukacs to resurrect and praise Manzoni's original goal in *I promessi sposi*. He calls Manzoni a great historical realist who captured in prose "the critical condition of the entire life of the Italian people resulting from Italy's fragmentation . . . the story of . . . the tragedy of the Italian people as a whole."[25]

The original theories of Lukacs on the historical novel did not receive an enthusiastic reception in Italy. In the 1950s, at the height of the neorealist movement, a militant Marxist critical establishment arguing for a realistic and committed "workers' literature" was quick to reject the Hegelian idealism in Lukacs's work. In the sixties, when Lukacs's image as an existentialist, negative thinker won more followers, enthusiasts of structuralism again dismissed Lukacs's work on the historical novel as another example of criticism of content.[26] When Elsa Morante's historical novel entitled *La storia* appeared in 1974 and unleashed a markedly divisive polemic over the form, Lukacs's name was heard again but this time as part of her defense. Catholic and non-Marxist critics alike used his name to buttress their arguments for the validity of Morante's aesthetics of history, so radically different from the poetic narratives for which she was known. If Morante's bitter vision of reality can still be found in La storia, the magical realism and incandescent, allusive style of previous novels is gone, states Joy Potter. Although Potter credits Morante for taking a committed, political position similar to other Italian Marxists, La storia's, "literary worth is minimal."[27]

In Morante's La storia, Manzoni's "umili" reappear. The main character is Ida Ramundo, a widowed elementary schoolteacher in Rome during World War II. Ida, a simple, good-hearted woman struggling to raise her only teenage son, Nino, is tormented both by the physical harshness of the life of the poor during wartime and by the fact that, because of her Jewish mother, she could end up in a concentration camp. Morante weaves her tale of power and the oppression of official History, written with a capital H and recounted by the narrator at the beginning of various chapters, around a clearly melodramatic plot.[28] History is not a reflection of providential will that rewards the good and the innocent, as is the case in I promessi sposi. Rather it has become the nemesis of our century, a demogogical machine bent on increasing its impregnability by crushing all those who cross its path. In Morante's view, the poetic imagination, and the utopian vision it incarnates and inspires, represented by Ida's son Useppe, is the only defense one has against oppression and all variations of (fascist) history. Useppe and poetry represent a positive, anarchistic force that unveils the atrocities of chronological, official History—defined by Morante in her subtitle as "uno scandalo che dura da diecimila anni" ("a scandal that has lasted 10,000 years")—and prefigures its demise.

In an article comparing La storia with historical novels by Elena Garro and Isabel Allende, James Mandrell claims that the prophetic, poetic voice that Useppe personifies is the most significant innovation contemporary women writers have introduced into the historical novel: prophecy, creativity, and the feminine enable these writers to defeat history, usually represented as a crushing, repetitive force.[29] Mandrell views Isabel Allende's House of the Spirits (1982) as the novel most successful at circumventing history because the voice functions as an "anticipation of history itself" (242), but he undercuts his own theory somewhat when he admits that, in Morante's case, it is not clear how the "utopian view of the individual can be reconciled with a patently dystopian presentation of society" (239). Mandrell defines the historical novel as a primarily representational form, and his analysis takes into account both the shaping and the limiting influences of form on message:

That this *new reality cannot be represented within the boundaries of the historical novel is one of the limitations of the genre itself.* Yet the fact that change is suggested—even negatively—must be seen as positive, if depressingly remote. (239, emphasis added)

The bitter polemic that followed *La storia*'s publication showed that Italian critics, too, were bothered not by Morante's accordance of a material, concrete power for poetry but rather by the form of *La storia*, which denied this same power by negating the possibility of progress and change. As Gregory Lucente points out in his detailed review of the debate, the Italian avant-garde of the time overwhelmingly rejected the ability of traditional forms and structures to do anything other than recapitulate and reinforce society's existing structures.[30] Traditional forms were equated almost naively at times with a type of "bad" subjectivity—that is, one not reducible to a collective movement against capitalism—whereas the negation of traditional character, plot, and causality in literature put into play a "good" subjectivity that was radical, political and, oppositional.[31] A letter written by Elisabetta Rasy, Nanni Balestrini, Letizia Paolozzi, and Umberto Silva three weeks after the appearance of *La storia* used the text as an example of how traditional representational systems fail to induce change in the organization of power in society, where a reorganization of linguistic and literary structures could succeed.[32]

More sympathetic critics defended Morante's poetic language and its power to offset her representation of history's hapless victims.[33] Critic Rossana Dedola argues, in terms reminiscent of Feuchtwanger's warnings, that the form of the popular novel effectively undermines Morante's vision of anarchy that she wants to oppose to bourgeois values, such as those that produced fascism. It is the paternalist, pathetic, and populist ideology inherent in the novel's form that preaches for such a vision at the same time that Morante's characters confess to Communist or anarchist tendencies.[34] Nevertheless, Dedola argues that there are strong, effective moments in the narrative, especially when the story is told through the eyes of Useppe: Useppe's viewpoint changes *La storia* from representation to symbol and the work becomes a modern psychological investigation into humans and their destiny (264–265).

The debate over *La storia* in Italy, though certainly comparable to feminist arguments over the value and possibilities of representational fiction, still picks up the main themes of discord over the historical novel form since its inception: its ability to express a higher form of poetic truth and to represent some kind of progress and development on the part of human beings. The historical novel appeared on the literary scene as a result of a new philosophy of history. Manzoni, taking his cue from Giambattista Vico, viewed history as a continuous process which, in his case, reflected a just providential order. When included in narrative forms, however, history most often undertakes the fictional role of causality, that is, the constellation of problems, events, and social, economic, or psychological forces that keep the plot moving forward and to which the characters must respond. It is here that the choice of narrative form in which the text is cast becomes important, since many of the possible generic forms have causal systems that conflict with the ideological view of history the author may claim to want to represent.

I promessi sposi itself is a case in point. I have argued elsewhere that Manzoni's choice of the romance form for his story, with its attendant rules of character portrayal, motivation, and causality, inevitably conflicted with the organic view of history the novel was supposed to represent.[35] Although Manzoni effectively reduced the role of religion in his narrative to one of consolation, albeit a necessary one, and depicted his characters as sprightly, inventive types, his implementation of the romance system of causality results in the depiction of history as an ultimately impenetrable as well as overwhelming force. Manzoni's insistence on a type of realism based on generalizing laws to validate events and character motivation is still within the realm of romance and only temporarily masks what Gérard Genette has called "l'arbitraire du récit."[36] His characters are never really in a position to resolve the action through knowledge gleaned from their adventures, and when external powers such as chance or Providence terminate the plot, human dependency and limits are again asserted.

It is not surprising that the criticism of *I promessi sposi* has been, at times, very similar to that of *La storia*. Manzoni's paternalistic moral at the end, which exhorts the humble to suffer in resignation the unavoidable and arbitrary injustices in history, seems to negate any analyses in the book that show humans to be responsible for their fate and capable of improving their lot alone.[37] Although form interferes with the portrayal of poetry's efficacy in *La storia*, it enhances Morante's critique of History. Manzoni's and Morante's narratives are both documented historical novels: they are works in which known and well-documented historical events serve as a backdrop for invented characters and plot. Morante, though, has changed certain elements so as to make her piece a critical commentary on the contradictions inherent in the historical novel in general and in Manzoni's work in particular.

In both narratives, external causal forces are seen as the ultimate determining forces. If Manzoni, in the interests of keeping a realistic narrative, allows for some freedom of action to make his characters appear more realistic and less stereotypical, Morante unmasks this tactic by allowing her characters none. In both works, history is the main character, the primary governing factor that insures unity and meaning to the characters' experiences. In *I promessi sposi*, Providence appears at the end to show that history was only the realistic *cause occasionelle* for its progressive work, but Morante exposes this *discorso segreto* by displaying the contradictions between form and ideology in the historical novel only too clearly. History is not an externally guided, beneficent force but a man-made causal system that has now turned into a monster feeding on its victims to extend its power.

Morante's characters, totally incapable of resistance, expose the question of free will and development in historical novels as a tragic farce. The emphasis on repetition as a major force in history reveals the historical novel's claim to present the possibility of change and demonstrates it to be a scandalous sham of the powerful. Therefore, in contrast to Manzoni and other epigones of the historical form, Morante emphasizes the helpless downward spiraling toward self-destruction inherent in the romance form and the popular novel and refutes Manzoni's discourse of history. Lucente argues that the regenerative plot of *I promessi sposi* teaches its protagonist, Renzo, "the ability to use language and other forms of behavior to make one's way *in the world of men* in what is now a symbolically and literally purged society."[38] If this is so, Morante's emphasis on poetic language could be interpreted as yet another critical overturning of the master's message, because Morante's poetic language admits to no such compromise.

Morante, dubbed *la grande solitaria*, never participated in any aspect of the feminist movement or showed any sympathy for the type of literature it was producing. Nonetheless, recent criticism emphasizes the feminine nature of the poetry and poetic language found in all of her works.[39] Despite Morante's almost legendary antagonistic relationship to other women writers, Paola Blelloch links the Morante of *La storia* to other, older women writers of historical fiction, such as Anna Banti and Maria Bellonci, all of whom "refute History with a capital *H*, made by man and woven through with his prejudices, and who write 'her story,' primarily composed of tears and humiliation, then of silence and finally of overt rebellion."[40] Valeria Finucci, in her reading of Banti's *Artemisia*, corroborates the view that these women writers, even if they were not conscious of "writing as a woman," as the phrase goes, could not ignore their own desire to explain the historical oppression of women.[41] Finucci describes Banti's story about how Artemisia Gentileschi, born in 1598 in Rome, overcame the shame of a rape trial and the rejection by her father to establish herself as a painter as a eulogy for thousands of women "whose destinies are doomed or vilified by sexual catastrophes" (171).

In contrast to Morante's *La storia*, the historical fictions of Banti and Bellonci recreate the psychological past of history's forgotten, misunderstood, or maligned women.[42] Although these women undoubtedly share a negative view of official History, their representations of it vary. Close readings of the novels of these older writers reveal a variety of techniques that many women critics now praise, though their works were previously given short shrift by the younger generation of women writers who considered them too traditional.[43] In her reading of Banti's *Artemisia*, Deborah Heller shows how Banti's complicated narratological techniques make her story a way of reaching into the past to create an empowering bond with another woman. The author-narrator and Artemisia take turns telling the story, which Banti changes at crucial points to emphasize the need for female solidarity if women are to become artists in their own right. The narrative also allegorizes the "reemergence of the writer's enduring cultural heritage, as an Italian and as a woman, in the face of the present destruction of her homeland following two decades of Fascist rule that have led to this debacle."[44] In Banti's novel, art and writing are major components of the private haven where the self can break the hold of history and destiny.

The retreat from life into art is not necessarily a female and/or feminist theme, although Banti is clearly protesting a stereotypical female destiny in *Artemisia*. Recent feminist studies corroborate Banti's depiction of Artemisia as the archetype of the oppressed female imagination that can overcome all odds to affirm female courage and achievement.[45] Painstaking research, artistically modified, and a powerful female survivor are also the main ingredients of Maria Bellonci's *Rinascimento privato* (*A Private Renaissance*), winner of the 1985 Strega literary prize.[46] Bellonci recreates the psyche of the well-known and admired Isabella d'Este, daughter of the powerful Ercole d'Este of Ferrara and wife of Francesco Gonzaga of Mantua. Isabella presided over a brilliant Renaissance court, acting as diplomat and informant for her husband, who was primarily concerned with saving the integrity of his military reputation.[47] The novel covers the tumultuous years from 1500 to 1533, a period which included numerous French and Imperial invasions that resulted in the fall of Florence, Venice, and Milan, the infamous reigns of Popes Julius II and Leo X, the rise of Martin Luther, and the sack of Rome. Isabella keeps in touch with the events of official History through the letters of an invented character, a cleric named Robert de la Pole who adores her from afar and writes secretly to warn her of the ever-impending dangers. His function is not only to report the facts but to effect a visible separation in the text, similar to the one in *La storia*, between historical facts and Isabella's personal interpretation of them.

If on the level of History, however, the period is one in which Italy changed from a composite of autonomous states into a dominated country, the private renaissance, as the title indicates, is the story of the struggles of an astute woman to ensure the survival of her family and thus fulfill what feminists have called her ahistorical destiny. On this level, Isabella achieves some success. At his death, her husband bequeaths to her all legal rights to govern the court of Mantua. She obtains the prestigious cardinal's hat for her son Ercole, and, after many intrigues and setbacks, she defies Emperor Charles V's choice of a marriage partner for her son Federico to insure an heir for the Gonzaga house.

Isabella's high intellect and overwhelming pragmatism make her superior to the men who govern historical events and even to the men in her family, for whom she must constantly fight by using her political acumen. After she wins her long battle to marry Federico to a member of an Italian aristocratic family, instead of to his mistress who had already born him a son, Isabella's cardinal son Ercole declares emphatically, "Mother . . . one thing is certain: none of your sons could ever defeat you" (527).[48] The adoring Robert de la Pole concludes in his final letter that Isabella personifies the consummate female intellect that can think independently of the body, yet her modest victories show she still retains her links to a pragmatic, earthly existence.[49]

Despite this reaffirmation of Isabella's essential female self, which reflects a topical feminist theme, she is successful because she denies rather than asserts her feminine nature. To be sure, Bellonci has her protagonist-narrator rail against those men who refuse to heed her advice and who advise her husband to do so as well because she is a female and thus, by definition, inferior. Yet Isabella knows that she will be victorious only by playing male games better than the men. She has no relationship to her mother, whom she considers weak, or to her female offspring, who are ignored and then placed in convents where they justifiably complain that their mother never comes to visit. Isabella fights for her sons in order to fulfill successfully the destiny of a woman and mother, a fate she admits a mother cannot escape. Thus, in order to critique man's base machinations which, in turn, fuel History's catastrophes, Isabella struggles to save herself, her husband, and her oldest son from any tendencies toward the weaker *femminile*, which would insure their early destruction.

The relationship of Isabella and Artemisia to prejudices against their own sex reflects Bellonci and Banti's uneasiness and anger with these biases. The debate over the superiority of poetry to history that has long plagued the form reinforces Bellonci and Banti's gender bind. Like Morante, Bellonci and Banti see history as a humanly made tyrannical force which can only be displaced through the affirmation of a poetic imagination. If poetry depicts a truth superior to that of history, however, it is only by first proving themselves to be competent, objective, and neutral historians that these women can begin to criticize the corruption and pettiness of man's history that is represented as an exaggeration of limiting male traits. If men must learn to rise above mundane history, so must women who, like Isabella, represent an androgynous human subject, the ideal mixture of both genders. Through the character of Isabella, Bellonci reaffirms her belief in the power of the human personality to rise above history. The novels of these women do not, as in the case of *La storia*, seek to destroy the form. Nonetheless, History will repeat itself again here and have the last word concerning these exceptional women. Despite Isabella's success in linking her family with the victorious Hapsburgs, the Gonzaga line died out in 1627 when the political defeat of Italy finally penetrated into Isabella's personal realm.

Historiographic Metafiction and Gendered Subjectivity

A somewhat different role for and representation of history is found in an early narrative by the literary critic Maria Corti, *L'ora di tutti* (1962).[50] Insofar as Corti claims to be recounting "the universal story of suffering" ("la storia universale dei dolori"), she appears to be following the recommendations of Lukacs to concentrate on the sufferings of the humble, the "umili" who, unlike Isabella d'Este, do not exert any real control, however temporary, over the historical events that threaten to annihilate them. The particular historical event that structures this novel is the successful Turkish invasion of Otranto on July 22, 1480. The Turks controlled the town for almost a year before the army of Don Alfonso d'Aragona returned to defeat them. The first two sections of the book deal with how three townspeople, a fisherman named Colangelo, the army captain Zurlo, and the beautiful peasant woman Idrusa, meet their death. The third section is divided into two chapters, the first of which depicts the massacre of those Christians who refused to renounce their faith in front of the Turkish soldiers. In the final chapter, another character describes the town after the restoration of Spanish order in Otranto.

The exact meaning and importance of *L'ora di tutti* is open to debate. The book jacket of the 1977 edition states that the book is first and foremost about the confrontation of a variety of people with death. On a deeper level, however, the story can be read as an allegory of any communal struggle of people held together by a "popular ethic," and thus can be related to the contemporary struggle of the much-maligned southern Italians. Blelloch's analysis concentrates on the story of Idrusa, which includes many topical feminist themes. Frustrated in her marriage to a simple fisherman whose death she indirectly causes, Idrusa revolts against the community by engaging in a satisfying sexual relationship with a handsome Spanish soldier. When she learns that she is being used by him as well, she demands his transfer from the town's mayor who has long admired Idrusa from afar. Idrusa dies a heroic death by taking her life in order to stop Turkish soldiers from raping her in a church where she, along with the other townspeople, had taken refuge in the final hours of the invasion. Blelloch reads the story as an allegory of the contemporary struggle of southern Italian women for whom love is usually depicted as something "obscure, violent, heroic and, in the end, tragic."[51]

The main subject of *L'ora di tutti* is, however, historicity itself. Rather than playing the role of a character gone mad, as in *La storia*, or a series of antagonistic events the protagonist must overcome, history here is more akin to the Annales school concept of *histoire de longue durée*, that is, the enduring social, economic, and psychological structures that inform the slowly changing *mentalités collectives*. The characters in *L'ora di tutti* are brought together by the equalizing experience of death, a subject which has itself been studied in depth by the social and cultural historians of the Annales school.[52] But, if the Annales group emphasized quantitative and serial data to confirm their findings, Italian historians, such as Carlo Ginzburg and Carlo Poni, developed an "evidential paradigm"—the reading of exceptional documents and records to identify in detectivelike fashion the secret and concealed discourses of the inarticulate. Although Ginzburg insisted on elucidating a "dead history" with no connections to the present, his method for explaining historical causality on the level of small groups focused, like Corti in her novel, on expressing the experiences of people lost by history's quantifying process.[53]

Rather than offering a profound analysis of various attitudes toward death, Corti uses culture and tradition here as the primary motivating factors for the characters' actions, thereby replacing Manzoni's providential plan for development with a more contextualized model of history. The anonymous narrator of the introductory paragraphs proposes to delve imaginatively into the past to explain the deep structural continuities in attitudes, language, and certain customs in contemporary Otranto, a town little changed by the major historical events comprising *l'histoire événémentielle*, that is, descriptions of wars and the lists of kings or government leaders. Duke Alfonso tells Aloise de Marco, the final narrator in *L'ora di tutti*, that these chronological events do not denote change: "The small things, not the big ones, point to the real changes" (326).[54]

Philippe Ariès states that modern-day historians have discovered that traditional cultures tend toward stasis; because their demographic and economic balance do not evolve, extraordinary events cause such cultures to regress even more forcefully to their initial beliefs and habits.[55] Likewise, if the characters in *L'ora di tutti* derive their strength from their historical culture, culture hinders the very change Duke Alfonso pretends to see and makes its representation unnecessary. The duke comments on the real nature of change after inviting himself to lead the opening dance at the first peasant wedding to take place after his liberation of Otranto. His participation not only embarrasses the peasants but also interferes with their custom of having the bride and bridegroom start the dancing with a bright kerchief that they then throw to the crowd. Duke Alfonso justifies his actions by announcing that the kerchief is a symbol of past servitude which he has ended: "We no longer dance with kerchiefs but hand in hand. And let this be a sign that servitude has ended. Have you men understood?" (331).[56]

Servitude is precisely the structure that has not changed and which accounts the most for the similarity between past and present in Otranto. Aloise de Marco's final question, "Has anything changed?" is a purely rhetorical one the introductory chapter had already answered in the negative. If History's repetitive nature is here openly emphasized, rather than disguised through the depiction of a series of partial victories by strong individuals, this same repetitive nature empowers the author-narrator to concentrate less on the representation of causal determining factors—the reasons for the historical fact—and more on how a subjective consciousness perceives and orders the world. Questions of progress and development, usually linked to the representation of official History in a way that hindered the individual development of the characters, are suspended. Consequently, lack of change paradoxically functions to permit the author to rewrite the episode in terms of the present, which is really the object of investigation in *L'ora di tutti*.

The shift in interest from what actually happened in the past to how we can come to know and experience it is, according to Linda Hutcheon, the distinguishing element in postmodern sensibility and the one that informs the plethora of historiographic metafictions appearing in many national literatures. Hutcheon points out that historiographic metafiction revives the old debate over truth of history and truth in fiction:

Historiographic metafiction refutes the natural or common sense methods of distinguishing between historical fact and fiction. It refuses the view that only history has a truth claim, both by questioning the ground of that claim in historiography and by asserting that both history and fiction are discourses, human constructs, signifying systems, and both derive their major claim to truth from that identity.[57]

The tenuous differences between history and fiction are collapsed, but not simply in an effort to deny the possibility of knowledge and to argue for ahistoricity. The study of historiographic metafiction can provide just as solid a basis for the materialistic study of the subject called for by Teresa de Lauretis in *Alice Doesn't*, because in historiographic metafiction a heterogenous subject is placed into the context of its *parole*, that is, the signifying activities that engender it as a subject (Hutcheon, 166–167, 172–173). Fiction's latest challenge to history's truth has again provoked historians to detach themselves even more from literature by initiating a closer association with the quantitative sectors of the social sciences.[58] Historiographic metafiction does not deny the veracity of the historical fact. By privileging interpretation, however, it both forces the narrating consciousness to reveal itself and its interests and validates the worth of such partial, reinterpretive vision. According to Hayden White, "historical inquiry is born less of a necessity to establish that certain events occurred than of the desire to determine what certain events might mean for a given group, society, or culture's conception of its present tasks and future prospect."[59]

As we have seen in an outline of the debates (Chapter 1), feminists and deconstructionists, despite many similar interests, are separated on questions of the necessity of positing some agency for the subject who can describe and analyze his or her experiences. In her work, Hutcheon makes a few brief references to the work of philosophers Gianni Vattimo and Pier Aldo Rovatti, creators of *il pensiero debole*, which can be translated as "weak epistemology," or more commonly "weak thought." Hutcheon describes *il pensiero debole* as the method closest to postmodern paradoxes because it deals with the need to think and criticize from inside a system in which one is necessarily implicated:

Fundamentally contradictory and provisional, this is a philosophy which knows it cannot dismiss "reason-domination" because it is implicated in it, but neither does it seek to avoid the challenges to the Enlightenment project, as some have accused Habermas of doing. (191)

In their various works, Vattimo and Rovatti present weak thought as an antidote to deconstructionist insistence on the loss of the referent and its decentering of subjectivity.[60] Weak thought, like French post-structuralism, opposes efforts to ground the human sciences in any foundations that claim a unifying principle. A main concern of the supporters of weak thought is how to preserve a positive concept of Being with a critical capacity while, at the same time, to avoid falling back into metaphysics, the traditional histories of Being. Giovanna Borrodori maintains that Vattimo's redefinition of Being as a "direction" avoids both the idealist and Marxian necessity of a "critical overcoming." Critical thought should direct itself at a "re-writing of metaphysics itself." Vattimo interprets this particular sense of Being, already suggested by Martin Heidegger in *Being and Time*, as a direction in which Being and beings happen to be on the same path, involved in a common movement that will lead them not to a stable basis but to a further dislocation, in which they will find themselves deprived of any center. Tradition so viewed is not something to be overcome dialectically, but which has to be "re-collected, re-used, re-accepted."[61]

Vattimo develops a theoretical perspective based on Heidegger's concept of *Verwindung* (overcoming), although for Heidegger this mode was considered an "improper" overcoming since it did not include the critical characteristics of the dialectical *Aufhebung* (sublation) and did not leave behind the past. Vattimo again borrows Heidegger's concept of *Andenken*, which literally means to re-collect: *Andenken* allows one to look at tradition from the point of view of *Ge-Schick*, that is, being sent back to review destiny or historical destination. Vattimo argues that only by adopting these concepts can postmodernism evolve without falling back into the traps of modernism itself. Postmetaphysical thought, although it cannot grasp Being as "presence," does not then necessarily have to move away from the content of metaphysics to another "object." Instead, it rethinks the history of metaphysics, which it perceives from a different, even distorted (*verwunden*) point of view.

Theories of weak thought are, as Peter Carravetta states, "a repositioning of the question of interpretation."[62] This process of reinterpretation or re-signing of events does not avoid the term "experience": in fact, it searches for a way that would allow a reconceptualization of the issue in terms of experience. The experience of history—or history's "errors," as theoreticians of *il pensiero debole* put it—links the feminist project in these works to contemporary philosophical probes into the inscription of subjectivity and problems of reference in a more textual manner. For Vattimo, experience is something we create, a rhetorical appeal, as he explains in his example of Friedrich Nietzsche's statement "God is dead." The death of God is in no way comprehensible as a metaphysical assessment of the nonexistence of God. It is, however, a real announcement of a fact, or an "experience," that Western culture has undergone.

Theoreticians of weak thought insist that we are still speaking of being and that by redefining the theoretical bases of modernism itself, by reliving the experience of the "necessity of the error," we come closer to understanding being's (written with a small *b*) hermeneutical nature. The struggle of Vattimo, Rovatti, and others to continue to study Being (the subject), to lay contradictions bare without proposing another "truth," and to recognize the difficulty if not impossibility of any "definitive farewell to reason" (Borrodori, 1) is certainly comparable to contemporary feminist struggles to justify the study of women and experience, including those "lost" in the past. Like many feminist redefinitions of experience and the interpreting subject, weak thought assumes a contradictory subject engaged in rethinking his or her historical past, albeit as error, because a complete break with it and with reason is impossible. The connection between the two systems of thought was suggested by Aldo Gargani, who termed the process of weak thought *la voce femminile*, defining it as the voice of sense and difference, the recall of signs, traces, and voices that have been forgotten by mainstream History.[63] In their historical narratives, Marisa Volpi and Marta Morazzoni resemble practitioners of weak thought in their effort to regain a setting for narration, a circumscribed domain of referentiality in which a certain knowledge can operate.

However compatible these theoretical desires may seem, practice has produced the predictable discontents and failures. In 1978 and 1980, two issues of the philosophical journal *aut aut* placed essays by male philosophers such as Vattimo, Rovatti, and Gargani side by side with those of feminist philosophers including Luisa Muraro and Lea Melandri.[64] Although in both issues the main theme is the crisis in subjectivity, especially the demise of Marxism's essentializing categories, the different sexes follow diverse itineraries. Paola di Cori notes that in these articles men lament the crisis of reason in moral terms and call for the need to examine other oppressed subjectivities, whereas women speak of creating a framework in which they can conceive of themselves as (gendered) subjects.[65] Maurizio Viano also notes the shared theories of weak thought and feminism. In practice, however, men ignore the corporality they claim to want to add to their theories; therefore Viano accuses weak thought practitioners of simply renaming their own subjectivity as weak in order to be able to continue playing games with the masculine symbolic, which is still assumed to be the only possible one and still masquerades as neuter and complete.[66]

Although the philosophers of weak thought most certainly can be faulted for ignoring gender, the influence of this theory, like that of cultural historians, on historical narratives has been to facilitate the depiction of gendered subjectivities. In Morazzoni's *La ragazza col tur-*

bante and Volpi's *Il maestro della betulla*, history is akin to the description by Michel Foucault of Nietzsche's effective history as "forces operating in history uncontrolled by destiny or regulative mechanisms but which respond to haphazard conflicts, a host of errors and phantasms."[67] Once again, although this particular concept of history may have its disadvantages for feminist historians, its representation in fiction enables a narrating subjectivity to represent itself differently from the previous historical narratives that linked history's progress to character development. This viewpoint also reverses the gender bind in which women writers like Bellonci and Banti found themselves. These writers would not need to disguise their alterations of historical fact in order to depict a victorious woman and thus risk diminishing their reputation as "objective writers"; nor would history's presence in the narrative force them to depict again the inevitable defeat and marginalization of women. This concept of history would enable these women writers to distance themselves from their personal experiences and, at the same time, to write these gendered experiences into a framework where history's overpowering destiny is reduced to "erroneous events" subject to interpretation.

Both Volpi's and Morazzoni's collections of stories include familiar themes found in feminist narratives and women's writing in general, such as female degradation, solitude, marginalization, the objectification of women by men, and the resultant regressive and dependent behavior. The historical figures that Volpi, an art critic, and Morazzoni, a specialist in German literature, depict are overwhelmingly chosen from the artistic milieu. The return to depicting lesser-known historical personages is not just an attempt to recuperate lost or misunderstood genius; it also mirrors Vattimo's aesthetic model of historical transformation. Vattimo, like Ginzburg and Foucault, denies traditional notions of continuity and progress, and he claims that the histories of both art and science succeed in the same discontinuous fashion. History and art are united in their similar rhetorical traits that persuade people to act according to one paradigm rather than the other. In Vattimo's aesthetic model of historical transformation, the work of art is a historical event in that we are changed by our efforts to interpret it and recover its truth.[68]

Six of the nine stories in Volpi's *Il maestro della betulla* are based on a known historical referent. The author flaunts the fictitious, personal nature of her historical inquiry through intermittent comments from a first-person narrator. This narrator, who personifies a *voce femminile*, openly admits her use of an "inventive memory" ("memoria inventiva") which, she warns, will be as inconsistent as any "human endeavor" (44). The formation of this voice is the topic of the first short story, "Caminito," which recounts the tale of a female student's relationship with her mentor, an English professor named Villalba. Their intellectual relationship is tinged with sexual innuendo, and the narrator speaks of Villalba as the father who is necessary to give form and stability to her life and work. The narrator describes herself as an educated woman who has had ample opportunity to realize herself professionally, but as a woman she feels helpless and lost when confronted with language and life:

I felt like a typical woman, incapable of creating a meaning for my life. Weak and subject to uncontrollable emotions, instinctively caught up in the need to have a man on my horizon, a man to compete with, even surpass, albeit one ready to help my weak fantasy and my even weaker spiritual determination. (17)[69]

Although this situation, in itself, is certainly neither new nor uncommon in women's writing, Volpi's persona unabashedly presents her feelings of dependency and inadequacy as precisely those that inform and empower her specific critical gaze. She interrupts this "confessional" statement, however, in order to stop her slide toward the self-destructive "mirror of introspection" and finishes the chapter by recounting her discovery of her professor's possible homosexual activities. As a result of this knowledge, the narrator realizes that the professor has also been the object of her own creative fantasies. His perceived identity, a result of encounters with indifference, solitude, and alienation, is no more fixed than hers.

The narrating voice then proceeds to recount the title short story, which portrays the experiences of a male outsider. The painter of birch trees is Gaspard Dughet, the now almost forgotten brother-in-law of the French classical painter Nicolas Poussin. Gaspard attacks the consoling nature of Poussin's classicism: "Your canvasses service those who study rational philosophy to exorcise their fears" (44).[70] Gaspard's own paintings, however, are dismissed as excessive, disorderly, and "feminine" (33). The recuperation of a misunderstood artist is not only linked to feminist outrage (similar to that of Martelli in *Chi perde la sua vita*) at the use of the epithet "feminine" to trivialize and marginalize difference. In addition, the narrating voice announces here that her conceptualization of Gaspard's exclusion, oppression, and revolt is based on her subjective experience of these same emotions.

The third short story, "Esilio" ("Exile"), is also replete with feminist themes and motifs that function as valid explanations for character motivations. "Esilio" recreates the ill-fated love affair of painter Anselm Feuerbach and his beautiful Roman model, Anna Risi. Upon arriving in Rome, Anselm is both inflamed and inspired by the sight of

Anna at a window holding her child. Soon afterward the couple is living together. Anna allays in the artist the sense of exile he feels from his country, his mother, and history (51); he gives form to this feeling in the representations of her as a series of Greco-Roman heroines. Anna, for her part, is also aware of the idealized, ethereal role she must play which, while guaranteeing that her beauty resist the ravages of time, divides her from her material, corporeal desires and existence. Eventually, the narrator tells us, both the artist and his model can know joy only through "fantasy and memory" (63). Anselm returns home at the request of his stepmother, Henriette, whose suppressed sexual feelings for him now cause her to take on the stereotypical role of guardian of his moral values. When Anselm is able to break from his stepmother and finance his return to Rome, neither he nor Anna is able to continue the relationship due to the many misunderstandings and misconceptions on which it had been founded. In this "historic recasting" of feminist theories on male idealization of the female, art is the medium that expresses the inexpressible feelings of the protagonists and narrator as well as the indicator of change in them. Furthermore, their experience of these sentiments is caused by the continuous and complex intertwining of gender relationships.

The solitary historical figures in Morazzoni's *La ragazza col turbante* are depicted through their experiences with cruelty, indifference, and revenge, three general themes that bring the diverse narratives together. In contrast to *Il maestro della betulla*, here there is no female authorial voice to interrupt the text. Art, however, continues to be the primary medium through which one can re-present history, causality, and character development. The title story in this collection concerns not an artist but a painting, Jan Vermeer's *Girl in a Turban*. This portrait is being sold by a well-known Dutch art dealer to a rich Dane around 1658. Both the eccentric Dane and the Dutch art connoisseur who brings him the portrait appear oblivious to women in real life. At the same time, they are learned adorers of the female image in the painting, the inanimate object of exchange upon which they can freely project their theories and emotions. Three other stories in the collection concern the degradation and oppression of historical figures in their private lives: a conversation between Wolfgang Mozart and his wife in his final hours; the story of the majordomo of Carlo V whose vendetta is to burn the memoirs the emperor had entrusted to him; Lorenzo DaPonte's humiliation at the hands of court musician Antonio Salieri. The last story, the only nonhistorical text, recounts the silent revenge of Karl Köllner, who has refused to die after a totally incapacitating stroke, consequently remaining an embarrassment to his family.

Given that the protagonist in each story is male, women initially appear to be absent from Morazzoni's collection of five short stories. One reviewer of *La ragazza col turbante* correctly comments that the title story, besides showing art's relationship to cultural and aesthetic values, also represents art's changing relationship to the new mercantilism, and thus the changing social and economic hierarchies, in the seventeenth century.[71] Neria de Giovanni suggests that the method and language of investigation is decidedly feminine since it validates what Luce Irigaray has defined as the basis of woman's creativity in language: her ability to reinvent the world through gossip, digressions, and the weaving together of seemingly unrelated (story) lines or threads.[72] Morazzoni herself describes her work as "gossip" concerning the past, and her gossip recreates all types of people. Although the stories appear to focus on male historical figures, women stereotypes fill the backgrounds of these stories: the lonely, resentful, pregnant wife the merchant leaves behind, since she cannot possibly understand "the pleasure which the thought of the journey roused in him at the moment and in those circumstances" (60); the slightly frivolous Mrs. Mozart, whose careless comments interfere with her husband's work in his final hours; the witchlike gypsy, for whom Carlo V's steward steals food in his initial revenge for having been separated from his own wife; the haughty Mrs. Köllner, who is determined not to allow her older, distant, and now disabled husband to renege on his promise to her to lead an elegant life, and thus fights to keep him in permanent seclusion.

Variations on these female types appear in those works we have classified as romance and *Bildungsroman*, and explanations for the behavior of these women have been treated at length in feminist treatises. Thus, although in these narrative tableaux Morazzoni leaves final explanations, if there are any, up to the reader, the vindictive, frivolous, trivial behavior of the female types has already been explained. In the text, Morazzoni's narrator attributes the characters' actions and reactions to general human needs and emotions: self-defense, survival, jealousy, anger, frustration, and so on. These emotions, however, produce different behaviors in males and females which are constantly being misinterpreted. On the representational level, the consistent lack of communication between both male and female protagonists suggests the separate and silenced "prehistory" of women condemned to marginal and stereotypical behavior. Yet the persistently generalizing viewpoint, which is now returning to experience this solitude and separation, constantly calls into question the partial nature of histories that have denied the influence of these women in those gray areas where "thought and reality unite" through the representation of interpretive errors.[73]

In Morazzoni's second novel, *L'invenzione della verità* (*The Invention of Truth*), the lack of communication between men and women parallels the structure of the narrative and reinforces the general theme that "man" can never completely comprehend the past. In alternating chapters, Morazzoni reinvents two separate stories that refuse to come together: that of an anonymous female tapestry-weaver in the Middle Ages and John Ruskin's later research into the same tapestry. Ruskin's frustration with the tapestry reveals his own partial vision, though Morazzoni stops short of directly attributing this deficiency to gender. History, as the title of the book underlines, is an inventive contemplation of a fact (or artifact) we can never fully recuperate. Yet its invention and reinvention are necessary human activities that both genders practice, as Morazzoni herself demonstrates by her very act of recreating, reordering, and reperceiving these historical vignettes.

History as Personal and Communal Autobiographies

In contrast to the circular narratives of Volpi and Morazzoni, Rosetta Loy's *Le strade di polvere*, Dacia Maraini's *La lunga vita di Marianna Ucrìa*, and Maria Rosa Cutrufelli's *La briganta* proceed in chronological order and return to a relatively objective and representational view of history more directly linked to character change and development. Nonetheless, in these full-length narratives the authors again develop and validate feminist themes by showing how they contribute to explaining the lacks, voids, and errors in male history. Despite differences among these works, the recreation of historical fact parallels the creation of a female authorial viewpoint that experiences history in both personal and general terms.

Loy, whose father came from near Monferrato, claims her interest in writing a historical narrative was sparked by a desire to bring to life a part of her family's past. Loy's previous novels deal with history insofar as they usually include a narrator who attempts to establish some continuity with a past that harbors unspeakable horrors and fears. Loy, who speaks very little of her own personal fears and goals, does write that, besides the early years of the feminist movement (discussed in *L'estate di Letuché*), the other most influential factor in her life and writings was witnessing fascist rule as a child.[74] In her historical novel *Le strade di polvere*, Loy retreats again behind an omniscient narrator. She recounts in detail the knowable realistic data—the births, deaths, family relationships, harvests, reappearances and disappearances of characters—of four generations of a Piedmontese peasant family in the last century, which leads the work to resemble some of the narrative histories produced by Ginzburg and his followers. The characters are initially defined by their stereotypical roles: some men go to fight, others stay home; some women marry, others go into the convent; some women die in childbirth, others live extremely long and healthy lives; some men and women find ways to circumvent the social norms that deny them personal satisfaction, others choose to embody these norms.

Loy is clearly not interested in linking character development to the social and political changes that were taking place at the end of eighteenth century. The main "events" in the text are a series of misplaced and misunderstood emotions that somehow form people's lives. Official History is not experienced by Loy's characters as something totally external to them, however, since historical events do have an effect on their main interpretive framework, the family. For these characters, the events of recorded history are as "real" and as important as the reappearances of dead family members and other unverifiable portents in Loy's recreation of a family's struggle for survival.

Indeed both personal and official history, depicted as a series of haphazard chance forces coupled with certain recognizable feminist motifs, together enable the characters, who develop within the parameters of their stereotypical destinies, to become somewhat individualized. The story begins with the family patriarch asking his sons to make a choice of wives from a family with two marriageable young women, Matelda and the very attractive Maria. Both sons fall in love with Maria, who picks the younger son, il Giai. Giai dies soon thereafter, however, and his wife marries the brother she had refused and who now accepts her as a wife, in the interest of continuing the family line. The theme of the wife or any woman as a transferable possession has received much attention in feminist inquiry. Yet, any polemical intent is tempered by the ironic variations on this theme developed in the narrative. Maria had chosen Giai because he was the more artistically oriented and sensitive of the brothers, although these same interests caused him to ignore his wife and prefigured a solitary destiny for her. The more pedestrian marriage to Pietro saves Maria from one fate and provides her with the children and the trials and tribulations that attend her station and class. Maria's development into a strong matriarchal figure in the narrative follows predictable lines, and her development, as well as that of the other characters, is explained by recognizable topical theories which replace psychological explanations for the characters' motivations and reactions. Although the lack of introspection on the part of the characters emphasizes their distance from and ultimate incomprehensibility to the narrator, the use of generalizing feminist themes, and the aura of objectivity they create in an admittedly fictional narrative, validate these female viewpoints as interpretive and explanatory categories of a past that can only be partially recaptured through subjective fantasy.

In several interviews, Maraini has openly admitted that her latest and most obviously literary narrative, *La lunga vita di Marianna Ucría*, is also inspired by a personal motive.[75] Maraini spent the first years of her life in Japan with her family. During their final three years the family was interned in a concentration camp with nine other Italians who refused to recognize officially the military rule in Japan. In 1947, the family returned home to live with Maraini's maternal grandmother in Bagheria, Sicily. Maraini describes her childhood in Sicily as characterized by a deeper, more oppressive type of suffering than the physical deprivations of the Japanese concentration camp. Although she was raised by open-minded, Leftist parents, Maraini was shocked by the backward nature of the laws, manners, and mores defining the role of women in society, marriage, and sexual relationships. Maraini emerged from her childhood, in her own words, paralyzed and dumb.[76] The female protagonist in the novel, an eighteenth-century deaf-mute duchess, was inspired by a Bagherian portrait of a woman with a pen and notebook in hand which reminded Maraini of her own liberating relationship to writing.

All of Maraini's fiction has had both personal and communal feminist goals. Maraini outlines the themes that link her latest fiction to her other writings and to her personal life: unrequited love for the father, frustrated maternity, the importance of writing, and the discovery of books. *La lunga vita* includes several of the standard themes, plot events, and character types found in previous works. Themes of women's sexual frustration at the hands of unthinking and unfeeling men, hints at lesbian relationships, portraits of women as degraded possessions of men, alienated from themselves and each other, are found in all of Maraini's feminist works. After giving the work a favorable review, Bruce Merry notes how the plot turns on another common topos, that of rape, and says, "In this sense, the life of Marianna Ucrìa is another picture in a nightmare gallery about the persecution of girls, in respectable families, by men who ought to know better."[77] In *La lunga vita*, the male rapist is none other than Marianna's maternal uncle whom she is forced to marry at age thirteen and to whom she bears six children. After the death of "il signor marito zio," Marianna learns that her deafness was a result of the rape that occurred when she was five. Marianna's father organizes her marriage to this pathetic, eccentric man as a fitting punishment for the crime and a pragmatic solution to the problem of what to do with his handicapped daughter.

Rossana Rossanda places *La Lunga vita* in the tradition of the classical *Bildungsroman* (*romanzo di formazione*) and compares Marianna's tenacious resistance favorably with the unenlightened tenacity of Morante's Ida.[78] Nonetheless, she registers her unease with the personal, solitary, even somewhat elitist nature of Marianna's developing consciousness, which she explains as a result of Maraini's desire to express her difference and felt exclusion from the feminist movement in the late 1980s. In *La lunga vita*, Marianna's destiny, especially as a female, appears sealed from the beginning. As in *Le strade di polvere*, however, a few chance variations on her female destiny, especially her deafness, turn out to be beneficial. Her handicap inspires pity and guilt in her father, who presents her with a pen and notebook and allows her to learn to read and write. On a narrative level, her ability to read and write justifies the acute observations made by the solitary child who is ignored if not mocked by other family members. This talent does not make Marianna a rebel, though, and she submits to her female destiny of subservience and abuse by exhibiting the trait she shares with Morante's Ida, Loy's Maria, and many of Maraini's previous female protagonists, that of patient endurance.

Despite Marianna's dissatisfaction with her relationship to her mother, who spends most days in a depressed, drugged stupor, she relates to her own children by repeating the same models of behavior she observed as a child. Marianna preaches obedience and subservience to her daughters and pardons the extravagant ways of her sons. The only child for whom she feels any special affection is a last, very sickly son who dies. Although this scene could be read as a prefiguration of the rebirth of Marianna's sensuality, which will lead to her affair with a younger male servant in the house, it also underlines Marianna's ineffectiveness in her dealings with adults. Revolt in such an environment is impossible, and Marianna's only refuge is literature.

Rossanda's unease with certain nostalgic, solitary tendencies in *La lunga vita* derive from the book's similarities in representations of history and destiny with more traditional historical novels. Marianna's quiet revolt against her destiny bears some similarity to that of Giuseppe Lampedusa's aloof but sensitive prince in *Il gattopardo* (*The Leopard*), a novel set during the time of Italy's reunification. Detractors of that book claimed that the beautifully written depiction of the disintegration of an aristocratic family and its replacement by a materialistic, rapacious, and reactionary bourgeois class not only denied the importance and possibility of historical change and progress but also inspired an unhealthy nostalgia for a romanticized past.[79] Marianna likewise witnesses the rise of the landlord class, which is poised to replace her family and against whose growing power her husband struggles in order to continue to care for his own land. Although Marianna as a female is demeaned and degraded, her survival is a question of class, as indicated by the many scenes contrasting the wealth of the Ucrìa family to the squalor and filth of the peasants. Marianna learns of the privileges of her class through the story of one uncle who, after attempting to depose a Spanish ruler, was able to pay for his pardon. This is not the case for the thirteen-year-old peasant boy accused of brigandage, whose public hanging Marianna witnesses at her father's side in the first chapter. In the final chapters, Maraini notes the resemblance of her narration to other historical novels by having the now personally liberated Marianna wistfully comment on the demise of her class with some of the same nostalgia felt by Lampedusa's prince.

Despite formal and thematic similarities to Lampedusa, however, if Marianna can be accused of any celebration of her past, it is primarily because that is precisely what it is—the past. Although Maraini does not hide the autobiographical tendencies of her work, the story is not solely one of personal liberation. Bruce Merry suggests that all of Maraini's previous novels can be read as updates of the archetypal story of women's oppression, emancipation, and rebirth told by Sibilla Aleramo in *Una donna*.[80] *La lunga vita di Marianna Ucrìa* recasts the story of Vannina's survival and emancipation told in *Donna in guerra* in a historical context. A forty-year-old, widowed Marianna with grown children is now free to read and explore even more on her own. Her true liberation comes, as in the case of Vannina in *Donna in guerra*, through a dream. The final scenes showing Marianna finding sexual satisfaction or traveling to other cities to continue her education link her again to the reborn Vannina ready to embark on a new course. In this historical fiction, though, the tortured face of the duke restores Marianna's memory, which is what enables her to overcome the past. The duke's reappearance to Marianna causes her to suspect the truth about her deafness, a truth she then forces her brother to validate. The discovery of how her father had sacrificed and betrayed her allows her to break with her past self, the martyred daughter, and announce a new beginning.

Although the "feminist" message of Maraini's previous works is repeated in *La lunga vita*, most male reviewers find it less offensive and woman-centered: in his review, Cesare de Michelis notes that the context chosen by Maraini takes her momentarily off the barricades. Her carefully documented historical framework and evocative language has made this version of "her-story" more palatable to reviewers, who feel more at ease with Maraini's historical and egalitarian depiction of oppression and the force of destiny in this narrative. All of the characters are caught in the webs of fate and history. Descriptions of the "signor marito zio," his love and concern for the land and family, allow a more in-depth and somewhat sympathetic (or pathetic) side to the man than the descriptions of his sexual activities. Throughout *La lunga vita di Marianna Ucrìa*, Maraini's feminist themes of female servitude and the physical and mental degradation of women are reviewed against the broad panorama of an enslaved, intellectually impoverished and flamboyantly contradictory Sicilian society. Such connections in traditional historical novels usually deny the possibility of change and progress in representational terms and, here, as in previous novels, the second, liberated part of Marianna's long life is not depicted. The final image of Marianna as a homeless traveler roaming around Italy connects with other feminist works by evoking the disappearing narrators of recent *Bildungsromane*. Yet here the protagonist's wanderings are desired and earned for she, like Maraini and other women writers who use the historical novel form, has found a positive way to reconnect with and build on her personal, literary, and collective past.

The historical framework chosen by Cutrufelli in *La briganta* highlights the themes of rebellion and revolt. *La briganta* recounts the fictional memoirs of Margherita, a female bandit from Palermo who joins one of the peasant brigand bands during Italy's unification. Margherita learns to read and write from her mother, the daughter of an impoverished aristocratic family from Palermo who had married a man from the upper middle class. As in the betrothal of Maraini's duchess, Margherita's marriage is also arranged. When her husband confiscates her books in order to facilitate her acclimation to a more subservient female destiny, Margherita murders him in his sleep and follows her admired brother into the bush to become part of the band of the peasant Carmine Spaziante. As can be expected, after a series of victories, the band is ambushed and most members are killed. In order to avoid being shot, Margherita bares her chest to the attacking soldier and is spared, only to be placed on trial and then sentenced to life imprisonment.

This rather simple story can be read on several levels. *La briganta* describes how the peasants, originally fighting for Giuseppe Garibaldi, became disenchanted and paradoxically ended up fighting for their previous oppressors, the landowners and nobility who wanted to reinstate the reactionary government of Ferdinando II. Like *La lunga vita*, the narrative includes real place names and descriptions of events that have been historically documented. Margherita's description of how she was treated as a biological anomaly by scientists who came to prison to measure her brain is based in fact as well.[81] *La briganta* also includes allusions to the historical novel tradition in Italy. Just as *La lunga vita* recalls ironically its resemblance to *Il gattopardo*, Cutrufelli ends her narrative with a reference to Manzoni's novel, when the narrator attributes her failed revolution to the seemingly unavoidable reinstatement of the providential order.

The final statement of an imprisoned Margherita brings us back to the long-standing negativity and denial of progress that has been part of the historical novel tradition and results from its chronological plot development and the linking of character development to plot events, realistically portrayed. In *La lunga vita*, Maraini addresses the formal problem by recalling the similarity of her text to *Il gattopardo* and then reestablishing links with her own and other feminist narratives. Throughout *La briganta*, Margherita's psychological development coincides with certain plot events; her different subjective states also follow the trajectory of feminism's theoretical coming to consciousness in the seventies and eighties. *La briganta* is not only the story of forgotten female bandits, but also a version of the history of Italian feminism in recent years. Margherita, like many feminists, believed that a series of superficial changes (here Margherita's shedding of women's clothes to dress like a man) would facilitate her participation in social change. She experiences feelings of liberation after escaping a stifling female destiny. Her "descent into terrorism" in the second chapter parallels the radical upheavals of the late sixties, the participation of women in mass demonstrations, and their total renunciation of any traditional female identity and destiny. Through her complex relationship with her protective brother and the courageous yet chauvinistic Carmine, Margherita progressively becomes aware of her essential difference. Although Margherita dresses like a man and strives to become a true *briganta*, a visit to a brothel with the men to relax crystallizes the feelings of insecurity and loss this assimilation produced in her. Despite feelings of solidarity and admiration for Carmine Spaziante, based on her identification with him as a member of an oppressed and exploited class, her revolution must follow a different path.

Margherita's coming to consciousness is, to be sure, validated by its similarity with official, historical fact. The constantly changing allegiances of the nobles and rich proprietors were essentially incomprehensible to the landless peasants who mainly fought to improve their own situation. This lack of self-consciousness made them the pawns of those for whom they were fighting, especially when their leaders returned their allegiance to conservative, reactionary forces. Margherita's transformation also parallels another story, however, that of the insistence on the recognition of gender categories in Italian feminist theory. Thus, after witnessing the shooting of Carmine's young, pregnant wife in a final rout by government forces, the Margherita who had wanted to leave behind her feminine identity bares her breast to the accosting soldier, who immediately lowers his gun. Despite her rejection of any stereotypical, historically defined feminine destiny and identity, Margherita still cannot leave behind her difference as a woman. The decision to bare her breast is not motivated by fear or capitulation to the old identity she had cast aside when she joined the brigands. Rather, as she states, it marks her refusal to become a victim in a revolution that is not hers and that still needs to be defined.

Rossana Ombres has said that a great women's literature would be one in which the female experience is absorbed to the point of non-recognition.[82] Variations in the representations of history and causality have turned the historical novel into a framework where women's partial truth can be represented in discourse rather than outside of it, as well as being a framework in which women continue to speak to one another of their similarities and differences. The viewpoint found in the works of Volpi, Morazzoni, Loy, Maraini, and Cutrufelli permit a shift away from the traditional sphere of women's personal, self-referential writing while avoiding the overtly metanarrative nature of much feminist theoretical and experimental discourse. Yet the goal of all these texts is precisely to describe the formation of a new subjectivity. The historical novel, despite its tradition of controversy over concepts of truth and representation, progress and destiny, provides possibilities excluded by romance and the *Bildungsroman*. This is not to say, however, that historical prose narratives will or should dominate women's literary efforts in the future. If this recently emerging women's tradition is to avoid becoming the one-sided and oppressive voice it seeks to question and displace, it will need the continued input of themes and ideas derived from all forms of writing that analyze the innovations and permutations caused by the ongoing feminist cultural revolution. In this process, women's literature must constantly redefine its relationship to both the mainstream and the margins, since women's writings now contribute to the creation of both spaces. The recent historical fictions discussed in this chapter use feminist themes to write the story of a developing feminist consciousness explored in the context of its experience with gender, class, and textual limits—a "lost" experience that needs to be "overcome," in Vattimo's sense, if one is ever to put a different feminine or any other subject into discourse.

Notes

1. Neria de Giovanni, "La sfinge cantatrice—Realtà come specchio nella narrativa femminile italiana post-neorealismo," *Romance Languages Annual* 1 (1989): 105–110.

2. De Giovanni borrows the term "first-generation writers" from Marina Zancan's essay "La donna" in *Letteratura italiana*, ed. Alberto Asor Rosa, vol. 5 (Turin: Einaudi, 1986), 765–827.

3. Rosetta Loy, *The Dust Roads of Monferrato*, trans. William Weaver (New York: Knopf, 1990). In 1988, the Campiello prize was awarded to Francesca Duranti for her fifth novel, *Effetti personali* (*Personal Belongings*), which is discussed in Chapter 7.

4. Rosetta Loy, *La bicicletta* (Turin: Einaudi, 1974) and *L'estate de Letuché* (Milan: Rizzoli, 1982).

5. See Loy's brief and typically cryptic self-portrait in Felice Piemontese, ed., *Autodizionario degli scrittori italiani* (Milan: Leonardo Editore, 1989), s.v. "Loy, Rosetta."

6. See Carol Lazzaro-Weis, "Dacia Maraini," in *Italian Women Writers*, ed. Rinaldina Russell (Westport, CT: Greenwood, 1993).

7. For example, Adele Cambria, *L'Italia segreta delle donne* (Rome: Newton Compton, 1984). This book includes chapters on mythical amazons and other legendary and literary figures as well as historical figures such as Beatrice Cenci. The book is well-documented, although Cambria presents each chapter in imaginative narrative style, as suggested by the book's subtitle: "Tormented Loves, Political Intrigues, Revolutionary Passions and Abandoned Romantics: Between Goddesses, Heroines, Poets, Noblewomen, a Voyage Through the Places Where the Protagonists of Our History Lived and Acted." In 1986, Cambria, a feminist journalist and activist whose arguments against traditional language and form in women's fiction have already been noted, published a highly personal confession, *Nudo di donna con le rovine* (*A Nude Woman Among the Ruins*) (Catania: Pellicanolibri) with the subtitle *Novel*. Armanda Guiducci, author of a series of now classic feminist sociological essays on the female condition—including *La donna non è gente* (Milan: Rizzoli, 1977), *La mela e il serpente* (Milan: Rizzoli, 1974), *Donna e serva* (Milan: Rizzoli, 1983), and one experimental feminist psychological novel, *A testa in giù* (Milan: Rizzoli, 1984)—has also recently published two noteworthy volumes on women's history: *Perdute nella storia: Storia delle donne dal I al VII secolo d.c.* (*Lost in History: The History of Women from the First to the Seventh Century A.D.*) (Florence: Sansoni, 1989), and *Medioevo inquieto: Storia delle donne dall' VIII al XV secolo d.c.* (*The Troubled Middle Ages: The History of Women from the Eighth to the Fifteenth Century A.D.*) (Florence: Sansoni, 1990). These books, less polemical than previous works but no less documented, are comparable in method and style to works such as the two volumes by Bonnie Anderson and Judith Zinsser, *A History of One's Own: Women in Europe from Prehistory to the Present*, 2 vols. (New York: Harper and Row, 1988). Joan Kelly's famous question of whether or not women had a renaissance has motivated much recent research on the question by Italian women historians. See *Rinascimento al femminile*, ed. Ottavia Nicoli (Rome: Laterza, 1991). A good bibliography available in Italian of works on Renaissance women, both scholarly and literary, is found in *Leggere Donna* 36 (1992): 4–5. In English, see Marilyn Migiel and Juliana Schiesari, eds., *Refiguring Woman: Perspectives on Gender and the Italian Renaissance* (Ithaca, NY: Cornell University Press, 1991).

8. Paola di Cori, "Soggettività e storia delle donne," in *Discutendo di storia: Soggettività, ricerca, biografia*, ed. Maura Palazzi and Anna Scattigno (Turin: Rosenberg and Sellier, 1990), 23–44. See also in the same volume, Marina D'Amelia, "A proposito di storiche, di madri, e di alcuni miti di fine secolo," 55–63. In her article in *Reti* (6 [1990]: 19–23), "Fare storia, non politica," D'Amelia uses the recent Italian translation of volume 3 of Georges Duby and Michelle Perrot's *Histoire des femmes en Occident* (Paris: Plon, 1991) to point out, however

carefully, the problems political stances cause in historical inquiries. Duby's series, which is under the direction of Natalie Zemon Davis and Arlette Farge, has evoked both praise from feminist historians for its factual accumulation of detail and inclusion of essays by women academics (although no Italian women historians have written for the collection) and criticism from some feminists still wary of joint endeavors.

9. Paola di Cori, "Prospettive e soggetti nella storia delle donne: Alla ricerca di radici communi," in *La ricerca delle donne: Studi femministi in Italia*, ed. Maria Cristina Marcuzzo and Anna Rossi-Doria (Turin: Rosenberg and Sellier, 1988), 96–111.

10. The bibliography on this subject is immense. Hayden White's theory was initially developed in his book *Metahistory: The Historical Imagination in Nineteenth-Century Europe* (Baltimore, MD: Johns Hopkins University Press, 1973). See also Dominick La Capra, *History and Criticism* (Ithaca, NY: Cornell University Press, 1985), and Hayden White, "The Question of Narrative in Contemporary Historical Theory," *History and Theory* 23, 1 (1984): 1–33.

11. E. L. Doctorow, *Ragtime* (New York: Random House, 1975); John Banville *Copernicus* (New York: Norton, 1976), and *Kepler* (London: Secker and Warburg, 1981). The film *Amadeus*, directed by Milos Forman, was released in 1984. Linda Hutcheon, *A Poetics of Postmodernism: History, Theory and Fiction* (New York: Routledge, 1988).

12. Marisa Volpi's *Il maestro della betulla* (Florence: Valecchi, 1986) was awarded the Premio Viareggio in 1986. Marta Morazzoni's *La ragazza col turbante* (Milan: Longanesi, 1986) has been translated into eight different languages; the English translation, *Girl in a Turban*, by Patrick Creagh was published by Knopf in 1988.

13. Sergio Pautasso, *Gli anni ottanta e la letteratura: Guida all'attività letteraria in Italia dal 1980 al 1990* (Milan: Rizzoli, 1991), 205–206.

14. Quoted in Paola Bono and Sandra Kemp, eds., *Italian Feminist Thought: A Reader* (London: Blackwell, 1991), 19.

15. Conference held at Circolo della Rosa, Rome, November 12, 1990.

16. See Laura Granatella, "Manzonismo e antimanzonismo nella critica," *Italianistica* 5 (1976): 11–117. Ignazio Silone, in an article in *La stampa*, April 2, 1972, called the lesson of "servitù volontaria" an example of the Italian lack of sense of civic duty. This latter viewpoint continues Antonio Gramsci's analysis of the work, which according to Donald Meyer shows how little value *I promessi sposi* has for the modern democrat: Gramsci likened Manzoni's outlook to the "aristocratic Catholicism" Italian intellectuals had for the people, a condescending benevolence rather than a shared humanity. Donald Meyer, *Sex and Power: The Rise of Women in America, Russia, Sweden and Italy* (Middletown, CT: Wesleyan University Press, 1987), 447.

17. See Sandra Bermann's excellent introduction to the translation of Alessandro Manzoni's *On the Historical Novel*, trans. Hannah Mitchell and Stanley Mitchell (Lincoln: University of Nebraska Press, 1984), 15–21.

18. Bermann, *On the Historical Novel*, 31–35.

19. Robert Scholes and Robert Kellogg, *The Nature of Narrative* (London: Oxford University Press, 1966), 12–15.

20. See Natalino Sapegno's introduction to *I promessi sposi* (Milan: Feltrinelli, 1968).

21. Lion Feuchtwanger, *The House of Desdemona or the Laurels and Limitations of Historical Fiction*, trans. Harold A. Basilius (Detroit, MI: Wayne State University Press, 1963).

22. Helen Cam, "Historical Novels," Pamphlet of the British Historical Association (London: Oscar Blackford, 1961), 20.

23. David Carroll, *The Subject in Question: The Languages of Theory and the Strategies of Fiction* (Chicago: University of Chicago Press, 1982), 99–109.

24. An analysis of *I promessi sposi* as an example of this limitation is given by Ann Rosalind Jones in her article "Manzoni's *I promessi sposi* and Lukacs' *Theorie des Romans*," *Arcadia* 11 (1976): 126–138. Jones sees the lack of clarity concerning the role of Providence, the narrator's intrusion and satirical remarks, and Manzoni's historicity as examples of Lukacs's theory about novelistic intrusions in a formal representation that desires to be epic.

25. Bermann, *On the Historical Novel*, 70.

26. Stefano Gensini, "Lukacs théoricien de la littérature en Italie," *Europe* 600 (1979): 154–166.

27. Peter and Julia Bondanella, eds., *Dictionary of Italian Literature* (Westport, CT: Greenwood Press, 1979), s.v. "Morante, Elsa."

28. Nine months after being raped by a drunken German soldier, Ida gives birth to Giuseppe (Useppe). When Allied bombings destroy the family's modest residence near San Lorenzo, the whole family is forced to move to a shelter. Throughout the narrative Useppe represents the power of poetry: his innocence, imagination, and love for life leave him strangely untouched by the horrors of the world around him. Ida's older son, Nino, first becomes involved with the fascists but later becomes a *partigiano* (resistance fighter) when he realizes, like any shrewd street boy, that all chiefs are the same and all ideologies are amoral. Nino then gets involved in the black market and is eventually killed in a street brawl. In the shelter, Ida and Useppe make the acquaintance of Davide, a Jewish anarchist, who is unable to expel the fascist tendencies in himself. Davide spends most of his time in a drugged stupor before he eventually dies of an overdose. After Nino's death, Useppe's epilepsy, which he inherited from Ida, becomes even more apparent and he dies from an attack. When Ida returns to the shelter to find Useppe dead, she goes mad and is institutionalized until her death nine years later.

29. James Mandrell, "The Prophetic Voice in Garro, Morante and Allende," *Comparative Literature* 42, 3 (1990): 227–246.

30. For an excellent review of this polemic in English, which includes a bibliography of the Italian articles on the debate over *La storia*, see Gregory Lucente, "Scrivere o fare altro: Social Commitment and Ideologies of Representation in the Debates over Lampedusa's *Il gattopardo* and Morante's *La storia*," *Italica* 61, 2 (1984): 220–251.

31. Di Cori, "Soggettività e storia delle donne," 26.

32. Elisabetta Rasy, Nanni Balestrini, Letizia Paolozzi, and Umberto Silva, letter to *Il manifesto*, July 18, 1974.

33. Vittorio Titone, "La critica e il caso Morante," *Nuova antologia* 523 (1975): 80: "In this poetic environment it is even possible that the dog Bella speaks to the child [Useppe] of his past, that Useppe speaks to the dog, and that both of them stay together all the time and understand each other perfectly. The distinction between fable and reality no longer holds. Every distinction dissolves in poetic cadence, that is, in the essence and truth of poetry" ("In questa clima di poesia è anche possibile che la cagna Bella parli al bambino e gli racconti del suo passato, che questo le parli e che tutti e due s'intendano, sempre che stiano insieme. La distinzione tra favola e la realtà non ha più luogo. Ogni distinzione si è dissolta nella poesia e cioè nel canto: poiché non

altra è l'essenza della poesia e non altra la sua verità"). Marco Forti, "La storia senza mito," *Approdo letterario* 67–68 (1974): 156, writes that "the story's real resolution lies in its sublime maternal compassion, and in the piety of the characters, helpless in the face of tragedy" ("la sua vera soluzione è nella compassionamente sublimamente materna e nella pietà di fronte alla tragedia di nature disarmate"). For an excellent discussion of poetic imagery in *La storia*, see Gregory Lucente, *Beautiful Fables: Self-Consciousness in Italian Narrative from Manzoni to Calvino* (Baltimore, MD: Johns Hopkins University Press, 1986), 246–265.

34. Rossana Dedola, "Strutture narrative e ideologia nella *Storia* di Elsa Morante," *Studi Novecenteschi*, 15 (1976): 247–265.

35. Carol Lazzaro-Weis, "The Providential Trap: Some Remarks on Fictional Strategies in *I promessi sposi*," *Stanford Italian Review* 4 (Spring 1984): 93–106.

36. Gérard Genette, "Vraisemblance et Motivation," in Genette, *Figures 11* (Paris: Seuil, 1969), 64. See also Marshall Brown, "The Logic of Realism: A Hegelian Approach," *PMLA* 96, 2 (1981): 22–241, esp. 228–230. Brown argues that although realism is often associated with the development of natural causal forces, the generalizing laws and the *deus ex machina* of romance are the antithesis of novelistic realism. Romance realism is based on the concept of general intelligibility and applicability; what cannot be reduced to general categories is excluded from the "real."

37. Although some critics have argued that this is merely a reflection of Manzoni's Catholic romanticism, in the 1950s, Marxist-oriented critics blasted Manzoni's conservative, bourgeois view which, they claimed, preached voluntary servitude to the master who must always remain the master. See Alberto Moravia, *Alessandro Manzoni e l'ipotesi di un realismo cattolico* (Milan: Bompiani, 1964). This is not to say that all Marxist critics deplored the conservativism in Manzoni's masterpiece. Liberals as well as conservatives have always used parts of Manzoni's texts to prove almost opposite viewpoints. Somewhat more recently, critics such as Enzo Raimondi go so far as to reinterpret Manzoni's causality as a kind of "discorso segreto" that works to deconstruct the narrative in almost modern or postmodern ways. Raimondi, "Genesis and Structure of a Catholic Novel," in *Interpretation, Theory and Practice*, ed. Charles Singleton (Baltimore, MD: Johns Hopkins University Press, 1969), 123–152.

38. Lucente, *Beautiful Fables*, 57 (emphasis added).

39. Valeria Finucci, "The Textualization of the Female 'I': Elsa Morante's *Menzogna e sortilegio*," *Italica* 65 (1988): 308–328.

40. Paola Blelloch, *Quel mondo dei guanti e delle stoffe* (Verona: Essedue Edizioni, 1987): "rifiutono la Storia con la S maiuscola, fatta dall'uomo e intessuta dei suoi pregiudizi, e scrivono invece la storia al femminile, fatta prima di lacrime e di umiliazione, poi di silenzio, infine di aperta ribellione"(58).

41. Valeria Finucci, "A Portrait of the Artist as a Female Painter: The *Künstlerroman* Tradition in Anna Banti's *Artemisia*," *Quaderni d'italianistica* 8, 2 (1987): 167–193.

42. Anna Banti, the author of over fifteen novels, is best known for *Artemisia* (1947; repr. Milan: Mondadori, 1953), which was recently translated into English by Shirley D'Ardia (Omaha: University of Nebraska Press, 1988). Other English translations of her works include the title story from *Il coraggio delle donne*, trans. Martha King, in *New Italian Women*, ed. Martha King and Barbara Nucci (New York: Italica Press, 1989), 1–22. Maria Bellonci's historical novels about known figures such as the notorious Lucrezia Borgia, the

Gonzaga family, and Marco Polo enjoyed a much broader audience. Her *Delitto di stato* (Milan: Mondadori, 1981) was adapted for television. She and her husband founded the Bellonci Foundation and instituted the Strega literary prize in 1947.

43. Sandra Petrignani's series of interviews published in *Le signore della scrittura* (Milan: La Tartaruga, 1984) represents an attempt to repair the rift between the younger writers and their over-seventy models. Bellonci and Banti were interviewed. Since Elsa Morante was recovering from a suicide attempt and unable to be interviewed, Petrignani put together an imaginary interview with her culled from Morante's previously published statements and interviews. The younger writers' difficult relationship with these older women writers is the subject of Grazia Livi's short story "Maestra e allieva," published in *Racconta*, ed. Rosaria Guacci and Bruna Morelli (Milan: La Tartaruga, 1989), 17–26. Livi speaks here of her interviews with Anna Banti before the latter's death. She classifies Banti as a member of the disappearing class of *letterate*: afterward, Livi states, one would have "just women who write" (25).

44. Deborah Heller, "History, Art and Fiction in Anna Banti's *Artemisia*," in *Contemporary Women Writers in Italy: A Modern Renaissance*, ed. Santo Arico (Amherst: University of Massachusetts Press, 1990), 44–60.

45. See Mary Garrard's recent book-length study, *Artemisia: The Image of the Female Hero in Baroque Art* (Princeton, NJ: Princeton University Press, 1989).

46. Maria Bellonci, *Rinascimento Privato* (Milan: Mondadori, 1985).

47. Reinhold Schumann, *Italy in the Last Fifteen Hundred Years: A Concise History* (Lanham, MD: University Press of America, 1986), 140.

48. "Madre . . . una cosa è certa: nessuna dei vostri figli potrà mai vincerla su di voi."

49. "Un intelletto femminile indipendente in sé, pur accettando tutti i legami con la vita terrena" (544).

50. Maria Corti, *L'ora di tutti* (Milan: Feltrinelli, 1962; repr. 1977). All parenthetical references are to the later edition.

51. Blelloch, *Quel mondo dei guanti*, 77.

52. Over a dozen of the essays of historian Philippe Ariès on the subject, some of which postdate the publication of Corti's novel, are republished in *Essais sur l'histoire de la mort en Occident du Môyen Age à nos jours* (Paris: Seuil, 1975).

53. Carlo Poni and Carlo Ginzburg edited *Quaderni storici*, an influential journal in which several women historians, including Gianna Pomata, published their work. Several important essays from the journal have recently been translated by Eren Branch and appear in *Microhistory and the Lost Peoples of Europe*, ed. Edward Muir and Guido Ruggiero (Baltimore, MD: Johns Hopkins University Press, 1991).

54. "Le piccole cose, e non le grandi, segnano i veri cambiamenti."

55. Ariès, "La mort apprivoisée," in *Essais sur l'histoire de la mort en Occident*, 21, n. 1.

56. "Non più fazzoletti, ma si balli da mano a mano, alla libera. E questo sia il segno che voi non avete più servitù. Avete inteso uomini?"

57. Linda Hutcheon, *A Poetics of Postmodernism: History, Theory and Fiction* (New York: Routledge, 1988), 93.

58. Linda Orr, "The Revenge of Literature: A History of History," *New Literary History* 18, 1 (1986): 1.

59. Hayden White, "Historical Pluralism," *Critical Inquiry* 12 (1986): 487–493. The quote comes from page 487.

60. For a brief, pithy discussion of "weak thought" see Giovanna Borrodori, "'Weak Thought' and the 'Aesthetics of Quotationism': The Italian Shift from Deconstruction," Working Paper 6, University of Wisconsin-Milwaukee Center for Twentieth Century Studies (1986): 1–12; Borrodori quotes from *Il pensiero debole*, ed. Gianni Vattimo and Pier Aldo Rovatti (Milan: Feltrinelli, 1983). See also Gianni Vattimo, *La fine della modernità: Nihilismo e ermeneutica nella cultura postmoderna* (Milan: Garzanti, 1985); *The End of Modernity: Nihilism and Hermeneutics in Postmodern Culture*, trans. Jon Snyder (Cambridge: Polity, 1988); and see Iain Chambers, "Rolling Away from the Centre Towards X: Some Notes on Italian Philosophy, 'Weak Thought' and 'Postmodernism,'" in *Culture and Conflict in Postwar Italy: Essays on Mass and Popular Culture*, ed. Zygmunt Baranski and Robert Lumley (Houndmills, Basingstoke, Hampshire: Macmillan, 1990), 178–191.

61. Borrodori, "'Weak Thought,'" 8.

62. Peter Carravetta, "Repositioning Interpretive Discourse: From 'Crisis of Reason' to 'Weak Thought,'" *Differentia* 2 (1988): 83–127.

63. Aldo Gargani, "La voce femminile," *Alfabeta* 64 (1984): 16.

64. *aut aut* vol. 165–166 (1978); *aut aut* vol. 175–176 (1980).

65. Di Cori, "Soggettività e storia delle donne," 31–32.

66. "Sesso debole, pensiero debole," *Annali d'italianistica* 7 (1989): 394–422. In this highly amusing and astute article, Viano likens "weak thought" to the Pinocchio tale as another attempt to continue telling lies about the changing system in an attempt to preserve the status quo. Feminist theoreticians are cast in the role of a liberated Little Red Riding Hood, no longer afraid of this wolf in female clothing. See also Renate Holub, "Weak Thought and Strong Ethics," *Annali d'italianistica* 9 (1991): 124–143.

67. Michel Foucault, *Language, Counter-Memory, Practice: Selected Essays and Interviews*, trans. Donald F. Bouchard and Sherry Simon (Ithaca, NY: Cornell University Press, 1977), 154–155.

68. Jon Snyder, "Translator's Introduction," in Vattimo, *The End of Modernity* (Cambridge: Polity, 1988), xxv–xxxvi. In "'Weak Thought'" Borrodori states: "If re-making and re-writing become the poetic criteria of relating present artistic experience to history, art becomes a rhetorical predication of the Western tradition assumed as a linguistic tradition" (11–12). Rodger Friedman points out that philosophy according to weak thought, that is, philosophy in a nonmetaphysical mode, is itself a testing of Theodor Adorno's formulation that philosophy "dissolves into poetry." Rather than tending toward fabulation, fiction "pursues a mode of discourse which wields the texture of language in a recursive, reflexive manner" (Friedman, "After Deconstruction," *Differentia*, 1 [1986]: 282).

69. "E mi sentii davvero donna, incapace io di creare il significato della vita. Così labile, soggetta ad incontrollabili moti, istintivamente coinvolta in ogni aspirazione al bisogno di vedere un uomo nel mio orizzonte, un uomo da raggiungere e magari sorpassare, ma pronto a soccorrere la mia debole fantasia e l'ancora più debole volontà spirituale."

70. "Le tue cornici? Esse servono alla gente che studia elucidate filosofie per esorcizzare la paura."

71. Stephan Salisbury, "Girl in a Turban," *The New York Times Book Review*, May 7, 1989, 24.

72. De Giovanni, "La sfinge cantatrice," 108.

73. "Il pensiero e la realtà si uniscono" (Morazzoni, *La ragazza col turbante*, 24).

74. Piemontese, ed., *Autodizionario degli scrittori italiani*, 197.

75. See for example, Firella Fumagalli, "Marianna dei Miracoli," *Tutto Milano*, January 31, 1991, 94; Cesare de Michelis, "Marianna," *Il gazzettino*, June 23, 1990; Virginia Visani, "Tutta una vita da ribelle," *Anno*, July 26, 1990, 68–74; Dina D'Isa, "La liberazione attraverso la scrittura," *Il tempo*, May 11, 1990.

76. Grazia Sumeli-Weinberg, "An Interview with Dacia Maraini," *Tydskrif vir Letterkunde* 27, 3 (1989): 64–72.

77. Bruce Merry, "Dacia Maraini's *La lunga vita di Marianna Ucrìa*," *PEN International Bulletin of Selected Books* 42, 1 (1992): 33–35.

78. Rossana Rossanda, "Una sovrana solitudine come forma di vita," *Il manifesto*, June 29, 1990, 5.

79. See Gregory Lucente, "Scrivere o fare . . . altro," esp. 221–237. See also his chapter on *Il gattopardo* in *Beautiful Fables*, 196–221.

80. Bruce Merry, *Women in Modern Italian Literature* (Townsville: James Cook University of North Queensland Press, 1990), 223.

81. The character of Margherita is drawn from several real-life *brigantesse*: the picture on the book's jacket is that of Maria Olivieri, the only female bandit who wore a skirt and who was condemned to death as a result of her activities, although the sentence was commuted to life at hard labor. The mentioned historical events and situations are verifiable as well.

82. Michèle Causse and Maryvonne Lapouge, eds., *Ecrits, voix d'Italie* (Paris: Editions des femmes, 1977), s.v. "Rossana Ombres," 168.

Chapter 6
Cherchez la femme:
Feminism and the *Giallo*

Whereas the historical novel can be used to depict a developing feminist and female subjectivity within and despite the limits of gender and genre, the detective novel is a form that seems to have the opposite effect. Traditionally, women writers have made a sizeable contribution to detective fiction. Novels by the "queens of crime," such as Agatha Christie, continue to sell millions of copies worldwide. Besides practicing the genre, women writers like Christie herself, Dorothy Sayers, and Patricia Highsmith, among others, have actively participated in establishing the theory of the detective novel. Although in this branch of writing women seem to "reign supreme," as Martin Priestman observes, the form remains highly resistant to any "specifically feminist interpretation."[1]

Explanations given for the resistance of the detective novel to feminist interpretation or rewriting usually begin by noting the overtly misogynist tendencies in the representation of women in this genre. These portraits of women are then interpreted as indications of deeper psychological, social, and even mythical patriarchal prejudices. The American "hard-boiled" crime novel depicts women primarily as either "too good" or "too bad" and therefore obviously merit or could not avoid their predetermined fate of being eliminated or ignored. Although in the more civilized English crime and detective novel the rational mind, rather than the gun, is the guarantor of stability and justice, condescending exploitative attitudes toward women prevail. As Tony Hilfer writes, "Whereas the American protagonist may be blind to a woman's love, the English protagonist is more likely to presume upon it."[2] Hilfer relates the female devil or angel in the American crime novel to the archetypal myth of romantic love examined by Denis de Rougemont in *Love in the Western World* which equates passion with death; the hero must either conquer the vindictive, revengeful femme fatale or become a victim and dupe of his own culturally constructed fears (55). Nonetheless, although the representation of a male dupe in crime and detective novels may "undermine the purity of the [form's] misogyny," it only marginally improves the female image. Even if the powerful woman figure receives more sympathy than fear in the classical English detective novel, the influence of the Oedipal pattern on the form again locks her into the role of the strong mother-figure bent on conserving her socially accepted maternal role and powers.[3]

Another major ideological bone of contention between feminism and detective fiction is the hero-worship implicit in the depiction of the detective figure. Dennis Porter notes that the detective story

celebrates traditional heroic virtues and expresses many of the attitudes associated with an ideology of hero worship. Given that fact, the genre is potentially anathema to such ideological adversaries of heroic male action as certain religious leaders, libertarians, utopians, social collectivists, and *radical feminists*, whose purpose is to forge a new sensibility and new forms of human association.[4]

Feminist critic Kathleen Klein agrees that the two ideologies inevitably clash for many of the same reasons.[5] Feminist writing, Klein argues, should show intelligent, capable women who assume moral responsibility and reject female stereotypes by virtue of their psychological complexity (201). Detective fiction that portrays and depends on stereotypical characters who exhibit conventional attitudes is at structural odds with such a goal. Moreover, feminism

rejects the glorification of violence, the objectification of sex, and the patronization of the oppressed. It values female bonding, awareness of women without continual reference to or affiliation with men, and the self-knowledge which prompts women to independent judgement on both public and personal issues. (201)

Klein restricts her analysis to those works in which a professionally paid woman detective is portrayed, because these women, rather than amateur sleuths, are in a position to threaten the established social order. Ultimately, competent women detectives have to reinforce the establishment and concede to the patriarchy, whereas a truly feminist detective novel, such as M. F. Beal's *Angel Dance*, destroys the genre by showing that there is no justice: "Knowing the truth does not lead to justice or action; and radical feminism cannot work within the system" (220). She concludes that perhaps the two ideologies can never mesh without producing "an unsatisfactory version of both which has compromised all of their greatest attractions" (221).

Klein's final judgment on feminism and the detective novel eluci-
dates the double bind of women writers of mystery fiction if one reads
fiction anticipating a reinforcement in representation of feminism's
positive achievements. Women writers who choose not to follow the
rules, including the "queens of crime," are open to accusations of
writing "bad" detective fiction, whereas those who obey the conventions are necessarily guilty of portraying female oppression and thus
directly or indirectly sustaining attitudes and structures responsible for
that oppression. Not all feminist critics, however, choose to emphasize
the conservative aspects of the form and discount its critical and creative advantages. Although Nicci Gerrard warns that in the detective
novel, as is the case for any type of formulaic fiction, feminist ideology
runs the risk of being frozen into a parody of itself, she correctly points
out that it affords women writers the opportunity to "invent an alter
ego with impunity; a double-edged strategy of subversion and conceal-
ment."[6] In another study of many specifically feminist experiments
with the detective novel, Maureen Reddy sees in the genre an opportunity for women to "play around with the issue of narrative authority"
and use feminist viewpoints to highlight the many patriarchal convictions and myths that shape our society.[7]

Both Reddy and Klein could be faulted for reading literature as if it
could and should unambiguously reflect real life. Reddy's analyses,
however, which show how feminist writers can use the genre to play
with the issue of narrative authority to trick the reader in the same way
their male counterparts have done, seem more sympathetic to feminist
achievements because her orientation is more toward what the genre
can do as opposed to what it cannot. Reddy is amenable to the view that
the portrayal of a more "tolerant and fallible detective" has feminist
overtones that radically change the form, whereas Klein would tend to
condemn this representation as one showing women fulfilling society's
expectations of them as emotional and scatterbrained beings incapable
of the ratiocinative deductions of the truly unfeeling detective. As
Klein herself demonstrates on numerous occasions, though, the elimination of such "feminine" features does not solve the problem, either,
since strong detective women figures do not herald the creation of new
stereotypes but fall into the category of another established negative
female stereotype, that of the frustrated shrew, a permutation of the
archetypal mother figure.

In her review of Klein and Reddy, Sherri Paris gives more general
reasons for the emerging and powerful interest of women writers in
the genre despite its pitfalls. Besides the obvious fact that detective
novels are popular and sell, women who write and read detective
fictions are motivated by a desire for justice, which is as "persistent,

irrational and romanticized a human need as the search for Perfect Love."[8] The detective novel in all its variations, from the cerebral types to the "politically correct lesbian" mode, can be used to reflect radically diverse moral outlooks of particular social groups. According to Paris detective novels, including feminist ones, encourage us to contemplate if not resolve a major issue for contemporary women: "Is moral fairness achievable? Can it be attained within, or only by dodging or subverting, the sanctioned judicial system?" (9).

The popular success of Umberto Eco's *Il nome della rosa* and Leonardo Sciascia's detective works in Italy attests to the genre's ability to promulgate philosophical ideas, criticize society, and still sell. Furthermore, as Maria Rosa Cutrufelli points out, the detective novel in Italy enjoys an equal and relatively high readership by both sexes, unlike science fiction, of which until recently most readers were male.[9] This message has never been ignored by Italian publishers, who immediately resumed their *giallo* series after the fall of the fascist regime, which had banned the imported detective novels that many Italians read with interest and pleasure.[10] In 1984, the feminist press La Tartaruga launched La Tartaruga Nera, a series dedicated to encouraging the production and publication of mystery and detective fiction by women. To date, however, the series still favors translations of foreign (women) writers of the genre. Other smaller presses, such as Bariletti editore in Rome, now provide a possible outlet for women writers interested in detective fiction.[11]

Rather than expecting a feminization of the form or a clear victory of feminist over bourgeois or patriarchal ideology that the detective novel is widely assumed to perpetuate, we will first examine how two feminist Italian women writers, Fiora Cagnoni in *Questione di tempo* and Silvana La Spina in *Morte a Palermo*, include feminist themes, motifs, and ideas in their works and exploit generic conventions to do so. Italian women write detective novels for the same reasons they are returning to other literary forms—to come to terms with their own past images and to criticize the role of such images in their exclusion, marginalization, and forced complicity. The traditional themes of justice, equality, and the archetypal motif of the powerful mother-figure in detective fiction facilitate the inclusion of topical feminist ideas on these subjects. Cagnoni's *Questione di tempo* and La Spina's *Morte a Palermo* show that contemporary feminist authors of detective fiction have a variety of techniques, conventions, and expectations from which to chose. Both authors share the feminist commitment to unmask the inadequacies of male justice and the social, historical, and psychological ways in which it suppresses and oppresses women. The detective novel, a form based in the parodic questioning and reimposition of its own limits, absorbs ideas according to its own inherent contradictions. Therefore, form is the key to understanding the main differences between Cagnoni's consistent and overt use of feminist ideology, in a text cast in the traditional detective novel form, and La Spina's ironic response to Eco, in which she dismisses all theories and ideologies as entertaining but often dangerously reactionary and certainly always in need of constant questioning.

The chapter concludes with the discussion of Laura Grimaldi's popular psychological crime novel *Il sospetto*. Although Grimaldi announces her works as specifically nonfeminist, her examination of guilt and its relationship to justice in her depiction of a mother who kills her son after she mistakenly concludes that he is a murderer links her text to the other specifically feminist experiments in ways that inform a feminist reading of the text.

The Literary and Social Context

Most critics agree that the detective novel, at least in its purest form, relies on stereotypical figures, a straightforward logical plot development, a contemporary and realistic setting, and, of course, a detective who creates a coherent narrative out of a series of unrelated clues and solves the crime.[12] Violations of many of the detective novel's formal characteristics by various authors after World War II drew critical attention to the "metaphysical detective novel" which reversed the genre's reassuring function. According to Michael Holquist, the metaphysical detective novel primarily challenged the detective novel's ideology of "radical rationality," a belief that the mind, given enough time, can understand everything because the relationship between ideas and things is a totally rational one.[13] This ideology derives from the bourgeois Enlightenment and its essentially "democratic" belief in the possibility of truth, justice, and equality—a belief shared by the detective, the secularized God figure, and the reader. Although this description of the form's ideology has been used to buttress explanations of why the detective novel did not take root in societies that lacked a secular democratic Enlightenment tradition, notably Germany and Italy, both German and Italian writers have produced their share of the so-called metaphysical detective novels, in which the failures of the detectives to solve mysteries or disprove other rational theories called these same principles into question.

In the 1970s and 1980s, the detective novel with its strong, well-known conventions and privileged status as a natural paradigm for the hermeneutic act of reading was used to serve the goals of much postmodern fiction. In particular, it was employed to unmask or flaunt a text's narrative and linguistic structures and challenge the reader to participate directly in creating or conferring meaning(s).[14] Theoreticians of popular detective fiction show that its various subgenres, however, were always created through parody or subversion of its own formulas. For example, Hilfer claims that the crime novel is a variant produced by both English and American writers and which is based on the inversion and subversion of the detective novel's conventions. In the classical detective novel, the discovery of truth takes priority over justice and the function of the detective is to guarantee the reader's absolution from any feelings of guilt. The detective novel assuages the reader because it neither challenges the possibility of justice and equality for all nor negates the ability of universal logic to effect justice; rather it punishes those that threaten this potential.[15] The crime novel, in contrast, maneuvers the reader into various forms of complicity which question the universality or possibility of justice (Hilfer, 3–5). The crime novel thus shifts attention from the detective to other protagonists such as the killer, guilty bystanders, innocent victims, or the falsely suspected. Writers of such works exploit these narratological situations to spread guilt and cause the reader to ponder the problems involved in the equal distribution of justice.

Setting is also a distinguishing aspect of detective and crime novels. In the detective novel, the main action revolves around resolution of the crime, and theoreticians and writers of the form in the 1930s, the so-called Golden Age of the detective novel, warned that excessive attention to setting would redirect reader interest and sympathy from the detective's ratiocinative talents and the crime's solution to social criticism, as is the case in the melodramatic *romanzo d'appendice*. In order to represent the mind as superior to matter, detective novelists were advised to limit descriptions of matter; indeed, some extreme theoreticians claimed that the only true detective novel would be a purely theoretical puzzle. The excessive attention to formulas has always served to emphasize the genre's detachment from reality, no matter how much attention the author paid to realistic detail. Priestman notes that, in classic detective fiction, "in the context of the recurrent 'least-likely because-most-likely-formula,' such moments of scrupulously pretended realism simply aggravate the pastoral remoteness of the form from 'real life'" (152). The sanitized, isolated settings in many traditional detective novels and figures of detectives who never left their desk or office to solve the crime are parodied in Jorge Luis Borges's detective, Sandro Parodì, who solves his mysteries from a jail cell.

Nonetheless, many writers are aware that readers were attracted to the form not only to solve puzzles but to contemplate the contradictions therein between a theoretical perfect justice for all, which was never realized in the text, and the actions and psychology of characters who jeopardized this ideal. The tension between the existence of an ideal, universal justice and its practice, one of the major potential contradictions in the popular *giallo*, is brought to the fore in Leonardo Sciascia's works when detectives solve murders but cannot bring anyone to justice in the real world.[16] Despite different emphases in the detective novel and the crime variant, however, both restore order through the observance of key conventions. Motives for the crime must be ahistorical, personal ones such as sex, ambition, or greed, so that excesses against universal justice can be reduced by the logic of the detective and the reader to a proper, manageable size. This literary convention is usually linked to another necessary convention of the detective and crime novel, the surprise ending.[17]

In *Postscript to the Name of the Rose*, Eco places his novel in the tradition of the crime variant when he writes that the real accomplishment of the *giallo* is to make us see that "we are the guilty party."[18] We, the reader, (criminally) produce the object of study by imposing a certain discourse on it, by reconstructing the past and our relationship to it according to our interests, prior interpretations, and political inclinations.[19] In *Il nome della rosa*, Eco sculpts a plot around the demonstration of the process of signification itself. Although William of Baskerville is forced to conclude at the end that the theory on which he based his detection was false, he does solve the mystery with it, thus underlining the usefulness and necessity of such theories for man, the rational being. These theories are allowed to become unquestionable truths, as oppressive and one-sided as those they claim to overthrow, and only laughter can undo them. Baskerville concludes that the mission of those who love humankind, as he puts it, is to "make people laugh at the truth, to make truth laugh, because the only truth lies in learning to free ourselves from insane passion for the truth."[20]

This statement resumes Eco's usage of the popular detective form to communicate the philosophical message of postmodernity and demonstrates how semiotics can function as a permanent, radical demystifier of ideologies. In representing his philosophy on how meaning is constructed, Eco's detective, despite his erudition, is equally powerless to stop other, stronger forces. Eco himself partially confirms this reading as part of his deliberate attempt to fool the ingenuous reader who may not realize until the end that "this is a mystery in which very little is discovered and the detective is defeated."[21] The helplessness of semiotic theory and the detective that represents it is allayed in the film version by a change in script to show the *menu peuple* rising up against the evil priests, saving Adso's innocent love, and effecting a spectacular, melodramatic kind of justice.

The depiction of deduction as an amusing yet somehow irrelevant pastime has a precedent in the turn-of-the-century detective fiction of Arthur Morrison, E. C. Bentley, and G. K. Chesterton, whose works include a variety of techniques and themes imitated by both Eco and Sciascia. Chesterton's statement equating the criminal with the creative artist and characterizing the detective as his critic is often quoted by critics and writers in their defense of the metaphysical and philosophical potential of this popular form. Despite the obvious appeal of such a notion to postmodern sensibilities, however, Chesterton's statements linking crime, deduction, and art were part of a wider ambivalence about contemporary theories of "art" itself. As a parodic form, the detective novel functions as the explanatory, demystifying Other for many of the period ideas it absorbs. Priestman shows that the "aestheticizing of crime and the corresponding criminalization of the aesthetic" were common structuring themes in the fictional works of the "modernist" generation of writers that included Henry James, Joseph Conrad, and Oscar Wilde (136–150). Although Chesterton and the other authors play with such "intellectual *peripeteais*" in their works, these rapprochements are eventually condemned for inciting "criminal hubris" instead of the concentrated reasoning that brings the criminal to justice. These preclassic detective novel writers sustain their socially critical position—which is at most anti-capitalist and includes some socialist overtones—by having their detectives, such as Bentley's Trent in *Trent's Last Case*, solve a mystery only to find out that their theories and logical deductions were incorrect, however aesthetically pleasing they might have been. Ideas and ratiocinative thinking function as a way of training the reader and the detective in the art of deduction, but this, in itself, will not "equip us to confront the real problems of life . . . however much we have learnt, this should be for us, as for Trent, the last case" (Priestman, 123).

Feminist critic Teresa de Lauretis agrees that the theory of "radical" semiotics in Eco's detective novel discounts its own radicality, but for different reasons.[22] De Lauretis argues that in *Il nome della rosa*, Eco replaces the supposedly moribund word and master theory of the Father with the equally oppressive word of the fathers through endless references to other male texts. The result is the creation of a "homosexual" pedagogical link between Adso's adoration for the knowledge of the detective monk and his desire to recuperate and thus salvage the knowledge, vision, and power of the Master.[23] Thus, writes de Lauretis, Eco's semiotic logic is not universal but male and functions to ensure its own survival, whereas women detective novel writers exhibit a different logic. As an example, de Lauretis refers to Dorothy Sayers's *Gaudy Night*, a work she claims exploits the contradiction "constitutive of women as subjects in a social reality instituted in the name of the father, and points to the contradiction of the plot itself, the compromise of narrative discourse as it exists historically in that reality" (67).

Indeed, in *Gaudy Night*, Sayers manipulates the inherent separation of ratiocinative theories and their practice in the detective novel to elucidate some of the limits and fallacies of theory, here the "theory" of women's emancipation. When Harriet Vane is called in to investigate acts of violence against women in an all-female setting, a women's college in Oxford, the theme of how an intellectual woman can find equality outside of an isolated, single-sexed community is broached immediately. The impossibility of putting the theory of emancipation into practice is mirrored in Harriet Vane's love relationship with Peter Wimsey, whom she is afraid to marry for fear (and the knowledge) that she will lose her autonomous identity. It is precisely those contradictions caused by female autonomy and women's right to challenge female stereotypical roles that motivate the crime.

The female criminal in *Gaudy Night* (uncovered by Peter Wimsey's logic and not that of Harriet Vane) is the wife of a male graduate student whose unprofessional academic practices had been uncovered and publicly denounced by an academic woman scholar, Miss DeVine. DeVine's condemnation ended the plagiarist's academic career and he committed suicide, leaving his wife, Anna, and children unprovided for. Anna justifies her revenge on DeVine by arguing that the latter herself, by posing as an intellectual, committed a crime against all women. As a female, DeVine should have upheld women's traditional social role of supporter of men and family and remained silent. In Sayers's remarkable novel, equality and justice do not exist for the emancipated woman except in those isolated magic moments when universal logic shows us that despite differences we can all think alike. The concrete appearance of women on the scene, however, causes trouble in Paradise and reveals them to be the pathway to the gates of Hell.

As noted in Chapter 2, Italian feminist theories concerning the necessity of establishing a different feminine justice and ethics began with Carla Lonzi's critique of the limits and disadvantages that emerged when the theory of emancipation was put into practice. In *Sputiamo su Hegel*, Lonzi argued that since legal justice had always been based on the exclusion of feminine sensibilities, especially female sexuality, as long as the women's movement was based on the falsely universal concepts of emancipation and equality, the movement would essentially inhabit a powerless position nurtured by a rhetoric of victimization and desperate claims for rights from men. The female vindicators of a repressive status quo for women in detective fiction, who, like Anna, murder for men, are another permutation of the theorization and justification of the control men had previously acquired over women, their sexuality, and their autonomous desire. When women enter History, writes Lea Melandri, they come in as either an economic machine to reproduce the race or the eternal *Dea madre*, herself a general equivalent of money, the most abstract measure created by patriarchal ideology.[24]

In her article in *MicroMega* and the ensuing Campo Marzio debate on October 26, 1990, Miriam Mafai accused such theories as being essentially anti-democratic. Both Claudia Mancina and Maria Luisa Boccia refused to speak at the Campo Marzio debate on the grounds that Mafai's critique falsely posed the question women needed to ask, namely, whether democracy is anti-female.[25] Although Mafai's views received little enthusiastic support, feminist critics of theories of sexual difference centered their concerns on the figure of the symbolic mother and the difficulty in keeping this image separate from the projection of paternal authority usually found in the social or real mother. Grazia Zuffa argues that some aspects of the theories of sexual difference and the practice of *affidamento* may even paradoxically undermine the critical and radical force of feminist theory by running the risk of leaving women unable to recognize moments when they imitate patriarchal ideology and cooperate with it. Attempts to eliminate the gap between the theory of what we want to be and the practice of what we are, writes Zuffa, distance women from the fruitful contradictions that emerge from their concrete experience as women.[26]

In response to Eco's proclamation that the real accomplishment of the *giallo* is to make us acknowledge our guilt and complicity, de Lauretis writes: "Who's we, white man?"[27] In her criticism of *Il nome della rosa*, de Lauretis succeeds in exposing Eco's male logic posing as universal logic, something women have no reason to feel guilty about, but Zuffa brings up another problem. In *giallo* terms, would an ideal female justice leave us unable to recognize the very historical and social contradictions that de Lauretis credits Sayers with bringing to our attention, and which cause women to murder?

The Female Criminal

Cagnoni's *Questione di tempo* is a detective story about women. The plot bears a certain general resemblance to one of Sayers's novels recently translated in the Tartaruga collection, *Strong Poison* (*Veleno Mortale*). In this novel, Sayers introduces the love story between Harriet Vane and Peter Wimsey. Lord Wimsey comes to her rescue when Vane is accused, in a seemingly open-and-shut case against her, of killing her boyfriend. In contrast, in *Questione di tempo* women save other women: Alice Carta comes to the rescue of her best friend, Elena Noja, who, in an equally hopeless situation, is accused of killing her married lover, Michele, after his body is found on her terrace.

Detective Alice pursues her detective role methodically, interviewing all possible suspects and amassing all the evidence that could prove them innocent or guilty. Alice and Elena keep company with a group of women on whom they can count in times of need. All female characters drink whiskey like real men, but cook like real women. They are all stereotypes of a sort, although this in itself is an accepted convention of the *giallo*. Alice spends most of her time interviewing a certain Doctor Cassini, with whom Elena had spent the afternoon of the crime in Florence, and the widow of the deceased, Magda Saveri, the stereotypical strikingly beautiful, rich woman who is supposedly permanently crippled due to an automobile accident. Like Eco and Sciascia, Cagnoni critiques a justice system that relies on stereotypical prejudices to find easy solutions, and she has little difficulty demonstrating that such a system victimizes women more than men. Elena is presumed guilty and detained in prison after Magda announces that she had known her husband was having an affair with Elena and had demanded that he stop seeing her. Authoritative logic immediately categorizes Elena as the typical outraged "other woman" seeking revenge.

This situation is reversed when detective Alice traces to Cassini the disappearance of the raincoat Elena was supposedly wearing when fleeing her apartment after allegedly murdering Michele. Cassini frames his confession in an equally stereotypical situation. Hopelessly in love with the young maid who worked for Michele and Magda and was also having an affair with Michele, Cassini claims he detained Elena in Florence and drove to Milan that evening to kill Michele in her apartment. Authorities, familiar with this plot as well, accept it, free Elena, and it appears that all is well that ends well.

In the last few pages, however, we hear the real story. Alice visits the beautiful but wicked widow and, in typical ratiocinative fashion, reconstructs the crime, revealing yet another series of clichés and stereotypes. Magda, taking advantage of Cassini's actual undying love for her, had involved him and the maid, whom she blackmailed, to take part in her revenge against Elena and Michele. Magda herself, whose paralysis was faked, followed her unfaithful husband to Elena's apartment and killed him. She is now content to continue to manipulate the enamored Cassini, who will take the rap for her. After revealing her theory to the widow, who affirms her narrative, Alice admits she is content to let Cassini take the rap since she is disgusted by foolish, stereotypical men who allow themselves to be ruled by their excessive, romantic love. Alice's surprise twist is that she will not turn the widow in because she is not the typical detective who seeks absolute Truth and assumes that its discovery will insure justice. Her primary motivation for accepting the case was to free her friend Elena from all suspicion. The story ends with Alice's admission that she was falling in love with the beautiful widow all along, and they spend the night together.

The ending in *Questione di tempo* is hardly a reassuring one, but for reasons other than its depiction of the inequities of male justice. Alice's generic deductive speech at the end certainly demonstrates how easy it is to "think like a man," and shows how women can ensnare men by manipulating the same prejudices and stereotypical behavior patterns that subjugate them (for example, the widow had framed her husband by faking paralysis in hopes of provoking his infidelity). Although Cagnoni shows throughout how justice is male-oriented, she neutralizes her own critique by representing a world where women and by extension female justice would be no different from that of men. This less than revolutionary ending results from Cagnoni's observance of the *giallo* rules, especially the one demanding a personal motive for the crime so that the ending constitutes a surprise reversal of expectations.

Elena and Alice are relieved to find that trivial motives, such as sex and personal revenge, motivated the murder. They had initially suspected that the unexpected disappearance of Saveri's maid, who had befriended Elena, was due to some entanglement with the Red Brigade or drug dealers. If the denial of historical and social motives in the detective story is essentially what blunts the critical edge of the traditional detective novel, the potentially revolutionary feminist community inhabiting the patriarchal structure in *Questione di tempo* also appears to lack the ability and, more important, the interest to modify anything. Detective Alice summarily fulfills her generic function of absolving the (female) readers from all guilt with reference to *Non credere di avere dei diritti*, in which it is stated explicitly that women owe nothing to men, especially ones like Cassini; yet she also excuses Magda's crime on the generic grounds that its perfect execution should incite admiration rather than criticism. This latter reason is often given in the traditional detective novel to shift the reader's sympathy away from the victim and social issues and to glorify the detective's theoretical infallibility.[28]

Doubtless, one could argue that Cagnoni's observance of the rules is meant to suggest the inability of women to achieve real autonomy in a patriarchal form and the society it represents. In *Questione di tempo* the social irrelevance of the form is mentioned: Alice says she gave up writing her own detective novel because she finds its ratiocinative tendencies too detached from the problems encountered in real life. In following the detective novel's rules, however, Cagnoni reinforces a common ideological inference in the popular detective novel that the problem does not lie in the deficient logic that defined justice, but rather in the egotistical, personal interpretations of it by individuals. Their ideas only produce in them a criminal-type hubris that deserves to be punished.

Whereas Cagnoni's detective story shows the homologizing effect of integrating pieces of feminist theory, recognizable only to a select few, into an established generic structure, La Spina's _Morte a Palermo_ exploits the crime variant's traditional lack of connection between an ideal justice and its practice in a more complex way. In _Morte a Palermo_, La Spina criticizes Eco in a Sciascian context and, in so doing, more pointedly highlights the dangers inherent in favoring theory over practice. La Spina sets her story in a mysterious Palermo filled with superstition and archaic loyalties. In the first chapter, Professor Costanzo, who was about to publish a purportedly revolutionary work on ancient matriarchies in the Palermo area, is murdered. His death is followed by those of his wife, who is for a time a suspect, and of her lover, Eugenio Nitti, who was Costanzo's student and another possible suspect.

Direct and indirect references to _Il nome della rosa_ abound throughout. Maps of labyrinths are found near the body of the dead professor, who, like Eco's monk, is found upside-down in a large cistern. Besides several discussions on the nature of labyrinths, one of which is taken directly from Eco's _Postscript to the Name of the Rose_, the blind Argentinean poet Borges is again evoked as a character in the text. Blind poet and writer Bustos Domecq is in Palermo at the time of the murders which, he immediately notes, follow patterns akin to plots in his detective novels. Finally, for most of the text, the reader is led to believe that the ultimate criminal is a book—Professor Costanzo's work which contains important revelations on the Mediterranean Mother Goddess and mysteriously disappears after his death.

Unlike Eco's extremely erudite detective, Detective Santoro is a more-down-to-earth Sciascian type with a modest literary bent. He further distances himself from Eco with his ironic allusion to _Il nome della rosa_, which he has not read yet since he prefers to read works when they are no longer in fashion. Santoro searches for the person responsible for the bizarre murders primarily through the normal investigative channels, while Bustos approaches the mystery by isolating the mythical plot the criminal is following. Despite their different methods, they simultaneously discover the real murderer. To find the criminal, Bustos determines that the murders are patterned after the myth of Daedalus and Minos in Sicily: Daedalus had Minos killed by drowning him head-first in a cistern. The death of Costanzo's unfaithful wife, who is found hanged in a crypt, was modeled on the figure of Ariadne, who hanged herself either out of remorse for having betrayed her father, Minos, by helping Daedalus escape or for having been abandoned by Theseus. Theseus himself was eventually thrown off a cliff by his rival; the third victim, Eugenio Nitti, is killed in the same manner. Finally, Daedalus was an architect and so is the criminal, whose motive is a recognizable one. Out of fear that Costanzo's book on matriarchies would cause archaeologists to demand that a certain area be off limits for his building speculation project, the well-known architect De Castro organized these murders in a pretentious parody of the mythical theories Costanzo outlines in his book.

Although Bustos, like Baskerville, solves the mystery through literary means, the Argentinean poet is highly critical of De Castro's imitation of his fictional stories to construct his crime: "This, my dear architect, is bad literature."[29] In the final chapter, Detective Santoro, who had arrived in the nick of time to save Bustos from being murdered by De Castro, comments that Bustos's interest in the crime was motivated by his desire to avenge himself on the man (Eco) who had reduced him to the role of a foolish character in a novel (136). La Spina takes that same man to task by choosing her ancestors among authors like Israel Zangwill, Chesterton, Bentley, and Sciascia. These authors criticized the overuse of clever theories in detective fiction by demonstrating how such theoretical musings obscure the truth and obstruct the questioning of justice the form has the capacity to incite. Unlike Cagnoni's Alice, who is fascinated by crime, La Spina's Santoro and others are irritated by the arrogance of the criminal who constructs evidence in a way that makes detection resemble "criminal hubris" instead of being a means to uncover guilt.[30] The artful crime committed by De Castro facilitates his capture and only temporarily conceals his personal and base motive.

Although La Spina does not essay a representation of women effecting their own justice, she does deploy feminist theories to criticize the partial nature of democratic justice. In *Morte a Palermo*, the criticism of (male) democratic justice is effected through its contrast to mythical justice, a contrast that, not surprisingly, reveals more similarities than differences. De Castro sets up the murders according to myths that carry with them a theory of archaic justice based on self-interest, unquestionable loyalties and revenge. "Così giustizia è fatta, non è vero" ("This is how justice is done, isn't it?"), remarks sarcastically one character to Santoro after they discuss the myths that the criminal is most likely following (123). This type of justice, often associated with primitive matriarchal societies, is what democratic justice supposedly defeats; this is indeed the result when Santoro exposes the criminal's personal greed and egotistical motivations. The theory of the defeat of matriarchal justice and power by a patriarchal, juridical justice was first advanced in the last century by J. J. Bachofen. In his now classic *Mutterrecht*, Bachofen read Aeschylus's trilogy, the *Oresteia*, as an allegory of the defeat of matriarchal societies. Feminist theoreticians, notably Luce Irigaray and more recently Adriana Cavarero in *Nonostante Platone*, have extended his theory in their explorations of the appropriation of female sexuality and defeat of female autonomy by the patriarchy.

In her review of a recent Italian translation of Bachofen's classic work on matriarchies,[31] Eva Cantarella suggests that, although Italian feminists have traditionally rejected theories glorifying archaic matriarchies and the Mother Goddess—because they, like many French feminist theories on the power of the feminine in writing, reinforce the same stereotypical, anti-social qualities previously deployed to marginalize women—feminists should now re-read Bachofen in light of the recent theories on sexual difference.[32] Nonetheless, Cantarella is aware of the dangers of reading Bachofen as a champion of women's rights. Although in his autobiography he writes that democracy is not a sign of progress but rather one that barbarity is returning, when he lauds the return of the matriarchy he still repeats traditional dichotomies in which women represent earth and nature and men belong to the realm of light, spirit, and intellect (18).

The figure of the Mother Goddess that appears in *Morte a Palermo* is more akin to criticisms advanced by Melandri and Lonzi, who argue that the *Dea madre* is only a male construction that men use to further their own petty rivalries and exclude women. This feminist theory reverses the form's generic tendency to depict men's tendency to fear strong women whom they see as permutations of the powerful Oedipal mother. In *Morte a Palermo*, the men who ascribe to this theory, including the professor, are punished. Costanzo's scholarly enemy, Professor Lo Giudice, reinforces this connection between feminist critical theory and the form's displaced mythical paradigm, although he reinterprets it in terms of the problem of provincialism in Sicily. Lo Giudice, who was one of the suspects for Costanzo's murder since he had written negatively of Costanzo's book, calls Costanzo's theories on *la gran Dea Mediterranea* dangerous and regressive. He believes they reflect a pathological tendency to invent an autonomous historical past for Sicily as the cradle of civilization, out of a fear of admitting that Sicily was only "the crossroads of other civilizations."[33] Neither professor's theory is validated in the text; however, neither does their intellectual disagreement motivate the real crime, although architect De Castro had unsuccessfully tried to talk Lo Giudice into eliminating Costanzo on these ideological grounds.

The ending in *Morte a Palermo* affirms Bachofen's comment and La Spina's critique of the continued barbarity and partial nature of democratic justice and male construction of idealized females through more ironic allusions to Eco. Costanzo's book, like Aristotle's on laughter in *Il nome della rosa*, disappears at the end. Instead of being lamented as a text that could have changed the course of civilization (and literary criticism), its disappearance goes unnoticed since no one, including Costanzo's beautiful and docile female student, was ever looking for it. The book slides behind a dusty bookcase and finds its place beside a learned, but as yet undeciphered and now lost, Arabic text. Jesuit priest Don Saverio comments to Santoro that perhaps the work could have showed us how to re-read history so that we can understand what we were at one time and why we have become the way we are now. Santoro's response to this statement, which is taken from Eco's *Postscript to the Name of the Rose*, takes a final ironic swipe at Eco's detective: "This we can never know. And I don't need these certainties."[34]

The fear of the archetypal-mother figure which is expressed through extreme representations of women in crime fiction receives different treatment in Laura Grimaldi's *Il sospetto*, a chilling crime novel based on a series of brutal, sexual murders that took place in and around Florence. The press dubbed the unapprehended criminal "the monster" (*il mostro*). Grimaldi recognizes the tradition she is using when she claims to have written the novel to explore the concept of guilt from a political and social viewpoint.[35] Since her model is the "hard-boiled" crime novel, she includes many realistic and detailed descriptions of the "monster"'s sexual assaults and deformations of his victims. Sixty-five-year-old Matilde Monterispoli, the well-off widow of a respected surgeon, begins to suspect that her forty-eight-year-old son, Enea, who still resides with her, may be the *mostro* when she notices that her husband's surgical knife is missing on the same day that the police come to question her concerning Enea's firearms. In refusing to answer the routine questions of the police, Matilde exhibits the behavior typical of an overprotective mother who would never betray her station in life through the betrayal of her son (12). The policemen's visit, however, causes her to begin to question Enea's behavior and actions in a way that eventually leads her to condemn him.

Grimaldi plays with the reader's sympathies and suspicions throughout, as is typical in crime novels. Enea is a possible suspect since he exhibits several pathological behavioral patterns. The product of a domineering father and a doting mother, Enea demonstrated great sensitivity and intelligence as a child. His withdrawal from others, however, in part a result of his stifling upbringing, has a "scientifically" provable basis in his minor physiological and slightly deforming disorders that interfered with the completion of a law degree although he now works diligently in the law office of a family friend. A subplot depicts a lonely, impotent Enea befriending a teenage drug addict, Nanda, who steals from him and eventually commits suicide. His nocturnal outings to find and protect Nanda, and his depression after her death, deepen Matilde's and the reader's suspicion that Enea could indeed be committing the multiple murders, though Matilde lacks _la prova fatta_. This definitive proof comes when she is informed that the gun used in the "monster"'s last attack is a Winchester H, a rare gun purchased by her husband twenty years earlier. Matilde kills her son by increasing his diabetes medicine to a stronger dosage. Enea does not notice the change and dies immediately. Shortly thereafter, however, Matilde is informed that the _mostro_ has been apprehended and Enea's innocence is established.

The effectiveness of Grimaldi's manipulation of the reader's sympathies and guilt feelings is reinforced by its resemblance to the archetypal and unsettling Medea myth. Furthermore, Matilde's transformation from protective to murderous mother recalls recent feminist arguments in the much debated law on sexual violence still pending in the Italian parliament. Certain Italian feminists have demanded a law that would no longer condemn rape primarily as a moral crime but as one against the "inviolability" of a woman's body. In her article in _MicroMega_, Mafai attacks this law "advanced by certain (female) lawyers from Milan and Bologna" which, among other stipulations, requires a mother to testify against her son in cases of rape. This clause is clearly meant to counteract the situation that begins Grimaldi's novel and a scenario discussed in Italian feminist theory, namely where a mother, out of familial obligations, protects a male criminal and helps perpetrate a crime against her own sex.[36] Matilde's original and stereotypical desire to protect her son against all harm is progressively replaced in the text by what she understands as her duty to protect other women from her possibly depraved son. Her allegiances begin to change when she finds a carving of a bust of Nanda in Enea's room (which explains the theft of the surgeon's knife in the first chapter). She interprets Nanda's horrified face, which depicts her suffering from drug withdrawal, as a cry for help from the women her son is victimizing.

Obviously these parallels are not presented to argue that Grimaldi is condemning or endorsing any specific feminist theory, especially since this representation of the mother-turned-monster is ultimately a generic one that Grimaldi exploits to create situations that engage the readers' feelings of suspense, fear, and guilt. In fact, the real "criticism" effected in _Il sospetto_ is primarily the type that is determined by the form

Grimaldi chose and one consonant with the sort of detective novels that Alfieri notes always appealed to Italian readers. Priestman points out that the crime variants at the beginning of the century included an implicit critique of the powerful but useless upper class, who resisted social change as part of their protest against capitalists (106–111). Although Matilde is not a totally unsympathetic character, Grimaldi places her in that social class described by Enea's boss as one where the people are "all more or less rich and without problems except when they try to decide in sterile discussions what is good and what isn't, what is just and unjust," subjects they discuss with "skeptical claws" (162). No matter what reasons Matilde toys with in the narrative, her final decision is based on her complicity with her class and its conservative desire to avoid scandal. Caught between the fear of public scandal for herself, her son, and her class, Matilde makes the decision to distribute her own personal justice.

In killing her son, Matilde reverses her archetypal role as giver of life and becomes the female criminal who decides to take it away. Through the archetypal vengeful mother motif, however, Grimaldi brings us again to the narrative and historical compromise point that de Lauretis praises in Sayers and which feminists have analyzed in various types of writing. Matilde's isolation and acceptance of her ahistorical role of guardian of family and privilege led to her unknowing complicity with those unwritten rules that force her to become a criminal and make of her a victim as well. By following the rules, Grimaldi demonstrates the ability of the form to condemn and endorse conflicting theories in the readers' minds without freezing any theory into a parody of itself.

Postscript to the Crimes

Despite all differences, Cagnoni, La Spina, and Grimaldi use detective and crime fiction to demonstrate the distance between an ideal, equal justice and its application. In order to accomplish this, they call on various techniques that belong to the long tradition of detective and crime fiction. The books discussed obviously do not exhaust the possibilities for feminism and the *giallo*. Clearly, it would be a lot to ask of the *giallo* to solve the question of how justice and equality for women could be achieved, because traditionally the form reviews these questions through the representation of the shortcomings of a theoretical ideal that can only be glimpsed in the contradictory space between theory and practice.

In an article in *aut aut* published toward the end of the 1970s, Biancamaria Frabotta writes that the "political duty" ("il compito politico") of women's writing should be to privilege the category of contradiction over transgression. Whereas the latter category leads to generalizing a priori definitions of the "feminine," the former permits the writer to explore patiently the attempts of women to enter the historical mainstream and to discover the many contradictory situations in which each newly found freedom places women.[37] Detective and crime novel structures allow for women to explore both categories, albeit within limits since the form most often provides ostensibly simple answers to complicated questions. Nevertheless, of all the criminals figured in the fictions discussed here, feminist ideology is as incapable of killing the form as any other system of thought the *giallo* has absorbed, criticized, portrayed, or rejected in its continuing tradition. The *giallo* as a literary form has long risked extinction due to overdoses of ideology only to come back more popular than before, a popularity most likely due to the fact that discussions on the meaning of justice and equality in political as well as fictional representation are forever relevant. Indeed, the opposition between feminism and the *giallo* is producing more Italian women who, despite their differences, write detective novels to ask the questions that the genre poses to a general public and a society that—to paraphrase Bruce Merry—should know better.

Notes

1. Martin Priestman, *Detective Fiction and Literature: The Figure on the Carpet* (New York: St. Martin's Press, 1991), 167.
2. Tony Hilfer, *The Crime Novel: A Deviant Genre* (Austin: University of Texas Press, 1990), 72–73.
3. In his discussion of Agatha Christie's novels, for example, Priestman quotes Stephen Knight (*Form and Ideology in Crime Fiction* [London: Macmillan Press, 1980], 107–113, 115) to make this similar point: "As Knight points out, such powerful women are usually presented more sympathetically than their male counterparts, though with a similar stifling effect on their dependents: the Oedipal pattern so frequent in the genre seems to address itself to the strong mother-figure" (155).
4. Dennis Porter, *The Pursuit of Crime: Art and Ideology in Detective Fiction* (New Haven, CT: Yale University Press, 1981), 126 (emphasis added).
5. Kathleen Klein, *The Woman Detective: Gender and Genre* (Chicago: University of Chicago Press, 1988).
6. Nicci Gerrard, *Into the Mainstream: How Feminism Has Changed Women's Writing* (London: Pandora Press, 1989), 124.
7. Maureen Reddy, *Sisters in Crime: Feminism and the Crime Novel* (New York: Continuum, 1988), 10.
8. Sherri Paris, "Riding the Crime Wave," *The Women's Review of Books* 7, 7 (1989): 8–9.
9. Maria Rosa Cutrufelli, "Alla conquista delle lettrici: Un nuovo mercato per l'industria editoriale," *Scritture, Scrittrici*, ed. Maria Rosa Cutrufelli (Rome:

Longanesi, 1988), 125–134. Cutrufelli notes that narrative is the preferred form of women readers and that, in Italy, detective novels are read by an equal percentage of women and men—33 percent (129).

10. In fascist Italy, detective fiction, especially the crime novel variant, in both Italian and other languages, was banned. Government censors claimed detective works facilitated the importation of foreign ideas dangerous to the Italian mentality. According to Peter Alfieri in his unpublished dissertation (Ann Arbor, MI: University Microfilms, 1986), "Il romanzo poliziesco in Italia," fascists mainly objected to the implication in all detective fiction, including the Golden Age classics of Agatha Christie, that delinquency could appear in persons of all social levels (111–112). Although the *gialli* that did get past the censors had to be written by Italians and include the necessary praises of fascist power and glory, the ban presented a problem for publishers who knew that Italian readers had a long-standing preference for imported detective novels. Many of the Italian detective works surveyed by Alfieri retain obvious affinities with the melodramatic *romanzo d'appendice* and depend excessively on chance and irony rather than rational thought to drive the plot. Alfieri concludes that Italians preferred "il detective che era coinvolto nell'intreccio, e storie capaci di far trepidare e di strappare le lacrime, proprio come il vecchio 'feuilleton' dell'ottocentescho. All'acume intellectuale del 'detective,' che indaga ma non punisce, si sovrappongono le gesta del bandito generoso che salva i 'buoni' e uccide i 'malvagi,' gesta che risvegliano sentimenti immediati e un instintivo, ancora grossolano senso della giustizia radicato nella psiciologia delle masse, assopite, scriveva Gramsci, in 'lunghe fantasticherie sull'idea di vendetta, di punizione dei colpevoli dei mali sopportati' " ("the detective who was personally involved in the plot, and stories capable of frightening the reader or bringing tears to his eyes, exactly like the nineteenth-century *feuilleton*. Added to the intellectual acumen of the 'detective' who investigates but does not punish, are the deeds of the generous bandit who saves 'good people' and kills 'evil ones,' gestures that brought on an immediate emotional response and awakened an instinctive and still undeveloped sense of justice that was rooted in the psychology of the masses who were kept in this somnolent state by 'long daydreams concerning vendettas and the punishment of those responsible for all the evils they [the masses] had endured' " (119–120).

11. As of 1990, among the nineteen titles published by La Tartaruga Nera, only three are written by Italian women. Two out of five titles already published by Bariletti are by Italian women writers, but four more titles were announced for 1991.

12. The bibliography on detective and crime fiction continues to expand exponentially. Besides the theoretical works already mentioned, other important theoretical analyses include: Julien Symons, *Bloody Murder: From the Detective Story to the Crime Novel* (New York: Viking, 1985); and Stefano Tani, *The Doomed Detective: The Contribution of the Detective Novel to Postmodern American and Italian Fiction* (Carbondale: Southern Illinois University Press, 1984). Peter Alfieri's unpublished dissertation "Il romanzo poliziesco in Italia" provides a valuable overview of the tradition in Italy. Excellent bibliographies of the most recent critical works on the genre are found in the works of Priestman and Hilfer.

13. Michael Holquist, "Whodunit and Other Questions: Metaphysical Detective Stories in Post War Fiction," *New Literary History* 3 (1971): 135–186. Holquist discusses primarily the works of Vladimir Nabokov, Friedrich Dürrenmatt, Alain Robbe-Grillet, and John Barthes.

14. Carol Lazzaro-Weis, "The Metaphysical Detective Novel and Sciascia's *Il contesto*: Parody or Tyranny of a Borrowed Form?" *Quaderni d'italianistica* 8, 1 (1987): 42.

15. Porter, in *The Pursuit of Crime*, also writes: "The dimension that is missing from the formulaic works in the detective genre is, in fact, any recognition that the law itself, with its definitions of crimes and its agencies of law enforcement, is problematic" (121).

16. Lazzaro-Weis, "The Metaphysical Detective Novel," 45–47.

17. This convention was later defended by Raymond Chandler, the American writer of the "hard-boiled" or more violent crime novel variant. See also Symons, *Bloody Murder*, chaps. 1–3. Hilfer notes that in the crime novel, the reader usually knows who the criminal is and wonders how he or she will be brought to justice, whereas in the detective novel, the action centers around the revelation of the criminal's identity. In both forms, however, the ending should be unexpected (3–5).

18. Umberto Eco, *Postscript to the Name of the Rose*, trans. William Weaver (New York: Harcourt, Brace, Jovanovich, 1983), 81.

19. Teresa Coletti, *Naming the Rose: Eco, Medieval Signs and Modern Theory* (Ithaca, NY: Cornell University Press, 1988), 5ff.

20. Umberto Eco, *Il nome della rosa* (Milan: Bompiani, 1980), 495.

21. Eco, *Postscript to the Name of the Rose*, 54.

22. Teresa de Lauretis, "Gaudy Rose: Eco and Narcissism," in de Lauretis, *Technologies of Gender: Essays on Theory, Film and Fiction* (Bloomington: Indiana University Press, 1987), 51–69.

23. De Lauretis, "Gaudy Rose": "While Eco's gaudy *Rose* pretends to have no master plot and alleges to be a story of books, a game of conjecture in which the referent, historical reality, is always already infinitely mediated, and truth ultimately beside the point, what the book affirms is the truth of discourse, the *Name* of the rose, and thus the continuity of the very institution it seems to challenge" (67). In this article, de Lauretis again attacks deconstructionist theories, especially those of Derrida, Lyotard, and Baudrillard, for their appropriation of the term "feminine" as a revolutionary, semiotic category. Their definitions of the feminine, grounded in characteristics such as hysteria, pleasure, fertility, passivity, and jealousy, accord on the one hand a miraculous subversive power to these notions. This eternal feminine, called up from the depths of history to liberate the "master-warrior-speaker" from his illusions, represents a further marginalization and silencing of real women. For an example of the kind of reading that claims to demonstrate how the "repressed feminine principle intrudes upon the patriarchal monistic order" and liberates the men from the "repressive tendencies of the patriarchy" (and to which de Lauretis objects), see Thomas S. Frentz, "Resurrecting the Feminine in *The Name of the Rose*," *Pre/Text* 9, 3–4 (1988): 123–145.

24. Lea Melandri, *L'infame originaria* (Milan: L'Erba Voglio, 1977), 27. See also Luisa Muraro, "Il segno della differenza sessuale," *Passaggi* 1 (1989): 18–25.

25. Lidia Menapace, "Seppelliamo il Principe," *Rinascita*, November 18, 1990, 38–39.

26. Grazia Zuffa, "Tra libertà e necessità: A proposito di *Non credere di avere dei diritti*," *Reti* 1 (1987): 52.

27. De Lauretis, "Gaudy Rose," 68.

28. Hilfer, *The Crime Novel*, 5–8.

29. "Questa, architetto, è cattiva letteratura" (128).

30. Priestman, *Detective Fiction and Literature*, 109.

31. J. J. Bachofen, *Das Mutterrecht* (Stuttgart: Krais and Hoffmann, 1861); trans. G. Schiavoni, *Il matriarcato* (Turin: Einaudi, 1988).

32. Eva Cantarella, "Le fortune del matriarcato," *Reti* 3–4 (1988): 17–19.

33. "Una grande carovaniera di civiltà altrui," (43).

34. "Questo non lo sapremo mai. E poi non ho bisogno di queste certezze" (137). Eco describes historical novels, such as his own popular success, *The Name of the Rose*, as ways "not only to identify in the past the causes of what came later, but also trace the process through which those causes begin slowly to produce their effects" (*Postscript to the Name of the Rose*, 76).

35. Felice Piemontese, ed., *Autodizionario degli scrittori italiani* (Milan: Leonardo Editore, 1989), s.v. "Grimaldi, Laura." Grimaldi has been writing crime fiction under a series of pseudonyms since the fifties. In the sixties, she was an editor of several *giallo* series. *Il sospetto* is the first of a trilogy of crime novels in which Grimaldi proposes to analyze three sentiments that cause human irrationality: suspicion, guilt, and fear. *La colpa* (*Guilt*) (Milan: Leonardo Editore) appeared in 1991.

36. Miriam Mafai, "Le vedove di Lenin e la deriva femminista," *MicroMega* 4 (1990): 12: "Nel caso dello stupro, ad esempio, mentre il diritto maschile sarebbe ispirato ad una normativa 'repressiva del reato a tutela dell'ordinato svolgersi del rapporto tra i cittadini,' il diritto femminile dovrebbe preoccuparsi di garantire l'inviolabilità del corpo delle donne 'attraverso la valorizzazione della genealogia femminile, la responsibilità della donna-madre verso il proprio sesso, quindi verso il sesso della donna stuprato, la sottrazione della solidarietà al figlio stupratore come espressione di autorità materna esercitata in nome del proprio sesso'" ("In the case of rape for example, in contrast to male law which is inspired by the 'normative controlling of the crime in order to uphold traditional relationships between citizens,' female law should concern itself with guaranteeing the inviolacy of women's bodies 'by activating the power of the female genealogy to direct the responsibility of the woman-mother toward her own sex, that is the raped woman, and thus destroy her solidarity with her rapist son, an action viewed as an expression of maternal authority exercised in the name of one's own sex.'" Mafai goes as far as to blame the failure of passage of the law on this distinction made by certain feminists. Livia Turco, "Noi donne ancora deboli . . . ," *La repubblica*, October 9, 1990, retorts that the real reason has little to do with feminist theory but rather with the usual obstructive parliamentary procedure and the hostile attitudes of the conservative Christian Democrats.

37. Biancamaria Frabotta, "Contraddizione e trasgressione," Sulla specificità del femminile," *aut aut* 161 (1977): 71.

Chapter 7
Mainstreaming

In an article in *L'espresso* on February 24, 1991, Marisa Rusconi introduces several fictional works of a new generation of Italian women writers with mixed feelings. If previous generations had to wait and hope for discovery and recognition, these women, primarily between thirty and forty years of age, no longer have to play Cinderella to the still predominantly masculine editorial world. Instead, women writers who have previously published in smaller women's presses can even expect to be courted by publishing houses eager to welcome a new generation of "signore della scrittura" who no longer produce "letteratura femminista," that is to say, militant, nonliterary excursuses, but the new "letteratura femminile," defined by writer Marco Lodoli in an *Espresso* interview as one "born of the gifts of sensitivity and perception that women possess to a greater degree than men."[1]

The women authors Rusconi reviews claim to be returning to examine society critically.[2] She fears, however, that their "careful mastery of linguistic instruments and narrative techniques" and their self-distancing from the autobiographical and "realistic" narratives of previous feminist writers are less a reflection of female sensitivity than a more self-protecting, cynical, even "frigid" attitude of the younger generation. These new writers feel, in the words of author Valeria Viganò, "mature enough to treat this incandescent material [sentiments and sexuality] without burning ourselves, like a blacksmith who knows his trade" (99). Nonetheless, after voicing these doubts, Rusconi finishes her essay by quoting Dacia Maraini, who flatly denies a lack of continuity between feminist mothers and their writing daughters: "Women who are writing today almost always assume feminine subjectivity. What difference does it make if we don't call this 'feminism'?"

Some of the causes and effects of the distinction between "feminist"

and "postfeminist" literature and the signs of friction between generations of women writers are succinctly outlined by Nicci Gerrard in her
Into the Mainstream: How Feminism Has Changed Women's Writing. The
term "postfeminism," a result of the fragmentation of feminism in the
1980s and the inevitable rivalry between different generations of
women, is both annoying and dangerous because it implies that "feminism has done its job and is over": postfeminism denies feminism's
power "as an ever-evolving and dynamic process" (7). To an older
generation, postfeminists seem to want to make full use of the free-
doms won for them in the seventies and, in order to do so, they have
discarded the collective spirit for a liberated individualism, an asser-
tive, stylish, and self-possessed manner not totally unrelated to Thatch-
erism and Reaganism and oftentimes seemingly apolitical (7–8).

Gerrard also points out that in feminist hands postmodernism can
appear to be not about anything, since the methods of parody and
pastiche associated with it, "its overdeveloped irony, its fear of commitment and of culturally distinct and unreferential forms, seems to identify with reaction and reflect a throwaway, trivialised world" (120).
Despite this caveat, however, in her analyses of the works of several
generations of women writers, Gerrard writes that feminism's confessional and realistic modes have become too limiting and coercive for
women writers who are returning to literature and literary genres, with
mixed success, in order to widen their perspectives. If not all women
writers can use the "whole of Western Europe as a scrapyard" as deftly
as Angela Carter, an example she cites, the tendency of women writers
to loot multiple genres, structures, and styles is necessary and can
herald a new, more exploratory, ambitious world view that is not synonymous with "selling out" just because these women appear ready to
call into question aspects of what they themselves have helped to
create.

The foregoing comments reflect both the privileges and the dilemmas of women writers today. Freedom from a strong political and
moralistic feminist line conjures up new possibilities for women writers, but these possibilities are tempered by the hidden traps of traditional meanings and structures. Italian feminists of the 1980s allow for
the development of individual differences, yet they still exhibit fears of
complicity with external powers and of internal strife. Most of the
American, English, and Canadian authors Gerrard interviews corroborate the comments made at the Palermo convention in 1988: the
majority of contemporary women writers, regardless of age, now feel
empowered rather than victimized by their gender consciousness, although female subjectivity is no easier to define now than it was when
their writing primarily revolved around showing how its formation was

denied. As writer and journalist Lidia Ravera states, however, the time has come for women to accept their difference and the ambiguous results that female difference creates.

As Italian feminist theory shifts from analyzing women as objects to examining their constructive power as subjects, women's literature has begun to change its focus from representations of women as created beings to women as creators. Not surprisingly, the Pygmalion theme underlies many recent women's narratives, only a few of which will be examined here. The writers to be discussed are separated in age and writing styles but united by the common experience of the feminist movement.

Francesca Duranti, who published her autobiographical first novel, *La bambina*, in 1976 at age thirty-eight, become well known in Italy with her third novel, *La casa sul lago della luna* (*The House on Moon Lake*), which was marketed in fifteen countries.[3] Her fifth novel, *Effetti personali* (*Personal Belongings*, 1988), received the Campiello prize in 1988. Lidia Ravera, born in 1951, scandalized the Italian literary scene with her best-seller *Porci con le ali* (*Pigs with Wings*, 1976), an open diary of the sexual experience, desires, and fantasies of two adolescents, set against the background of student protests and increasing terrorist activity. Until the publication of *Per funghi* (*For Mushrooms*, 1987), a short story narrated by a child critical of the 1960s generation, Ravera's writings, some of which were adapted for television, were dismissed as *romanzi di genere*, or commercialized portraits of the problems of the baby-boom generation which were well-written but demonstrated few "literary" pretensions. In her most recent novel, *Voi Grandi* (*You, Adults*, 1990), Ravera again examines the generation gap and the problems and myths of the sixties era through a love triangle consisting of a feminist terrorist, her former *compagno*, and his twenty-year-old bride-to-be.

Sandra Petrignani's third novel, *Come cadono i fulmini* (*How the Lightning Bolts Fall*, 1991), also portrays the difficulties an aging generation has in coping with or even understanding the same myths and ideologies it helped to create. Although there are many differences in the texts to be examined, variations in the Pygmalion myth and the appearance of structures from different generic traditions provide a framework for these writers to include many similar feminist themes, situations, even stereotypes, as they write their stories against and into the more supposedly universal literary frame.

*   *   *

The most obvious adaptation of the Pygmalion myth appears in Duranti's *The House on Moon Lake*. In his review of Stephen Sartarelli's

English translation, Paul Hallam calls attention to the work's fictional framework and its general themes in his description of the narrative as a "chilling literary thriller . . . an elegant, old-fashioned well wrought tale, an attack on modern greed and speed."[4] Protagonist Fabrizio Garrone, an overly sensitive, somewhat dandyish aristocrat striving to create a singular name and identity for himself, is thrust into a cruel and ruthless modern world and forced to eke out a living as a translator after his father squanders the family fortune. Leafing through an essay at a bookstall in Milan, Fabrizio notes a reference to a possible master-piece written by a little-known, early twentieth-century Viennese writer, Fritz Oberhofer. Fabrizio sees his opportunity to place himself above quotidian chance and adversity by establishing his identity as the discoverer, chief critic, and translator of this masterpiece. He sets off for Vienna, partially financed by his independent, down-to-earth (read feminist) girlfriend, Fulvia, whose straightforwardness and self-assur-ance inspire both attraction and fear in him. After a few comical adventures, Fabrizio finds the novel by chance at a hotel on Moon Lake near Salzburg, translates the book, and is requested by the publisher—his childhood friend and son of the caretaker of the estate of Fabrizio's parents—to write Oberhofer's biography. He does so and invents the character of Maria Lettner as Oberhofer's lover and inspiration for his final novel. Maria, the fictional creation, captures the public imagina-tion and comes to life as a popular media figure to usurp both transla-tor and author.

At one point, the narrator in *The House on Moon Lake* briefly likens the quest of Fabrizio Garrone to find his identity by writing about Oberhofer to the archetypal Faustian pact against death that always turns out to be such a terrible bargain for the living (164). But Fabrizio's adventures, which are divided into three sections bearing the female names Fulvia, Maria, and Petra, follow more precisely the pattern of the Pygmalion myth. This myth originated in Ovid's *Metamorphoses*, one of the many variations on the theme of punishment incurred as a result of human hubris that annoys or angers the gods, who then exercise their power and right to interfere in human history. Punishment takes the form of the materialization of desire; as J. Hillis Miller notes, "Ovid's stories show that you always get some form of what you want, but you get it in ways that reveal what is illicit or grotesque in what you want."[5] From that perspective, the original Pygmalion story is an anomaly in that the materialization of desire brings the inanimate to life instead of the opposite. Furthermore, in Ovid's version, Pygmalion is not imme-diately punished. Miller points out, however, that the theme of punish-ment deferred links together many tales in the *Metamorphoses*, and Pyg-malion's case is most complicated.

In the story preceding Galatea's transformation, women are at war. Venus punishes the Propoetides who have challenged her divine nature and turns them into (literally) hardened prostitutes. Frightened of such types but unwilling to remain alone, Pygmalion creates Galatea. Although Venus brings the statue to life, his punishment materializes in his offspring, especially his granddaughter Myrrha, whose incestuous relationship with her father materializes the sin of incest implicit in Pygmalion's marriage to his own creation.[6] In this tale, however, even the divine Venus must pay for her fear of losing power over Pygmalion. When she falls in love with the product of this last relationship, Adonis, she is forced to suffer the pain of human loss to which she presumed herself divinely immune.

The extended Pygmalion tale, thus, develops the human "ethical" questions defined by Miller: punishment is delivered to those who try to avoid both the encounters with the human "other" and the loss associated with change and transformation. Attempts to avoid such loss lead to irresponsible behavior. Finally, the Pygmalion myth, especially in literary displacements, explores the cost of taking one's own creation, including what one has created with language, for the "real" (5–7).

The similarity of these general ethical problems to those examined in Italian feminist theory, especially the creation of a female-centered symbolic which would unite (female) desire with a material world, seems obvious. The difficulties encountered in creating a "different" female Other who is constantly revealing herself to be the same, the pain in leaving behind a past that continues to reappear or the contradictions that result from the creation of a new one, are important themes in the women's romances, *Bildungsromane*, and historical texts we have discussed here. Fantastic or tragic materializations of desire in and of language either express a temporary escape from reality or force an encounter with it. The Pygmalion theme allows women writers to reintroduce these themes from two opposing and thus seemingly more complete viewpoints in the text, the punisher and the punished, the creator and the created. Women occupy both spaces, which are no longer determined by gender, although the behavior, expectations, and actions of the characters continue to reflect the partial viewpoints of both sexes. In the detective novel, images of powerful females incite fear in men who eliminate them physically or, as in La Spina's novel *Morte a Palermo*, devise theories to do the same.[7] Thus, the Pygmalion theme also permits women an ironic or tragic distance from these traditional representations that appear in their texts.

From Ovid's time on, the Pygmalion myth merged with the story of Prometheus, the creator of humankind who was punished for the presumptuousness underlying his creative, narcissistic act, although he did not fall in love with his creation.[8] Since in the literary displacements of the myth both creator and created wear a variety of masks, the myth can be easily made to serve the purposes of social criticism or satire, tragedy, comedy, slapstick, or horror. In many examples given by Raymond Trousson, the myth is used as a vehicle for misogynist satire when the creator invents a selfish, troublemaking coquette. The innocence or ignorance of the created, male or female, could also be used to comment on the evils of life. This is the case, for example, in the work of the eighteenth-century French writer Madame de Genlis in her *Pygmalion et Galatée*, a work said to have influenced Mary Shelley's *Frankenstein*.[9] Despite variations, however, the standard paradigm demands that the creator love the created and that the created must flee and punish the creator.

Fabrizio invents Maria Lettner after Mario rejects his introduction to the book on the grounds that Fabrizio had identified too heavily with the author. He then suggests that Fabrizio write a short biography. Maria, the woman Fabrizio claims kept Fritz Oberhofer company in the last four years of his life before he died of pneumonia, is on the one hand his alter ego. On the other hand, she clearly represents, in Galatean fashion, the "abstract essence of womanhood" (112), although such an essence represents the impossible other, that "absolute rarity among creatures, a lovable woman" (110). Fabrizio's femme fatale is an amalgam of every possible stereotypical female characteristic ever attributed to women by men, as the ironic description of her complicated genesis indicates:

Thus Maria was *Laurus nobilus, Angelica Archangelica*: and yet at times she could be terrible, tempestuous—*Sturmschwalbe, Procellaria Gravis, Potentilla Tormentilla*. She was strong and courageous, someone in whom you could have faith: Kingfisher, Golden Eagle and even Levant Sparrow Hawk (who knows, perhaps a drop of Semitic blood—from this name he derived her nose, her demeanor and her unfathomable, disturbing psychological depth).

Then there was that special grace in the way she moved her hands, and in the delicate curve of her neck: *Demoiselle, Nigella damascena, Belladonna Lily*. She was also sweet and childish, almost silly at times: Willow Tit, Kittiwake, Peewit and Puffin. Suddenly she needed to be sheltered, protected: *Campanula fragilis, Erica gracilus*. But she was also the Little Owl, who in Latin became *Athena Noctua*; and here Maria revealed yet another aspect, silvery and nocturnal—*Lunaria Perennis, Silene pendula*. In the sun, her chestnut hair blazed fire-red: *Russula Aurata*. And of course Cattleya, *ça va sans dire*, but also *Narcissus poeticus*. (114)

Fabrizio is happy with his brilliant role as "creator and worshipper," leaving Maria to be his "creation and inanimate goddess," until, predictably, his creation begins to have a life of her own. Fashion designers invent a new Maria Lettner line and others start to add details to the past of Fabrizio's creation. This last development, which signifies that Fabrizio's Galatea is breaking away from him, causes him to consider killing his wayward offspring turned Other. A phone call from an Austrian woman, Petra, who claims to be Maria Lettner's granddaughter and to have love letters from Fritz to Maria, seals his fate. Fabrizio travels to Petra's house and becomes the sex slave of this self-appointed representative in the flesh of his own invented creation and wastes away, too weak even to alert Fulvia of his presence in Petra's house when she comes to rescue him in the final pages. Trapped by his own paranoid fears of modern society, from which he always felt excluded, as in the final paranoid demise of Armanda Guiducci's housewife ten years earlier, Fabrizio accepts his marginalization and immanent annihilation:

If only he could not see the millions of plastic bags produced every day and subjected to a very brief tryout (the hour it took to get home from the supermarket) before being immediately sent off to fulfill their true purpose: to cover the earth, to float on the sea, to taint the atmosphere with their poisonous fumes . . . not see the torrid Christmases and freezing Julys amid the sinister hums of heaters and air conditioners; not see the obscene greed that turns everything into vice, into drugs—even diets, even fasting a form of greed. (178)

In archetypal terms, Fabrizio has become the victim of his human (read masculine) attempts to appropriate the creative power of language. Generally speaking, *The House on Moon Lake* can be read as critical parody of consumerism and image-making in contemporary society. In feminist terms, however, he is also victimized here by his own paranoia, which, rather than creating a significant Other, has turned his fear of matriarchies into his final imprisonment in a "real" one of his own creation, paradoxically. All of these readings are effected by Duranti's parodic usage of feminist ideas on male specular desire, female objectification, and the theme of the vengeful and much feared Mother Goddess in the exaggerated figure of Petra. The theme of creation in these narratives is somewhat similar to the search for origins and recreation of the mother found in the feminist romances discussed earlier in Chapter 3: Petra searches to fuse with her grandmother and repossess her maternal lineage.

Duranti uses the Pygmalion theme and literary structures both to distance herself and to identify with her characters in a way that reflects no single ideological stance. She is not entirely unsympathetic to Fabrizio's nostalgic aspirations to find an identity or to his misgivings concerning the independent, unfaithful Fulvia who carelessly dismisses these aspirations and desires. Fulvia is a materialistic type, "not one to indulge in gratuitous meditation. She made good use of her intelligence, but only in the service of concrete goals" (78). Vestiges of a misogynist trend in the Pygmalion tradition also appear in Duranti's equally exaggerated portrait of Petra. Petra, a cold, hypocritical, church-going woman, is ready to sacrifice Fabrizio to recreate her maternal line. In this ironic commentary on the difficulty of establishing oneself as an individual in a consumer society, Duranti deploys the myth to highlight the different varieties of narcissistic presumptuousness, self-indulgence, and dangers involved on all levels of self-creation by both sexes.

In Duranti's *Effetti personali*, which takes place primarily in an unidentified city in the former Communist Eastern bloc, themes of individualism versus consumerism again seem to take center stage. Michele Prisco writes that the novel confronts the general theme of choice of life-style. The two styles are

the Western way of life, conditioned by a consumerism that wants to have it all even if a few basic values are lost along the way including that of one's own personal identity, and a way of life that denies well-being and tries to maintain fundamental values, even if it denies the fundamental principles of liberty and choice.[10]

As is the case in *The House on Moon Lake*, the plot of *Effetti personali* is built around the adventures of a protagonist searching to create an identity by discovering a writer. In *Effetti personali*, however, the individual who takes on a homologizing, superficial society is female. Valentina is a recent divorcée in her late twenties whose husband has taken away all the "personal belongings" that had determined her previous identity, including the brass nameplate from their front door.

Leaving behind her staunch and politically correct feminist mother and her hopelessly egocentric ex-husband, who had used her as an anonymous researcher for the books that brought him fame, Valentina crosses the Iron Curtain in search of an interview with Milos Jarco, a writer who had achieved a certain renown in the West. After her arrival in the East and her encounter with several stereotypical members of the official Union of Writers, Valentina begins her comic, Kafkaesque search for the author's whereabouts, a search constantly frustrated by contradicting claims. She develops a romantic attachment to a young Leftist poet named Ante Radek who will eventually disclose the artificial genesis of Milos Jarco—who turns out to be, like Maria Lettner, an invention. Jarco is the pen name given to the collaborative efforts of a few writers, including Ante, who himself is running from his own created identity that is now threatening to consume him.

In writing *Effetti Personali*, Duranti's use of a variety of literary structures and genres has caused some confusion as to how to categorize the text: one critic calls the novel a mixture of *Bildungsroman*, sentimental romance, Kafkaesque metanovel, spy novel, and finally both "un romanzo sessantottesco e post-femminista."[11] At the novel's end, Duranti recalls the *Bildungsroman* tradition when her protagonist declares that, as a result of the plot adventures, she has learned enough to cope with the world. After the mystery of Jarco's identity is solved, Valentina has to decide whether to stay with Ante and become a possession he can add to his "personal" authentic world, made up of a little shack in the midst of a mosquito-ridden swamp where he hides the personal belongings he is forced to disclaim in public. Rather than accepting the inverted consumerism of the East and again becoming a specular image and possession of another man, Valentina decides to return to her own disparate belongings that somehow make up her floating identity.

I know that nothing will be as before. This is a return after having spent a winter in the trenches, after a space odyssey. At the end of the voyage there is my house, my mother, my work, my few absent-minded friends, my ex, my house door without a name—but also a piece of paper and a pen to make a new temporary plate while I order a brass one. There are my six embroidered sheets and the six flowered cotton ones. There is my little bank account. My walnut night table. There is my membership to the alternative cinema of the priests. There are the people, streets, pots, trolley cars, stairs, trees which belong completely or partially to me. They are not "me" but points outside of me that line up in a reasonable enough way to form some contours that, from the Alpine hills, are clearly identifiable. There is the certainty of having learned almost nothing because there is almost nothing to learn, except for the fact that things could really be destined to roll in either one direction or the other, because a third choice doesn't exist in nature. (166)[12]

Valentina's generically determined conclusion that there is nothing to learn except that there is little to learn reiterates the traditional message of accommodation of the *Bildungsroman* and unmasks the claims of the many *Bildungsroman* protagonists of having found an all-encompassing answer to life. The ending both comments on and complements other female and feminist *Bildungsromane* of the 1980s as well. In *Effetti personali*, the narrator does not disappear as a result of not being able to find her identity or of having to refute a socially imposed one. Valentina returns from her trip after having concluded, in contrast to Bompiani's Sophie and the other narrators, that she does not need to be created by achieving recognition in someone else's eyes. Rather, Valentina's voyage allows her to use her past to create herself, or more precisely to accept the challenge of creating her own person composed of a series of ever-changing fragments and disparate collection of belongings.

Valentina learns that Ante refused to take on the identity Milos Jarco, since to do so, he would have had to renounce the authorship of his own book of poems. Against the Communist background, Ante's choice to remain true to his own identity is motivated by a desire to create personal possessions in a society that publicly denies their value. Valentina's definition of self, on the contrary, is a result of her formation in a society that defines people according to what they own and openly flaunt. Both characters' refusal to allow others to create identities for them is the quality that enables them to survive, albeit not without experiencing "human" solitude and loss.

*   *   *

The search for self and individualism in a materialistic world and the contradictory, even hypocritical fantasies people create for themselves and others inform Ravera's tragi-comic romance *Voi grandi* and Petrignani's tragic romance *Come cadono i fulmini*. Like *The House on Moon Lake*, *Voi grandi* has a tripartite structure that frames the Friday, Saturday, and Sunday during which the action takes place. Marianna, a thirty-nine-year-old terrorist, appears in the apartment of her former boyfriend Sergio, on the eve of his marriage to the twenty-year-old, rather well-off Laura, one of Sergio's former university students. Although Marianna has her face redone so that she can return incognito to Italy, where she is wanted on murder charges, her character remains as inflexible and vindictively ideological as before. Sergio still harbors inexpressible fears of Marianna, his former mistress and seductress, whom he describes as a "loaded bomb" ("una bomba innescata," 42). A mistress of disguises who speaks several languages fluently, Marianna returns after tiring of endlessly assuming the many fixed identities associated with being a social outcast, such as thief, pimp, prostitute, drug addict, and dealer. Marianna, an exaggerated misfit, could hardly be said to be the symbol through which Ravera either condones or condemns the radical and violent nature of the 1968 revolution, a theme treated in other women's novels including Frabotta's *Velocità di fuga*. Instead, Marianna's "totalitarian sentimentalism," which motivated her desire to save and change the world by refuting all possessions in the name of total freedom, represents the major illusion of a generation from which Sergio and others are now trying in various ways to disassociate themselves in this comic romance plot.

The "creative" endeavors of Sergio and Marianna in this text are attempts to avoid the loss and inevitable punishment for their previous creative errors. In presenting her characters in this Pygmalion framework, Ravera follows the rules of romance characterization.[13] Marianna, the former terrorist who hides behind her new face, and Sergio, the man who tries to resolve his mid-life crisis by marrying a younger and, he hopes, more malleable woman, are recognizable types who will act in predictable ways. In order to make the characters interesting to the reader, Ravera fleshes out their stereotypical frames by showing how their actions are motivated by a mixture of general human desires, here the need for stability and normality, and contemporary psychological, philosophical, even political ideas. Marianna, still determined to live a life-style consonant with her ideology of destruction and refutation of all belongings, ridicules Sergio's return to a bourgeois life-style. Sergio's inability to subscribe to Marianna's theories of total freedom and renunciation of all possessions derives from his poor, Southern background, which left him desirous of achieving some type of social standing and recognition. Thus Sergio is indeed the hypocrite Marianna accuses him of being: a complacent bourgeois who earns his living by nostalgically retailing Marxist and Hegelian theories in the classroom and whose most radical accomplishment is to use these theories to attract the attention of his student Laura, who falls in love with his eloquence. Sergio himself admits that his greatest achievements, the books he writes to stabilize his individual identity (as so many other characters in contemporary texts do), are compromised popularizations of these theories. To make matters worse, he published them through the editorial connections of his prospective father-in-law. Although Sergio describes Marianna as a person who tried to negate reality, he is one who compromises constantly with it, not necessarily out of Sartrian bad faith, but out of human weakness and a desire to be normal.

Although in contrast to Sergio's compromising nature Marianna seems more ideologically pure, she is also not immune to the need for stability and normality. Her ideological stance is not above suspicion, since it derived from her rebellious refutation of her rich, Northern, upper-class background where wealth and possessions were simply taken for granted. Marianna's return to Sergio is motivated by a desire to return to some identity in the past that is as unchanged and frozen in time as her new, surgically produced face and simultaneously avoid paying the price for that past. Her criticisms of Sergio and her attempt to block his marriage can be interpreted more simply as a manifestation of jealousy of a younger woman whose presence reminds Marianna of her inability to recreate the past and reactivate her control over Sergio.

The evening before the wedding, Marianna, who is trying to stop the marriage, enrages Sergio to the point that he strikes her and believes her to be dead. Nonetheless, he leaves her body in the apartment and goes through a satirical wedding scene that pokes fun at bourgeois weddings in general. After the ceremony, Sergio returns home with his annoyed wife. The possible tragic ending is averted and the tone changes to comedy when it appears that Sergio, as usual, had overestimated his strength. Marianna is gone and his new wife, who takes control of cleaning up the mess, coolly dismisses Sergio's adventure and apology on the grounds that she does not dismiss her commitments easily:

—According to me, you are crazy—said Laura.
—And you, what do you intend to do?
—Leave.
—With me.
—With you.
—Why, what if I'm crazy?
—Because I decided to. That's why. Because I don't do things just to undo them right afterwards. I want things to last. I want to enjoy them! (166)[14]

With these words and a refusal to say she loves him because "I told you that three years ago," Laura prepares for their sailing honeymoon paid for and arranged by her father. Thus Ravera ends her text in traditional romance style by having the blocking character (here female) eliminated so that the couple can marry and presumably live happily ever after. This ending also picks up the motif of punishment deferred, however, to point out differences and continuities between the generations of Laura and Marianna. Laura, like Fulvia, clearly represents the materialistic, self-assured next generation that neither refutes nor hypocritically acquires possessions; rather she simply seems to absorb them as a means to enjoy life. Although Marianna warrants no real affection from the reader throughout the narrative, Ravera does show that Marianna, as an aging woman, like Guiducci's prostitute and housewife, is not immune to the crisis that occurs when women lose the attribute that had given them a certain amount of power. Sergio appears to have an easier time at starting over because he can fall back on the traditional schema of marrying a younger woman and starting all over again. He contrasts Marianna's piercing and controlling eyes that indicate her unchanging nature underneath her new face to Laura's young and trusting gaze (12).

Sergio may delude himself that his seduction of and marriage to Laura is indicative of his ability to create a loving woman and a peaceful existence for himself, yet Laura is neither formed nor created by Sergio and his love. Her brusque dismissal of Sergio's near criminal act recalls the tone of misogynous Pygmalion satires when the devilish coquette starts to come into her own. In addition, Laura's genealogy is decidedly female. Formed by feminism and her successful, though slightly neurotic, film-making mother, she is linked in yet unknown ways to Marianna, despite the latter's elimination, or more precisely, disappearance. Laura's forty-four-year-old father admits to understanding neither his daughter nor his wife, these "new" women who laugh, talk about themselves, make films, write books, have careers and, above all, as feminist theory has told them to do, refuse to be victims and martyrs (119). He clearly states, however, he does know that Laura has little to do with Pygmalion (120). Laura's "revenge" against anyone who attempts to form her is not yet definable, but it is certainly inevitable. Sergio may have found a temporary port but the storm is not over yet. In contrast to the feminist romances of the 1980s in which women come face to face with creations of themselves, Ravera ends *Voi grandi* with Sergio facing feminism's newest unknown creation, the postfeminist.

*   *   *

In Petrignani's *Come cadono i fulmini*, the generational love triangle is presented in a tragic romance form. One oft-repeated motif in this story of Luigi Tomek, a famous contemporary musician, his girlfriend, directly formed by the feminist experience, and his much younger American wife, Gwen, is that of communication. Luigi Tomek tells the American woman (his future wife) interviewing him that his music is a way to communicate less his own personal self than the ideas and mood of a certain generation through communal forms (17). Luigi's description of the function of art is similar to Petrignani's own experience with narrative as a means of experimentation and communication. In her autobiographical sketch in the *Autodizionario degli scrittori italiani*, Petrignani writes that the fundamental problem for writers today is how to "recreate the act of narrating."[15] This can only be accomplished by activating our "historical memory . . . a recuperation and synthesis of what is behind us, including the failures and the funerals of our century (literally and artistically speaking), in order to move, somewhat innocently, into new terrains" (269).

Petrignani describes her first novel, *Le navigazioni di Circe* (1987), as an inquiry into the problem of how to write after the crisis of the avant-garde and its "final solutions" through the use of "the primitive form of the picaresque genre" (269–270). She describes her second novel, *Il catalogo dei giocattoli*, as an experiment with

the narrative possibilities evoked by a single object, the diverse appearances it assumes and the psychological and remembering effects it provokes. Description valued in and for itself tries to coincide with the architectural structure of the narration. (270)

Petrignani, though certainly never denying the role of gender in her childhood formation, refuses the descriptions of failure and victimization typical of many feminist *Bildungsromane* by returning to a seemingly objective narration in which both an individual and a communal past of a certain generation is reviewed in terms of its possessions, here its shared "toys."

These narrative experiments precede the more traditionally presented plot line found in *Come cadono i fulmini*. Rusconi describes the book as the most romantic of the novels she reviews but still one motivated by the same noncommittal philosophy of detachment and meaninglessness of life that the two guardian angels watching and commenting on the narrative represent: "Their observations from on high function to remind us that facts are insignificant, history a question of perspectives, human life an accident."[16] Although these topical generalizations are included in the narrative, Petrignani's romance could also be viewed as a response to Frabotta's evaluation of her own *Velocità di fuga* as a criticism of feminism's failure to communicate a new model for loving.[17] Indeed, Petrignani's description of the failed romance of Luigi Tomek and his girlfriend, Federica, includes the reasons given by Maraini and Frabotta in their romances of failed encounters, such as male egotistical attitudes and the many oppressive patriarchal myths and social structures that stifle female development and autonomy. Whereas Maraini's Vanna rejoices at a world to be constructed again and Frabotta's narrator renounces Eugenio when she comes face to face with the female image he wants her to be, Petrignani uses romance conventions to present a more general view of the ideas and illusions for which a generation must now take responsibility. In Luigi's words, "we are prisoners of ideas that do not belong to us but we are responsible for what horrible things these ideas have produced in reality" (144).[18]

Even if both Federica and Luigi agree on the idea of taking responsibility for one's fate, their ideas on how to do so differ, as Petrignani echoes another common theme in contemporary women's writing—the lack of communication between the sexes. Federica's response to Luigi's statement on responsibility, which comes late in the narrative, is that once again she does not understand to which ideas he is referring. The ill-fated love affair between the two starts in the late 1960s when she is fourteen and he sixteen. Federica, now in her thirties, still believes in political activism, which she sees as a way to make her life useful and to give it an ennobling purpose. Federica belongs to Marianna's generation of feminists for whom politics was perceived as (and still is) a way to close the gap between "thought and action," between becoming a woman and becoming an autonomous individual in society (53).

It is no coincidence that the angels' story of Federica emphasizes how her "personal" development began with her participation in *autocoscienza* groups and violent political demonstrations. The angels claim to be telling the story from Luigi's point of view, a more objective, impartial stance; as the narrative progresses, however, the gendered nature of all actions becomes obvious. Luigi watches with incomprehension Federica's interest in politics and her desire to use it as a means to restore the wholeness and integrity to her person. For Luigi, words are too important for these women, a reaction that indeed ironically recalls the impatience of Pygmalion figures when their creations start to talk.[19] He sees politics as something that threatens to flatten a person's originality by forcing him or her "to act and react with collective and predictable gestures" (49). Federica's faith in politics is the faith of an entire feminist generation: her belief in the power of ideas and ideologies to right certain historical wrongs is also generational. Thus, like Frabotta's narrator, her initial sexual experience with Luigi is part of a conscious strategy to lose her virginity before marriage in a gesture of revolt against the monitoring of female sexuality. These ideas and strategies, however, do not help Federica to cope with her real feelings for and attraction to Luigi.

The separation of the couple through ideas links Petrignani's text to the feminist romances analyzed in Chapter 3. In the romance, psychological, social, political, or philosophical ideas serve to depict the characters as believable, interesting types, although their actions are primarily governed by the passions and the higher powers. The higher powers here are the two guardian angels who interrupt the narrative five times to comment on their presentation. Petrignani's characters are determined to put their ideas into action, though, and Luigi accuses Federica with just cause on several occasions of replacing feelings with ideas. But although he is correct that Federica fights her feelings of love and dependency for him with stiff, uncompromising ideologies that recognizably derive from contemporary feminist theory, her arguments do have some validity. When Luigi, who is considering marrying Gwen, travels to Paris to find Federica and see if there is any hope for the relationship, Federica argues that his love for her is based in his desire to make of her his possession:

I think that the deepest love is the most unpredictable. . . . Aren't we here together speaking? And what difference does it make, now, if we saw each other two days, ten years or ten minutes ago? Don't we know each other as if we had lived every moment together? No, you want a wife who will shield you from strangers, who will produce happy, healthy children and who dedicates her life to you and them. You don't want to suffer. You want to sleep. You want to control nature. You fool yourself into thinking you are omnipotent. You think that happiness is having something to protect, an object in a glass jar to look at. Isn't it enough that you create music? Why do you want to create everything else in your image? (69)[20]

Luigi brusquely categorizes her by now well-known arguments for the existential nature of women as "theatrical" and returns home to marry Gwen.

Luigi's views, which may initially appear less ideological than those of Federica, are no less typical than hers, and many of Federica's accusations against him are validated by other characters. Luigi's comments on love and responsibility are indeed heavily informed by patriarchal ideology, as his reason for marrying Gwen shows—he claims he wants to give something back to society in the form of offspring (89). A close friend, Marcello, also remarks that Luigi's love for Federica is based in a desire to possess and dominate her and it is only this inability to do so that keeps the love alive (76). Luigi could never admit to himself that Federica served as an inspiration for him in composing his music because this would be an admission of some kind of dependency on her (12). His attraction and marriage to a younger woman is indeed formed by the Pygmalion mythology that lurks behind Sergio's marriage to Laura and that Federica rejects in refusing to be his wife.

Although Gwen is presented as a member of the younger, more materialistic generation, she is less self-assured than Laura or Fulvia. Gwen bases her desire to marry Luigi on a mixture of motives: she admires him and his music, she would like to live in his house, and she hopes, in contrast to Federica, that the marriage will offer some stability and meaning to her life. Therefore she willingly agrees to play the role of the stable, normal, faithful wife, although this role is clearly too stifling and confining for her. It is also not a role that completely satisfies Luigi, who continues his sporadic relationship with Federica, although every encounter results in a new separation. When Luigi runs away with Federica to Africa, Gwen realizes rather belatedly that Luigi could not create her, even though that is what they both desired:

She [Federica] has that advantage over me. She inspires his illusions. . . . Luigi thought he wanted my stability, my faithfulness, my normality. But he doesn't know what to do with that. . . . But what did he do for me? He expected everything and didn't think he owed me a thing. But, it's not important. I can't save myself blaming him. He is a gift in himself, he creates, but he can't create me. (131)[21]

The reason the couples fail to unite in *Come cadono i fulmini* is that the narrative is determined by another literary myth, that of romantic love. According to Denis de Rougemont, the myth originates in the Tristan and Iseult story and demands that the couple remain separated in order to keep their love alive, a love that is only consummated in death.[22] Whereas in the detective novel the reappearance of the myth enhances depictions of the male fear of women, here, in romance fashion, it perpetuates the separation of Federica and Luigi and keeps their love alive, a love that is indeed a romantic one underneath all the contemporary trappings. Thus Petrignani concludes the work in tragic romance style. Federica, who had contacted malaria in Africa, dies listening to Luigi's magisterial performance in the Colosseum to usher in the next millennium. Luigi himself is shot after his performance by a jealous admirer. His death leaves the grieving widow Gwen, now the mother of Luigi's two children, isolated and alone.

This and the other traditional endings neither refute nor laud the accomplishments of feminism or any other contemporary ideology. Petrignani, like Duranti and Ravera, among others, by putting some new wine in old bottles, uses these "old bottles" to write the history of the relationship of a generation to its own recent past in a larger, literary framework. For the three authors examined here, genre is certainly not the symbol of a repressive, external structure that needs to be overthrown. Rather, generic structures are the means by which these authors include the fruits of feminism in both the political and literary realms.

The possibility, and even the use of such integration actually started before the late 1980s. Feminist themes and motifs now have literary functions; they serve to depict characters, explain their actions, and cause plot events. This new role, rather than representing capitulation or "selling out" to the mainstream, is part of the process by which women writers everywhere are moving into a constantly changing mainstream that they themselves are helping to create. Nicci Gerrard welcomes the kind of literary integration exemplified by the texts examined here and claims it heralds a more radical move past the self-indulgent descriptions of suffering which indicated moral superiority. Gerrard describes contemporary women's writings as

more political, because they are in motion; more inventive because they are not confined by static, predetermined theories. . . . They are more feminist, because less policed by a repressive feminist ideology; more illuminating because the novel's spotlight casts a wider arc. And they are more mainstream because, quite simply, they are more enjoyable. (14)

Such general and generalizing statements need to be examined against the accomplishments of the individual texts now appearing. These works are undoubtedly more enjoyable, however, since they are in many ways influenced by a feminist revolution in progress. They may indeed refuse feminism's referential forms, but through the employment of traditional structures, women writers enter another realm of reference, that of no longer describing their isolation and oppression but showing how they think and act (differently) in a variety of so-called general situations. Empowered by feminist themes, images, and ideas, women writers no longer have to refute aggressively literary form that was assumed to be as mystical and oppressive as the patriarchy that produced it. As a result, their fiction does appear to be "coming down from the barricades."

Feminist fiction has often been defended for its explanatory and consoling roles, and these newer works continue to fulfill that same function. Gerrard's remark on their entertaining nature may prompt the question, "Entertaining to whom?" But it does indicate that the method of presentation therein, the "show" rather than the "tell," no longer places the female reader in a position of resistance to the "immasculation" process that occurs when one's own viewpoint is consistently missing or downgraded.[23] Gender is a source of a difference that can no longer be ignored, and literary structures provide the means to extend the feminist and female critical viewpoint outside its own domain. As women writers shift from being the material from which language and literature is made to creating their own errors, metaphors, types, and punishments, genre moves from being the force against which to formulate an opposite viewpoint to presenting the means to review what women have created in marginal or central positions. The return to general literary structures is also enabling women to create their own intertextual network of reinterpretation of those general literary themes which, like Pygmalion's Galatea, have a stubborn, unchanging life of their own. All of these functions exemplify what Adena Rosmarin has called the power of genre, a power that extends to writers, readers, and critics—a power that has enabled us in this volume to use our own partial vision to describe and participate in the multifaceted materialization of desire into experience that motivates and produces the writings of many contemporary Italian women writers.

Notes

1. Marisa Rusconi, "Le chances delle donne," *L'espresso*, February 24, 1991, 99: "Ecco la letteratura femminile nasce da doti di sensibilità, di percettività che le donne possiedono molto più degli uomini."

2. The authors and works reviewed are: Romana Petri, *Il ritratto del disarmo*; Susanna Tamaro, *Per voce sola*; Ippolita Avalli, *Storie di Nisse*; Valeria Viganò, *Il doppio regno*; and Sandra Petrignani, *Come cadono i fulmini*. All five works were published by Rizzoli in 1991.

3. Francesca Duranti, *La casa sul lago della luna* (Milan: Rizzoli, 1984), *The*

House on Moon Lake, trans. Stephen Sartarelli (New York: Random House, 1984). All English quotes in this chapter come from this edition.

4. Paul Hallam, "The House on Moon Lake," *New Statesman*, March 4, 1988, 26.

5. J. Hillis Miller, *Versions of Pygmalion* (Cambridge, MA: Harvard University Press, 1990), 1.

6. J. Hillis Miller, *Versions of Pygmalion*, 10–11.

7. Although the Pygmalion theme does not dominate Italian literature, clearly the literary creations of Laura and Beatrice and the images they have spawned continue to reinforce the idea that the creation of female images is a male domain. The Pygmalion theme does structure Tommaso Landolfi's short story "Gogol's Wife" (1954; in *Racconti* [Florence: Valecchi, 1961]). Landolfi is considered an eccentric in Italian literature, although his parodic and fantastic writings are sometimes compared to those of Italo Svevo and Italo Calvino. Male fear of women is highlighted in Landolfi's story of Nikolay Gogol's wife, an extremely sexy blow-up balloon he destroys after she becomes a repository of all his fears. (Landolfi did write a biography of the eccentric Gogol, who burned his own parodic works before taking his life.) For this reference and in the following discussion on the relationship of Duranti's Fabrizio to language, I am indebted to Ana Rueda, whose careful reading of this chapter and comments improved it considerably.

8. See Raymond Trousson, *Le mythe de Prométhée dans la littérature européenne* (Geneva: Droz, 1964).

9. See Burton Pollin, "Philosophical and Literary Sources of *Frankenstein*," *Comparative Literature* 17 (1965): 97–108.

10. Michele Prisco, "Un viaggio oltrecortina fra speranze e delusioni," *Il nostro tempo*, December 11, 1988.

11. Piero Cigada, "Particolari effetti personali," *Il sole*, December 18, 1988.

12. "So che niente sarà come prima. Questo è un ritorno dopo un inverno passato in trincea, dopo un'avventura spaziale. Alla fine del viaggio ci sono la mia casa, mia madre, il mio lavoro, i miei pochi e distratti amici, il mio ex marito, la mia porta di casa senza nome—ma anche un pezzo di carta e un pennarello per fare una nuova targhetta provvisoria intanto che ordino quello di ottone. Ci sono le mie sei lenzuola ricamate e le sei di cotone stampato. C'è il mio piccolo conto in banca. C'è il mio abbonamento al cinema d'essai dei preti. Ci sono persone, strade, pentole, tram, scale, alberi, che in tutto, o in parte, mi appartengono. Non sono 'me' ma sono punti fuori di me che si allineano in mode abbastanza ragionevole, tanto, insomma, da formare un contorno che finalmente mi appare, visto dalle pendici delle Alpi, bene identificabile. C'è la certezza di non aver imparato quasi nulla perché non c'è quasi nulla da imparare, salvo il fatto che le cose potrebbero davvero essere sempre inevitabilmente destinate a rotolare o da una parte o dall'altra, perché una terza scelta non esiste in natura."

13. Domenico Starnone notes the use of the romance form by Ravera, which, despite its stereotypical characters, allows Ravera to view her characters from an original angle: "Marianna, who comes from a past that has completely absorbed her, is a tough stereotypical terrorist. . . . Even the professor is the typical 'reformed' (social protester) type without too many surprises. However, it is precisely the use of the romance plot ('trama rosa') and its stereotypes that permits the author to look at the theme from an irregular and new angle" ("Pentimenti e brusche conversioni," *Tuttestorie* 2 [1991]: 68–70). Starnone

says that the topical theme Ravera is investigating here is that of repentant terrorists.

14. —Secondo me tu sei pazzo—disse Laura.

—E tu, che cosa ha intenzione di fare?

—Partire.

—Con me.

—Con te.

—Perché, se sono pazzo.

— Perché l'ho deciso. Ecco perché. Perché io non faccio le cose per disfarle subito dopo! Voglio che durino. Voglio godermele."

15. Felice Piemontese, ed., *Autodizionario degli scrittori italiani* (Milan: Leonardo Editore, 1989), s.v. Petrignani, Sandra.

16. Marisa Rusconi, "Le chances delle donne," 99. The quote, slightly modified, is from the book jacket of the March 1991 edition: "Il loro sguardo dall'alto sta lì a ricordare che le date sono insignificanti, la storia una questione di prospettive, la vita umana un incidente."

17. "We did not know how to transmit a new way of loving" ("Non abbiamo saputo trasmettere un modo diverso d'amare, noi femministe"). Interview with Silvia Neonato, "D'amore (forse) si muore: Due generazioni sullo sfondo femminismo," *Secolo XIX*, February 18, 1989.

18. "Siamo prigionieri di idee che non ci appartengono, ma siamo responsabili di tutto quanto di orribile quelle idee producono nella realtà."

19. In Landolfi's short story, Gogol's destructive anger is motivated by one sentence uttered by his usually passive wife, "I want to go poo-poo." The anonymous biographer, obviously a comic representation of Landolfi himself, is at first confused by this seemingly irrational judgment of the wife as overly loquacious. He does agree with Gogol, however, that this is a rebellious statement on her part since she could not possibly have such needs.

20. "Credo che l'amore più profondo sia il più provvisorio. . . . Non siamo qui a parlare, io e te, adesso? E che differenza fa, adesso, se ci siamo visti due giorni fa o dieci anni o dieci minuti? Non ci conosciamo come se avessimo vissuto insieme ogni istante? No, tu vuoi una moglie che faccia da schermo fra te e gli estranei, che ti fabbrichi bambini belli e sani, che annulli la sua vita in nome della tua e della loro. Tu non vuoi soffrire. Vuoi dormire. Vuoi domare la natura. Illuderti di essere onnipotente. Credi che esista la felicità come qualcosa da proteggere, un oggetto dentro una campana di vetro, da guardare. Non ti basta creare la musica? Perché vuoi creare a tua immagine anche il resto?"

21. "Ha questo vantaggio su di me. Che lei può dargli illusioni. . . . Luigi credeva di desiderare la mia stabilità, la mia fedeltà, la mia normalità. Ma non sa che farsene. . . . Lui si aspettava tutto, non pensava di dovermi niente. Ma non importa, non è incolpando lui che mi salvo. Lui è un dono in se stesso, lui crea, non poteva creare anche me."

22. Denis de Rougemont, *L'Amour et l'Occident* (Paris: Librairie Plon, 1939).

23. Judith Fetterley, *The Resisting Reader: A Feminist Approach to Modern Fiction* (Bloomington: Indiana University Press, 1978), 8.

Bibliography

Primary Sources

Aleramo, Sibilla. *Una donna*. Turin: Sten, 1906. Repr. Milan: Feltrinelli, 1976. *A Woman*. Trans. Rosalind Delmar. Los Angeles: University of California Press, 1980.

Banti, Anna. *Artemisia*. Florence: Sansoni, 1947. Repr. Milan: Mondadori, 1953. English translation by Shirley D'Ardia. Omaha: University of Nebraska Press, 1988.

———. *Un grido lacerante*. Milan: Rizzoli, 1982.

Bellonci, Maria. *Delitto di stato*. Milan: Mondadori, 1981.

———. *Rinascimento privato*. Milan: Mondadori, 1985.

———. *Tu vipera gentile*. Milan: Mondadori, 1972.

Belotti, Elena Gianini. *Il fiore dell'ibisco*. Milan: Rizzoli, 1985.

Bompiani, Ginevra. *L'attesa*. Milan: Feltrinelli, 1988.

———. *L'incantato*. Milan: Garzanti, 1987.

———. *Mondanità*. Milan: La Tartaruga, 1980.

———. *Specie del sonno*. Milan: Biblioteca Blù, 1975.

———. *Vecchio cielo, nuova terra*. Milan: Garzanti, 1988.

Cagnoni, Fiora. *Questione di tempo*. Milan: La Tartaruga, 1985.

Cambria, Adele. *Nudo di donna con le rovine*. Catania: Pellicanolibri, 1986.

Castelli, Silvia. *Pitonessa*. Turin: Einaudi, 1978.

Cerati, Carla. *Un matrimonio perfetto*. Padua: Marsilio, 1976.

Ceresa, Alice. *Bambine*. Turin: Einaudi, 1990.

———. *La figlia prodiga*. Turin: Einaudi, 1967.

Corsi, Carla. *Ritratto a tinte forti*. Florence: Astrea, 1991.

Corti, Maria. *L'ora di tutti*. Milan: Feltrinelli, 1962. Repr. 1977.

Cravetta, Maria Letizia. *Tutti sanno*. Rome: Edizioni delle donne, 1976.

Cutrufelli, Maria Rosa. *La briganta*. Palermo: La Luna, 1990.

Di Maggio, Marisa. *C'era una volta un re . . .* Rome: Il Ventaglio, 1985.

Duranti, Francesca. *La bambina*. Milan: La Tartaruga, 1976. Repr. Milan: Rizzoli, 1985.

———. *La casa sul lago della luna*. Milan: Rizzoli, 1984. *The House on Moon Lake*. Trans. Stephen Sartarelli. New York: Random House, 1984.

———. *Effetti personali*. Milan: Rizzoli, 1988.

Ferri, Giuliana. *Un quarto di donna*. Padua: Marsilio, 1973.

Frabotta, Biancamaria. *Velocità di fuga*. Triest: Reverdito Editore, 1989.

Guiducci, Armanda. *Due donne da buttare: Una donna di buona famiglia e una exprostituta confessano il fallimento della loro vita*. Milan: Rizzoli, 1976.

———. *A testa in giù*. Milan: Rizzoli, 1984.

Grimaldi, Laura. *Il sospetto*. Milan: Mondadori,1988.

———. *La colpa*. Milan: Leonardo, 1989.

La Spina, Silvana. *Morte a Palermo*. Milan: La Tartaruga, 1987.

Lilli, Laura. *Ortiche e Margherite*. Verona: Essedue Edizioni, 1987.

———. *Zeta o le zie*. Rome: Edizioni delle donne, 1980. Repr. Milan: Bompiani, 1989.

Livi, Grazia. "Maestra e allieva." In *Racconta*. Ed. Rosaria Guacci and Bruna Miorelli. Milan: La Tartaruga, 1989.

Loy, Rosetta. *La bicicletta*. Turin: Einaudi, 1974.

———. *L'estate de Letuché*. Milan: Rizzoli, 1984.

———. *Le strade di polvere*. Turin: Einaudi, 1987. *The Dust Roads of Monferrato*. Trans. William Weaver. New York: Knopf, 1990.

Magrini, Gabriella. *Una lunga giovinezza*. Milan: Mondadori, 1976.

Maraini, Dacia. *Donna in guerra*. Turin: Einaudi, 1975. *Women at War*. Trans. Mara Benetti and Elspeth Spottiswood. New York: Italica Press, 1988.

———. *La lunga vita di Marianna Ucrìa*. Milan: Rizzoli, 1990. *The Silent Duchess*. Trans. Dick Kitto and Elspeth Spottiswood. London: Peter Owen, 1992.

———. *Memorie di una ladra*. Rome: Bompiani, 1972. Repr. 1984. *Memoirs of a Female Thief*. Trans. Nina Rootes. Levittown, PA: Transatlantic Arts, 1974.

———. "Sekmeth." In *Racconta*. Ed. Rosaria Guacci and Bruna Morelli. Milan: La Tartaruga, 1989.

———. *Il treno per Helsinki*. Turin: Einaudi, 1984.

Martelli, Dacia. *Chi perde la sua vita*. Rome: Transmedia, 1982.

Morante, Elsa. *La storia*. Turin: Einaudi, 1974.

Morazzoni, Marta. *L'invenzione della verità*. Milan: Longanesi, 1988.

———. *La ragazza col turbante*. Milan: Longanesi, 1986. *Girl in a Turban*. Trans. Patrick Creagh. New York: Knopf, 1988.

Ombres, Rossana. *Principessa Giacinta*. Milan: Rizzoli, 1970.

———. *Serenata*. Milan: Mondadori, 1980.

Petrignani, Sandra. *Catalogo dei giocattoli*. Rome: Theoria, 1988.

———. *Come cadono i fulmini*. Milan: Rizzoli, 1991.

———. *Le navigazioni di Circe*. Rome: Theoria, 1987.

Ramondino, Fabrizia. *Althénopis*. Turin: Einaudi, 1980. English trans. Michael Sullivan. Manchester: Carcanet, 1988.

Ravera, Lidia. *Porci con le ali*. Rome: Savelli, 1976.

———. *Per funghi*. Rome: Theoria, 1987.

———. *Voi grandi*. Rome: Theoria, 1990.

Rossi, Rosa. *L'ultimo capitolo*. Rome: Lucarini, 1984.

Sanvitale, Francesca. *Madre e figlia*. Turin: Einaudi, 1980.

Schiavo, Maria. *Discorso eretico alla fatalità*. Florence: Giunti, 1990.

———. *Macellum: Storia violentata e romanzata di donne e di mercato*. Milan: La Tartaruga, 1979.

Villani, Tiziani. *Demetra*. Milan: Mimesi, 1989.

Volpi, Marisa. *Il maestro della betulla*. Florence: Valecchi, 1986.

Secondary Sources

Abba, Luisa, Gabriella Ferri, Giorgia Lazzaretto, Elena Medi, and Silvia Motta, eds. *La coscienza di sfruttata*. Milan: Mazzotta, 1972.

Abel, Elizabeth, Marianne Hirsch, and Elizabeth Langland, eds. *The Voyage In: Fictions of Female Development*. Hanover, NH: University Press of New England, 1983.

Alcoff, Linda. "Cultural Feminism versus Post-Structuralism: The Identity Crisis in Feminist Theory." *Signs* 13.3 (1988): 405–446.

Alfieri, Peter. "Il romanzo poliziesco in Italia." Unpublished diss. Ann Arbor, MI: University Microfilms International, 1986.

Anderson, Bonnie, and Judith Zinsser. *A History of One's Own: Women in Europe from Prehistory to the Present*. 2 vols. New York: Harper and Row, 1988.

Apter, Emily. "The Story of I: Luce Irigaray's Theoretical Masochism." *NWSA Journal* 2.2 (1990): 186–198.

Arico, Santo. *Contemporary Women Writers in Italy: A Modern Renaissance*. Amherst: University of Massachusetts Press, 1990.

Ariès, Philippe. *Essais sur l'histoire de la mort en Occident du Môyen Age à nos jours*. Paris: Seuil, 1975.

Bachofen, J. J. *Das Mutterrecht*. Stuttgart: Krais and Hoffmann, 1861. *Il matriarcato*. Trans. G. Schiavoni. Turin: Einaudi, 1988.

Barthes, Roland. *Critique et vérité*. Paris: Seuil, 1966.

Bassnett, Susan. *Feminist Experiences: The Women's Movement in Four Cultures*. London: Allen and Unwin, 1986.

Beauvoir, Simone de. *Le deuxième sexe*. Paris: Gallimard, 1949.

Belotti, Elena Gianini. *Amore e pregiudizio: Il tabù dell'età nei rapporti sentimentali*. Milan: Mondadori, 1988. Repr. 1990.

———. "Giovane scrittore, sì, giovane scrittrice, no." In *Una donna, un secolo*. Ed. Sandra Petrignani. Rome: Il Ventaglio, 1986.

Benhabib, Seyla, and Drucilla Cornell, eds. *Feminism as Critique*. Minneapolis: University of Minnesota Press, 1988.

Berg, Maggie. "Luce Irigaray's 'Contradictions': Poststructuralism and Feminism." *Signs* 17.1 (1991): 50–70.

Bermann, Sandra. Introduction. *On the Historical Novel*. Translation of Alessandro Manzoni's *Del romanzo storico*. Trans. Hannah Mitchell and Stanley Mitchell. Lincoln: University of Nebraska Press, 1984.

Birnbaum, Lucia. *Liberazione della donna: Feminism in Italy*. Middletown, CT: Wesleyan University Press, 1986.

Blelloch, Paola. "Francesca Sanvitale's *Madre e figlia*: From Reflection to Self-Invention." In *Contemporary Women Writers in Italy: A Modern Renaissance*. Ed. Santo Arico. Amherst: University of Massachusetts Press, 1990.

———. *Quel mondo dei guanti e delle stoffe*. Verona: Essedue Edizioni, 1987.

Boccia, Maria Luisa. *L'io in rivolta: Vissuto e pensiero di Carla Lonzi*. Milan: La Tartaruga, 1990.

———. "Le matrici culturali del neofemminismo: Appunti di lettura sulla presenza di riferimenti al marxismo nel pensiero femminista degli anni Settanta." In *Esperienza storica femminile nell'età moderna e contemporanea*. Vol. 2. Ed. Anna Maria Crispino. Rome: La Goccia, 1989.

———. "Percorsi della mente femminile e forme del sapere." In *Con voce di donna: Pensiero, linguaggio, comunicazione*. Siena: Centro Culturale Mara Meoni, 1989.

————. "Solitudine di un io femminile." *Reti* 3–4 (1989): 22–25.

Bompiani, Ginevra. *Spazio narrante*. Milan: La Tartaruga, 1978.

Bondanella, Peter, and Julia Bondanella, eds. *Dictionary of Italian Literature*. Westport, CT: Greenwood, 1979.

Bono, Paola. "Una sfida contro la moderazione: La quasi collana sulla differenza sessuale degli editori Riuniti." *Reti* 6 (1990): 24–26.

Bono, Paola, and Sandra Kemp, eds. *Italian Feminist Thought: A Reader*. Oxford: Blackwell, 1991.

————. *The Lonely Mirror: Italian Perspectives on Feminist Theory*. London: Routledge, 1993.

Borrello, Giovanna. "Il fondamento del pensiero della differenza sessuale." Group B, Workshop, June 11–12, 1988. Rome: Edizioni Centro Culturale Virginia Woolf, 1988.

Borrodori, Giovanna. "'Weak Thought' and the 'Aesthetics of Quotationism': The Italian Shift from Deconstruction." Working Paper 6. University of Wisconsin-Milwaukee Center for Twentieth Century Studies, 1986.

Braendlin, Bonnie Hoover. "*Bildung* in Ethnic Women Writers." *Denver Quarterly* 17.4 (1983): 75–87.

Braidotti, Rosi. *Patterns of Dissonance: A Study of Women in Contemporary Philosophy*. Trans. Elizabeth Guild. Oxford: Polity, 1991.

————. "Il triangolo della differenza." *NoiDonne: Legendaria* (May 1990).

Brown, Marshall. "The Logic of Realism: A Hegelian Approach." *PMLA* 96.2 (1981): 224–241.

Bruffee, Kenneth. *Elegiac Romance: Cultural Change and the Loss of the Hero in Modern Fiction*. Ithaca, NY: Cornell University Press, 1983.

Cam, Helen. "Historical Novels." Pamphlet of the British Historical Association. London: Oscar Blackford, 1961.

Cambria, Adele. *L'Italia segreta delle donne: Amori tormentati, intrighi politici, passioni rivoluzionarie e abbandoni romantici: Tra dee, eroine, poetesse e nobildonne, un viaggio attraverso i luoghi dove vissero e agirono le protagoniste della nostra storia*. Rome: Newton Compton, 1984.

————."Il neo-femminismo in letteratura: Dove sono le ammazzoni?" In *Una donna, un secolo*. Ed. Sandra Petrignani. Rome: Il Ventaglio, 1986.

Campanaro, Lidia. "La potenza generativa delle donne in un vuoto di immagini e di parole." *Il manifesto*. December 7, 1990.

Cantarella, Eva. "Le fortune del matriarcato." *Reti* 3–4 (1988): 17–19.

————. *Secondo natura*. Rome: Riuniti, 1988. *Bisexuality in the Ancient World*. Trans. Cormac Ò'Cuilleànain. New Haven, CT: Yale University Press, 1992.

Carravetta, Peter. "Repositioning Interpretive Discourse: From the 'Crisis of Reason' to 'Weak Thought.'" *Differentia* 2 (1988): 83–127.

Carroll, David. *The Subject in Question: The Languages of Theory and the Strategies of Fiction*. Chicago: University of Chicago Press, 1982.

Castelli, Silvia. "Miti, forme e modelli della narrativa nuova." In *La letteratura emarginata*. Ed. Walter Pedullà. Rome: Lerici, 1978.

Causse, Michèle, and Maryvonne Lapouge, eds. *Ecrits, voix d'Italie*. Paris: Editions des femmes, 1977.

Cavarero, Adriana, Christiana Fischer, Elvia Franco, Giannina Longobardi, Veronica Mariaux, Luisa Muraro, Anna Maria Piussi, Wanda Tommasi, Anita Sanvitto, Betty Zamarchi, Chiara Zamboni, and Gloria Zanardo. *Diotima: Il pensiero della differenza sessuale*. Milan: La Tartaruga, 1987.

————. "L'elaborazione filosofica della differenza sessuale." In *La ricerca delle donne: Studi femministi in Italia*. Ed. Maria Cristina Marcuzzo and Anna Rossi-Doria. Turin: Rosenberg and Sellier, 1987.

————. *Nonostante Platone: Figure femminili nella filosofia antica*. Rome: Riuniti, 1990.

Chambers, Iain. "Rolling Away from the Centre Towards X: Some Notes on Italian Philosophy, 'Weak Thought' and 'Postmodernism.'" In *Culture and Conflict in Postwar Italy: Essays on Mass and Popular Culture*. Ed. Zygmunt Baranski and Robert Lumley. Houndmills, Basingstoke, Hampshire: Macmillan, 1990.

Cigada, Piero. "Particolari effetti personali." *Il sole*. December 18, 1988.

Cixous, Hélène. "Le sexe ou la tête." *Cahiers du Grif* 13 (1976): 5–15. Trans. Annette Kuhn. "Castration or Decapitation." *Signs* 7.1 (1981): 36–55.

Cohen, Ralph. "History and Genre." *New Literary History* 17.2 (1986): 203–218.

Coletti, Teresa. *Naming the Rose: Eco, Medieval Signs and Modern Theory*. Ithaca, NY: Cornell University Press, 1988.

Colie, Rosalie. *The Resources of Kind: Genre Theory in the Renaissance*. Ed. Barbara Lewalski. Berkeley: University of California Press, 1973.

Corona, Daniela, ed. *Donne e scrittura*. Palermo: La Luna, 1990.

Corti, Maria, ed. *Opere di Elio Vittorini*. Milan: Mondadori, 1974.

Costa-Zalessow, Natalia. *Scrittrici italiane dal XIII al XX secolo*. Ravenna: Longo Editore, 1982.

Crispino, Anna Maria. "Autrici? Visto, si stampi." *NoiDonne: Legendaria* (May 1990): 10–11.

Culler, Jonathan. *Structuralist Poetics: Structuralism, Linguistics and the Study of Literature*. Ithaca, NY: Cornell University Press, 1975.

Cutrufelli, Maria Rosa. "Alla conquista delle lettrici: Un nuovo mercato per l'industria editoriale." In *Scritture, Scrittrici*. Ed. Maria Rosa Cutrufelli. Rome: Longanesi, 1988.

————. "Un mondo di parole che parte dal corpo." *NoiDonne: Legendaria* (June–August 1990).

————. "Scritture, scrittrici: L'esperienza italiana." In *Donne e Scrittura*. Ed. Daniela Corona. Palermo: La Luna, 1990.

————. "Sordità tra noi donne: Ecco che cosa può renderci più deboli." *L'unità*. October 30, 1990.

Daly, Mary. *Beyond God the Father*, Boston: Beacon Press, 1973.

D'Amelia, Marina. "Fare storia, non politica: Il successo de *La storia delle donne* apre interrogativi tra le storiche." *Reti* 6 (1990): 19–23.

————. "A proposito di storiche, di madri e di alcuni miti di fine secolo." In *Discutendo di storia: Soggettività, ricerca, biografia*. Ed. Maura Palazzi and Anna Scattigno. Turin: Rosenberg and Sellier, 1990.

Dedola, Rossana. "Strutture narrative e ideologia nella *Storia* di Elsa Morante." *Studi Novecenteschi* 15 (1976): 247–265.

de Giovanni, Neria. "La sfinge cantatrice—Realtà come specchio nella narrativa femminile italiana post-neorealismo." *Romance Languages Annual* 1 (1989): 105–110.

de Lauretis, Teresa. *Alice Doesn't: Feminism, Semiotics, Cinema*. Bloomington: Indiana University Press, 1984.

————. "The Essence of the Triangle or, Taking the Risk of Essentialism Seriously: Feminist Theory in Italy, the U.S., and Britain." *Differences* 1.2 (1990): 3–37.

————. "Feminist Studies, Critical Studies: Issues, Terms, Contexts." In *Feminist Studies, Critical Studies*. Ed. Teresa de Lauretis. Bloomington: Indiana University Press, 1986.

————. "Gaudy Rose: Eco and Narcissism." In *Technologies of Gender: Essays on Theory, Film and Fiction*. Bloomington: Indiana University Press, 1987.

————. "The Practice of Sexual Difference and Feminist Thought in Italy: An Introductory Essay." Introduction to her translation, with Patricia Cicogna, of *Non credere di avere dei diritti*. In *Sexual Difference: A Theory of Social-Symbolic Practice*. Bloomington: Indiana University Press, 1990.

de Michelis, Cesare. "Marianna." *Il gazzettino*. June 23, 1990.

Denham, Robert, ed. *Visionary Poetics: Essays on Northrop Frye's Criticism*. New York: Peter Lang, 1991.

de Rougemont, Denis. *L'Amour et l'Occident*. Paris: Librairie Plon, 1939.

Derrida, Jacques. "The Law of Genre." *Critical Inquiry* 7.1 (1980): 55–81.

Derrida, Jacques, and Christie McDonald. "Choreographies." *Diacritics* 12 (1982): 66–76.

di Cori, Paola. "Prospettive e soggetti nella storia delle donne: alla ricerca di radici communi." In *La ricerca delle donne: Studi femministi in Italia*. Ed. Maria Cristina Marcuzzo and Anna Rossi-Doria. Turin: Rosenberg and Sellier, 1988.

————. "Soggettività e storia delle donne." In *Discutendo di storia: Soggettività, ricerca, biografia*. Ed. Maura Palazzi and Anna Scattigno. Turin: Rosenberg and Sellier, 1990.

D'Isa, Dina. "La liberazione attraverso la scrittura." *Il tempo*. May 11, 1990.

di Stefano, Christine. "Dilemmas of Difference: Feminism, Modernity and Postmodernism." In *Feminism/Postmodernism*. Ed. Linda Nicholson. New York: Routledge, 1990.

Dominijanni, Ida. "Il femminismo degli anni Ottanta: Un nodo: Uguaglianza e differenza." In *Esperienza storica femminile nell'età moderna e contemporanea*. Vol. 2. Ed. Anna Maria Crispino. Rome: La Goccia, 1989.

————. "Le origini di fronte." *Il manifesto*, January 10, 1991.

————. "Politica sotto processo: Rifondazione comunista, democrazia, soggetti del cambiamento. Un seminario." *Il manifesto*. December 20, 1990.

————. "Una quasi-collana che sa la differenza." *Il manifesto*. November 9, 1990.

Donovan, Josephine. "Towards a Women's Poetics." *Tulsa Studies in Women's Literature* 3.1–2 (1984): 99–110.

Dubrow, Heather. *Genre*. New York: Methuen, 1983.

Ecker, Gisela, ed. *Feminist Aesthetics*. Trans. Harriet Anderson. London: The Women's Press, 1985.

Eco, Umberto. *Il nome della rosa*. Milan: Bompiani, 1980.

————. *Postscript to the Name of the Rose*. Trans. William Weaver. New York: Harcourt, Brace, Jovanovich, 1983.

Felski, Rita. *Beyond Feminist Aesthetics: Feminist Literature and Social Change*. Cambridge, MA: Harvard University Press, 1989.

Fetterly, Judith. *The Resisting Reader: A Feminist Approach to Modern Fiction*. Bloomington: Indiana University Press, 1978.

Feuchtwanger, Leon. *The House of Desdemona or the Laurels and Limitations of Historical Fiction*. Trans. Harold A. Basilius. Detroit, MI: Wayne State University Press, 1963.

Fink, Laurie. "The Rhetoric of Marginality: Why I Do Feminist Theory." *Tulsa Studies in Women's Literature* 5.2 (1986): 250–272.

Finucci, Valeria. "A Portrait of the Artist as a Female Painter: The *Künstlerro-man* Tradition in Anna Banti's *Artemisia.*" *Quaderni d'italianistica* 8.2 (1987): 167–193.

———. "The Textualization of the Female 'I': Elsa Morante's *Menzogna e sortilegio.*" *Italica* 65 (1988): 308–328.

Forti, Marco. "La storia senza mito." *Approdo letterario* 67–68 (1974): 149–158.

Foucault, Michel. *Language, Counter-Memory, Practice: Selected Essays and Interviews.* Trans. Donald F. Bouchard and Sherry Simon. Ithaca, NY: Cornell University Press, 1977.

Fowler, Alistair. *Kinds of Literature: An Introduction to the Theory of Genres and Modes.* Cambridge, MA: Harvard University Press, 1982.

Frabotta, Biancamaria. "L'identità dell'opera e l'io femminile." In *Donne e scrittura.* Ed. Daniela Corona. Palermo: La Luna, 1990.

———. "Contraddizione e trasgressione: Sulla specificità del femminile." *aut aut* 161 (1977): 67–73.

———. *Letteratura al femminile.* Bari: DeDonato, 1981.

Fraire, Manuela. "Una pratica per una politica." In *L'apprendimento dell'incertezza: I centri culturali delle donne.* Ed. Carla Cotti and Francesca Molfino. Rome: Edizioni Centro Culturale Virginia Woolf, 1989.

Frentz, Thomas. "Resurrecting the Feminine in *The Name of the Rose.*" *Pre/Text* 9.3–4 (1988): 123–145.

Friedman, Rodger. "After Deconstruction." *Differentia* 1 (1986): 281–287.

Frye, Joanne. *Living Stories, Telling Lives.* Ann Arbor: University of Michigan Press, 1986.

Frye, Northrop. *The Secular Scripture: A Study of the Structure of Romance.* Cambridge, MA: Harvard University Press, 1976.

———. "Varieties of Eighteenth Century Sensibility: Response." *Eighteenth Century Studies* 24.2 (1990–91): 243–249.

Fuderer, Laura Sue. *The Female Bildungsroman in English: An Annotated Bibliography of Criticism.* New York: MLA Publications, 1990.

Fumagalli, Firella. "Marianna dei Miracoli." *Tutto Milano.* January 31, 1991.

Furiani, P. L. "Di donna in donna: Elementi femministi nel romanzo greco d'amore." In *Piccolo mondo antico: Le donne, gli amori, i costumi, il mondo reale nel romanzo antico.* Ed. P. L. Furiani and A. M. Scarcella. Perugia: Edizioni Scientifiche Italiane, 1989.

Fusini, Nadia. "Commento alla relazione di Silvia Vegetti-Finzi." In *La ricerca delle donne: Studi femministi in Italia.* Ed. Maria Cristina Marcuzzo and Anna Rossi-Doria. Turin: Rosenberg and Sellier, 1988.

———. *La luminosa: Genealogia di Fedra.* Milan: Feltrinelli, 1990.

Gagliasso, Elena. "Articoli di fede? No grazie." *Reti* 3–4 (1989): 52–56.

Gallop, Jane. *The Daughter's Seduction: Feminism and Psychoanalysis.* Ithaca, NY: Cornell University Press, 1982.

———. "Quand nos lèvres s'écrivent: Irigaray's Body Politics." *Romanic Review* 74 (1983): 77–83.

Garrard, Mary. *Artemisia: The Image of the Female Hero in Baroque Art.* Princeton, NJ: Princeton University Press, 1989.

Gargani, Aldo. "La voce femminile." *Alfabeta* 64 (1984): 16.

Gelfand, Elissa. *Imagination in Confinement: Women's Writings from French Prisons.* Ithaca, NY: Cornell University Press, 1984.

Genette, Gérard. "Vraisemblance et motivation." In *Figures 11.* Paris: Seuil, 1969.

Gensini, Stefano. "Lukacs théoricien de la littérature en Italie." *Europe* 600 (1979): 154–166.
Gerrard, Nicci. *Into the Mainstream: How Feminism Has Changed Women's Writing.* London: Pandora Press, 1989.
Gertz, Clifford. *The Interpretation of Cultures.* New York: Basic Books, 1973.
Gilbert, Susan, and Sandra Gubar. *The Madwoman in the Attic.* New Haven, CT: Yale University Press, 1979.
———. *No Man's Land.* New Haven, CT: Yale University Press, 1988.
Giorgio, Adalgisa. "A Feminist Family Romance: Mother, Daughter and Female Genealogy in Fabrizia Ramondino's *Althénopis.*" *The Italianist* 11 (1991): 128–149.
Girard, René. *Deceit, Desire and the Novel: Self and Other in Literary Structure.* Baltimore, MD: Johns Hopkins University Press, 1976.
Gramaglia, Mariella. "Sesso e democrazia." *La repubblica.* October 9, 1990.
Granatella, Laura. "Manzonismo e antimanzonismo nella critica." *Italianistica* 5 (1976): 110–117.
Grasso, Laura. "Madre e figlie." In *Il filo di Arianna: Letture della differenza sessuale.* Ed. Franca Bimbi, Laura Grasso, and Marina Zancan. Rome: Utopia, 1987.
Grimshaw, Jean. *Philosophy and Feminism.* Minneapolis: University of Minnesota Press, 1986.
Gubar, Susan. "The Birth of the Artist as Heroine: (Re)production, the *Künstlerroman* Tradition and the Fiction of Katherine Mansfield." In *The Representation of Women in Fiction.* Ed. Carolyn Heilbrun and Margaret Higonnet. Baltimore, MD: Johns Hopkins University Press, 1983.
Guiducci, Armanda. *La donna non è gente.* Milan: Rizzoli, 1977.
———. *Donna e serva.* Milan: Rizzoli, 1983.
———. *Medioevo inquieto: Storia delle donne dall' VIII al XV secolo d.c.* Florence: Sansoni, 1989.
———. *La mela e il serpente.* Milan: Rizzoli, 1974.
———. *Perdute nella storia: Storia delle donne dáll' I al VII secolo d.c.* Florence: Sansoni, 1990.
Guillen, Claudio. *Literature as System: Essays Toward the Theory of Literary History.* Princeton, NJ: Princeton University Press, 1971.
Gunn, Janet. *Autobiography: Towards a Poetics of Experience.* Philadelphia: University of Pennsylvania Press, 1982.
Hallam, Paul. "The House on Moon Lake." *New Statesman.* March 4, 1988.
Heilbrun, Carolyn. *Reinventing Womanhood.* New York: Norton, 1979.
Heiserman, Arthur. *The Novel Before the Novel: Essays and Discussions About the Beginnings of Prose Fiction in the West.* Chicago: University of Chicago Press, 1977.
Heller, Deborah. "History, Art and Fiction in Anna Banti's *Artemisia.*" In *Contemporary Women Writers in Italy: A Modern Renaissance.* Ed. Santo Arico. Amherst: University of Massachusetts Press, 1990.
Hellman, Judith. *Journeys Among Women: Feminism in Five Italian Cities.* New York: Oxford University Press, 1987.
Hermann, Claudine. *La voleuse des langues.* Paris: Editions des femmes, 1976.
Hilfer, Tony. *The Crime Novel: A Deviant Genre.* Austin: University of Texas Press, 1990.
Hirsch, Marianne. *The Mother-Daughter Plot: Narrative, Psychoanalysis, Feminism.* Bloomington: Indiana University Press, 1989.

————. "The Novel of Formation as Genre: Between *Great Expectations* and *Lost Illusions*." *Genre* 12 (1979): 293–311.

Hite, Molly. *The Other Side of the Story: Structures and Strategies of Contemporary Feminist Narrative*. Ithaca, NY: Cornell University Press, 1989.

Holquist, Michael. "Whodunit and Other Questions: Metaphysical Detective Stories in Post War Fiction." *New Literary History* 3 (1971): 135–186.

Holub, Renate. "For the Record: The Non-Language of Italian Feminist Philosophy." *Romance Languages Annual* 1 (1990): 133–140.

————. "The Politics of Diotima." *Differentia* 5 (1991): 161–173.

————. "Weak Thought and Strong Ethics." *Annali d'italianistica* 9 (1991): 124–143.

————. "Towards a New Rationality? Notes on Feminism and Current Discursive Practices in Italy." *Discourse* 4 (1982): 89–107.

Hutcheon, Linda. *A Poetics of Postmodernism: History, Theory and Fiction*. New York: Routledge, 1988.

Irigaray, Luce. *Ce sexe qui n'en est pas un*. Paris: Minuit, 1977. *Questo sesso che non è un sesso*. Trans. Luisa Muraro. Milan: Feltrinelli, 1978.

————. *Sexes et parentés*. Paris: Minuit, 1987. *Sessi e genealogie*. Trans. Luisa Muraro. Milan: La Tartaruga, 1989.

Irving, Katrina. "(Still) Hesitating on the Threshold: Feminist Theory and the Question of the Subject." *NWSA Journal* 1.4 (1989): 630–643.

Izzo Francesca. "Immagini del soggetto moderno: Etica e soggettività." *Reti* 3–4 (1989): 304–306.

————. "Il materno tra origine e storia." *Reti* 2 (1989): 23–26.

Jameson, Fredric. *The Political Unconscious*. Ithaca, NY: Cornell University Press, 1981.

Jardine, Alice. *Gynesis: Configurations of Women in Modernity*. Ithaca, NY: Cornell University Press, 1985.

Jehlen, Myra. "Archimedes and the Paradox of Feminist Criticism." *Signs* 6.4 (1981): 575–601.

Jelinek, Estelle, ed. *Women's Autobiography*. Bloomington: Indiana University Press, 1980.

Johnson, Barbara. *The Critical Difference*. Baltimore, MD: Johns Hopkins University Press, 1980.

————. "Gender Theory and the Yale School." In *Rhetoric and Form: Deconstruction at Yale*. Ed. Robert Con Davis and Ronald Schiefer. Oklahoma City: University of Oklahoma Press, 1985. Repr. in *Speaking of Gender*. Ed. Elaine Showalter. New York: Routledge, 1989.

Jones, Ann Rosalind. "Inscribing Femininity: French Theories of the Feminine." In *Making a Difference: Feminist Literary Criticism*. Ed. Gayle Green and Coppélia Kahn. London: Methuen, 1985.

————. "Julia Kristeva on Femininity: The Limits of a Semiotic Poetics." *Feminist Review* 18 (1984): 56–73.

————. "Manzoni's *I promessi sposi* and Lukacs' *Theorie des Romans*." *Arcadia* 11 (1976): 126–138.

Kennard, Jean. "Convention Coverage or How to Read Your Own Life." *New Literary History* 13.1 (1981): 69–88.

King, Martha, and Barbara Nucci, eds. *New Italian Women*. New York: Italica Press, 1989.

Klein, Kathleen. *The Woman Detective: Gender and Genre*. Chicago: University of Chicago Press, 1988.

Knight, Stephen. *Form and Ideology in Crime Fiction*. London: Macmillan, 1980.
Kofman, Sarah. *L'énigme de la femme*. Paris: Galilée, 1980.
———. "Supplément rhapsodique." *Discourse* 4 (1982): 37–52.
Kristeva, Julia. *La révolution du langage poétique*. Paris: Seuil, 1974.
———. "Le temps des femmes." *Cahiers de recherche des sciences de textes et de documents* 5 (1979). "Women's Time." Trans. Alice Jardine and Henry Blake. *Signs* 7.1 (1981): 13–35.
La Capra, Dominick. *History and Criticism*. Ithaca, NY: Cornell University Press, 1985.
Laillou-Savona, Jeannette. "Dé-lire et délit/ces: Stratégies des lectures féministes (Coward, de Lauretis, Moi, Cixous, Broussard, etc.)." *Canadian Review of Comparative Literature* 15.2 (1988): 220–253.
Lang, Berel. "Postmodernism and Philosophy: Nostalgia for the Future, Waiting for the Past." *New Literary History* 18.1 (1987): 209–224.
Lasch, Christopher. *The Culture of Narcissism: American Life in an Age of Diminishing Expectations*. New York: Norton, 1978.
Lazzaro-Weis, Carol. "Dacia Maraini." In *Italian Women Writers*. Ed. Rinaldina Russell. Westport, CT: Greenwood, 1993.
———."The Experience of Don Juan in Italian Feminist Fictions." *Annali d'italianistica* 7 (1989): 382–393.
———."The Female *Bildungsroman*: Calling It into Question." *NWSA Journal* 2 (1990): 16–34.
———. "From Margins to Mainstream: Some Perspectives on Women and Literature in Italy in the 1980s." In *Contemporary Women Writers in Italy: A Modern Renaissance*. Ed. Santo Arico. Amherst: University of Massachusetts Press, 1990.
———. "Gender and Genre in Italian Feminist Literature in the Seventies." *Italica* 65.4 (1988): 293–307.
———. "The Metaphysical Detective Novel and Sciascia's *Il contesto*: Parody or Tyranny of a Borrowed Form?" *Quaderni d'italianistica* 8.1 (1987): 42–52.
———."The Providential Trap: Some Remarks on Fictional Strategies in *I promessi sposi*." *Stanford Italian Review* 4.1 (1984): 93–106.
Lentricchia, Frank. *After the New Criticism*. Chicago: University of Chicago Press, 1980.
Lilli, Laura, and Chiara Valentina, eds. *Care compagne: Il femminismo nel PCI e nelle organizzazioni di massa*. Rome: Riuniti, 1978.
Lonzi, Carla. *Sputiamo su Hegel: La donna clitoridea e la donna vaginale, e altri scritti*. Milan: Rivolta femminile, 1974.
Lucente, Gregory. *Beautiful Fables: Self-Consciousness in Italian Narrative from Manzoni to Calvino*. Baltimore, MD: Johns Hopkins University Press, 1986.
———. "Scrivere o fare altro: Social Commitment and Ideologies of Representation in the Debates over Lampedusa's *Il gattopardo* and Morante's *La storia*." *Italica* 61.2 (1984): 220–251.
Lukacs, Georg. *The Theory of the Novel*. Trans. Anna Bostock. Cambridge, MA: MIT Press, 1971.
Mafai, Miriam. "Compagne, l'ideologia adesso non basta più." *La repubblica*. February 20, 1991.
———. "Le vedove di Lenin e la deriva femminista." *MicroMega* 4 (1990): 7–15.
Mancina, Claudia. "Perché non si può imporre per statuto la politica della differenza." *L'unità*. February 17, 1991.

————. "Praticare la differenza come categoria politica: Il caso delle donne nel PCI." *Passaggi* 1 (1989): 25–32.

Mandrell, James. "The Prophetic Voice in Garro, Morante and Allende." *Comparative Literature* 42.3 (1990): 227–246.

Maraini, Dacia. "Quale cultura per la donna?" In *Donna, cultura e tradizione*. Ed. Pia Bruzzichelli and Maria Luisa Algini. Milan: Mazzotta, 1976.

Marx, Elaine. "Women and Literature in France." *Signs* 3.4 (1978): 832–842.

McKeon, Michael. *The Origins of the English Novel 1600–1740*. Baltimore, MD: Johns Hopkins University Press, 1987.

Melandri, Lea, ed. *L'infame originaria*. Milan: L'Erba Voglio, 1977.

Menapace, Lidia. "Seppelliamo il Principe." *Rinascita*. November 18, 1990.

Merivale, Patricia. "Through Greene-Land in Drag: Joan Didion's *A Book of Common Prayer*." *Pacific Coast Philology* 15 (1980): 139–152.

Merry, Bruce. *Dacia Maraini and Her Place in Contemporary Italian Literature*. Oxford: Berg, 1993.

————. "Dacia Maraini's: *La lunga vita di Marianna Ucrìa*." *PEN International Bulletin of Selected Books*. 42.1 (1992): 33–35.

————. *Women in Modern Italian Literature: Four Studies Based on the Work of Grazia Deledda, Alba de Céspedes, Natalia Ginzburg and Dacia Maraini*. Capricornia 8. Townsville: James Cook University of North Queensland, 1990.

Meyer, Donald. *Sex and Power: The Rise of Women in America, Russia, Sweden, and Italy*. Middletown, CT: Wesleyan University Press, 1987.

Migiel, Marilyn, and Juliana Schiesari, eds. *Refiguring Woman: Perspectives on Gender and the Italian Renaissance*. Ithaca, NY: Cornell University Press, 1991.

Miller, J. Hillis. *Versions of Pygmalion*. Cambridge, MA: Harvard University Press, 1990.

Miller, Nancy. "Authorized Versions." *French Review* 61.3 (1988): 405–413.

————. "Feminist Writing and the History of the Novel." *Novel* 21.2–3 (1988): 310–321.

————. *The Heroine's Texts: Readings in the French and English Novel 1722–1781*. New York: Columbia University Press, 1980.

————. "Men's Reading, Women's Writing: Gender and the Rise of the Novel." *Yale French Studies* 75 (1988): 40–55.

Moi, Toril. *Sexual/Textual Politics*. New York: Methuen, 1985.

Molfino, Francesca. "Fedeltà a se stesse e testimonianza reciproca." In *L'apprendimento dell'incertezza: I centri culturali delle donne*. Ed. Carla Cotti and Francesca Molfino. Rome: Edizioni Centro Culturale Virginia Woolf, 1989: 12–21.

————. "Psicoanalisi e femminismo: Le radici culturali del neofemminismo." In *Esperienza storica femminile nell'età moderna e contemporanea*. Vol. 2. Ed. Anna Maria Crispino. Rome: La Goccia, 1990: 63–75.

Montefoschi, Silvia. "Il ruolo materno e l'identità personale: Riflessioni sul movimento femminista e la psicoanalisi." *Nuova DWF* 6–7 (1978): 143–173.

Morandini, Giuliana. *La voce che è in lei: Antologia della narrativa femminile italiana tra '800 e '900*. Milan: Bompiani, 1980.

Moravia, Alberto. *Alessandro Manzoni e l'ipotesi di un realismo cattolico*. Milan: Bompiani, 1964.

————. "Paura del benessere." *Corriere della sera*. September 2, 1989.

Moretti, Franco. *The Way of the World: The Bildungsroman in European Culture*. Norfolk, VA: Verso, 1987.

Muir, Edward, and Guido Ruggiero, eds. *Microhistory and the Lost Peoples of Europe*. Baltimore, MD: Johns Hopkins University Press, 1991.

Muraro, Luisa. "Il concetto della genealogia femminile." Rome: Edizioni Centro Culturale Virginia Woolf, 1988.

———. *Diotima: Il pensiero della differenza sessuale*. Milan: La Tartaruga, 1987. (Authored with Adriana Cavarero, Cristiana Fischer, Elvia Franco, Giannina Longobardi, Veronica Mariaux, Anna Maria Piussi, Wanda Tommasi, Anita Sanvitto, Betty Zamarchi, Chiara Zamboni, and Gloria Zanardo.)

———. *Guglielmo e Maifreda*. Milan: La Tartaruga, 1985.

Neera [Anna Radius Zuccari]. *Le idee di una donna* (1903); *Le confessioni letterarie* (1891). Published in one volume. Florence: Vallecchi, 1977.

Neonato, Silvia. "D'amore (forse) si muore: due generazioni sullo sfondo del femminismo." *Secolo XIX*. February 18, 1989.

Nicoli, Ottavia, ed. *Rinascimento al femminile*. Rome: Laterza, 1991.

Nozzoli, Anna. "La donna e il romanzo negli anni Ottanta." Proceedings of the conference "La donna nella letteratura italiana del 900." Ed. Sergio Gensini. Empoli: Rivista di cittadina, 1983.

———. *Tabù e coscienza: La condizione femminile nella letteratura italiana del Novecento*. Florence: La Nuova Italia, 1978.

Orr, Linda. "The Revenge of Literature: A History of History." *New Literary History* 18.1 (1986): 1–22.

Pacifici, Sergio. *The Modern Italian Novel: From Capuana to Tozzi*. Carbondale: Southern Illinois University Press, 1973.

———. *The Modern Italian Novel: From Pea to Moravia*. Carbondale: Southern Illinois Press, 1979.

Pagels, Elaine. *Adam, Eve and the Serpent*. New York: Random House, 1988.

Pallotta, Augustus. "Dacia Maraini: From Alienation to Feminism." *World Literature Today* 58 (1984): 359–362.

Pampaloni, Geno. "Introduzione." *I giovani hanno riletto per voi: 40 anni di narrativa italiana (1940–1954)*. Vol. 1. Rome: Mondadori, 1991.

Paris, Sherri. "Riding the Crime Wave." *The Women's Review of Books* 7.7 (1989): 8–9.

Pautasso, Sergio. *Gli anni Ottanta e la letteratura: Guida all'attività letteraria in Italia dal 1980 al 1990*. Milan: Rizzoli, 1991.

Pedullà, Walter. *La letteratura emarginata*. Rome: Lerici, 1978.

———. "Scrittori d'oggi: Un promettente esordio." *Avanti*. May 23, 1989.

Perrotta-Rabissi, Adriana, and Maria Perucci, eds. *Perleparole: Iniziative a favore dell'informazione e della documentazione delle donne europee*. Rome: Utopia, 1989.

Petrignani, Sandra, ed. *Una donna, un secolo*. Rome: Il Ventaglio, 1986.

———. *Le signore della scrittura*. Milan: La Tartaruga, 1984.

Petroni, Franco. "La narrativa della 'contestazione.'" *Belfagor* 33.5 (1978): 599–606.

Piemontese, Felice, ed. *Autodizionario degli scrittori italiani*. Milan: Leonardo Editore, 1989.

Pollin, Burton. "Philosophical and Literary Sources of *Frankenstein*." *Comparative Literature* 17 (1965): 97–108.

Poovey, Mary. "Feminism and Deconstruction." *Feminist Studies* 14 (1988): 51–65.

Porter, Dennis. *The Pursuit of Crime: Art and Ideology in Detective Fiction*. New Haven, CT: Yale University Press, 1981.

Portinari, Folco. *Le parabole del reale: Romanzi italiani dell'Ottocento*. Turin: Einaudi, 1986.

Potter, Joy. "The Ideological Substructure in *Conversazione in Sicilia*." *Italica* 52.1 (1975): 50–69.

Pratt, Annis. *Archetypal Patterns in Women's Fiction*. Bloomington: Indiana University Press, 1981.

Priestman, Martin. *Detective Fiction and Literature: The Figure on the Carpet*. New York: St. Martin's Press, 1991.

Prisco, Michele. "Un viaggio oltrecortina fra speranze e delusioni." *Il nostro tempo*. December 11, 1988.

Raimondi, Enzo. "Genesis and Structure of a Catholic Novel." *Interpretation, Theory and Practice*. Ed. Charles Singleton. Baltimore, MD: Johns Hopkins University Press, 1969.

Rasy, Elisabetta. *Le donne e la letteratura*. Rome: Riuniti, 1984.

——. *La lingua della nutrice*. Rome: Edizioni delle donne, 1978.

Re, Lucia. "The Debate on the Meaning of Literature in Italy Today." *Quaderni d'italianistica* 7.1 (1986): 96–111.

Redaelli, Paola. "Se la notte viene alla luce." *Lapis* 5 (1989): 65–66.

Reddy, Maureen. *Sisters in Crime: Feminism and the Crime Novel*. New York: Continuum, 1988.

Rosmarin, Adena. *The Power of Genre*. Minneapolis: University of Minnesota Press, 1985.

Rossanda, Rossana. *Le altre: Conversazioni sulle parole della politica*. Milan: Bompiani, 1979. Repr. Milan: Feltrinelli, 1987.

——. "Introduzione" to *Antigone*. Trans. Luisa Biondetti. Milan: Feltrinelli, 1987.

——. "Riconoscersi per negazione: Storie di un apprendistato femminile." *Il manifesto*. February 9, 1989.

——. "Una sovrana solitudine come forma di vita." *Il manifesto*. June 29, 1990.

Rossi, Rosa. *Le parole delle donne*. Rome: Riuniti, 1978.

Rowe, John Carlos. *Henry Adams and Henry James: The Emergence of a Modern Consciousness*. Ithaca, NY: Cornell University Press, 1976.

——. "To Live Outside the Law, You Must Be Honest: The Authority of the Margin in Contemporary Theory." *Cultural Critique* 1 (1985–86): 35–68.

Rusconi, Marisa. "Le chances delle donne." *L'espresso*. February 28, 1991.

Salisbury, Stephan. "Girl in a Turban." *New York Times Book Review*. May 7, 1989.

Sammons, Jeffrey. "The Mystery of the Missing *Bildungsroman* or What Happened to Wilhelm Meister's Legacy?" *Genre* 14.2 (1981): 229–246.

Sanvitale, Francesca. "Madre e figlia." In *Vivere e pensare la relazione madre-figlia*. Proceedings of a seminar held in Milan, March 19, 1990. Milan: Edizioni Associazione Culturale Melusine, 1990.

Sapegno, Natalino ed. *I promessi sposi*. Milan: Feltrinelli, 1968.

Sarrasini, Bia. "Sulla soglia, la madre." *NoiDonne: Legendaria* (December 1990): 64–66.

Schacherl, Bruno. "Il mito di Useppe e il romanzo popolare." *Rinascita*. August 28, 1974.

Scholes, Robert, and Robert Kellogg. *The Nature of Narrative*. London: Oxford University Press, 1966.

Schumann, Reinhold. *Italy in the Last Fifteen Hundred Years: A Concise History*. Lanham, MD: University Press of America, 1986.

Schweickart, Patrocinio. "Reading Ourselves: Toward a Feminist Theory of

Reading." In *Speaking of Gender*. Ed. Elaine Showalter. New York: Routledge, 1989.

Sennett, Richard. *The Fall of the Public Man*. New York: Knopf, 1977.

Showalter, Elaine. *A Literature of Their Own*. Princeton, NJ: Princeton University Press, 1977.

———, ed. *Feminist Criticism: Essays on Women, Literature, and Theory*. New York: Pantheon, 1985.

Spacks, Patricia Meyer. *The Female Imagination*. New York: Knopf, 1975.

Starnone, Domenico. "Pentimenti e brusche conversioni." *Tuttestorie* 2 (1991): 68–70.

Steiner, George. *Antigones*. Oxford: Oxford University Press, 1984. Italian translation, Milan: Garzanti, 1991.

Sumeli-Weinberg, Grazia. "An Interview with Dacia Maraini." *Tydskrif vir Letturkunde* 27.3 (1989): 64–72.

Swales, Martin. "The German *Bildungsroman* and the Great Tradition." In *Comparative Criticism*. Ed. Elinor Shaffer. Cambridge: Cambridge University Press, 1979.

———. *The German Bildungsroman from Wieland to Hesse*. Princeton, NJ: Princeton University Press, 1978.

Symons, Julien. *Bloody Murder: From the Detective Story to the Crime Novel*. New York: Viking, 1985.

Tamburri, Anthony. "Dacia Maraini's *Donna in guerra*: Victory or Defeat?" In *Contemporary Women Writers in Italy: A Modern Renaissance*. Ed. Santo Arico. Amherst: University of Massachusetts Press, 1990.

Tani, Stefano. *The Doomed Detective: The Contribution of the Detective Novel to Postmodern American and Italian Fiction*. Carbondale: Southern Illinois University Press, 1984.

Tatafiore, Roberta, ed. *A prova di donna: Interviste sulla svolta del PCI*. Rome: Cooperativa Libera Stampa, 1990.

Titone, Vittorio. "La critica e il caso Morante." *Nuova antologia* 523 (1975): 71–80.

Tompkins, Jane. *Sensational Designs: The Cultural Work of American Fiction*. New York: Oxford University Press, 1985.

Trousson, Raymond. *Le mythe de Prométhée dans la littérature européenne*. Geneva: Droz, 1964.

Turco, Livia. "Noi donne ancora deboli. . . ." *La repubblica*. October 9, 1990.

Vaihinger, Hans. *The Philosophy of 'As If': A System of the Theoretical, Practical and Religious Fictions of Mankind*. Trans. C. K. Ogden. London: Routledge and Keagan Paul, 1924.

Vattimo, Gianni. *La fine della modernità: Nihilismo e ermeneutica nella cultura postmoderna*. Milan: Garzanti, 1985. *The End of Modernity: Nihilism and Hermeneutics in Postmodern Culture*. Trans. Jon Snyder. Cambridge: Polity, 1988.

Vattimo, Gianni, and Pier Aldo Rovatti, eds. *Il pensiero debole*. Milan: Feltrinelli, 1983.

Vegetti-Finzi, Silvia. *Il bambino della notte: Divenire donna, divenire madre*. Milan: Mondadori, 1990.

———. *Storia della psicoanalisi*. 2 vols. Milan: Mondadori, 1986.

Vendler, Helen. "Feminism and Literature." *New York Review of Books*. May 30, 1990.

Viano, Maurizio. "Sesso debole, pensiero debole." *Annali d'italianistica* 7 (1989): 394–422.

Villani, Tiziana. "Demetra." In *Vivere e pensare la relazione madre-figlia*. Proceedings of a seminar held in Milan, February 26, 1990. Milan: Edizioni Associazione Culturale Melusine, 1990.

Visani, Virginia. "Tutta una vita da ribelle." *Anno*. July 26, 1990.

Warner, Marina. *Alone of All Her Sex: The Myth and Cult of the Virgin Mary*. New York: Knopf, 1976.

Watt, Ian. *The Rise of the Novel: Studies in Defoe, Richardson and Fielding*. Berkeley: University of California Press, 1957.

Weedon, Chris. *Feminist Practice and Postructuralist Theory*. Oxford: Basil Blackwell, 1987.

Wells, Susan. *The Dialectics of Representation*. Baltimore, MD: Johns Hopkins University Press, 1985.

White, Hayden. "Historical Pluralism." *Critical Inquiry* 12 (1986): 480–493.

———. *Metahistory: The Historical Imagination in Nineteenth-Century Europe*. Baltimore, MD: Johns Hopkins University Press, 1973.

———. "The Question of Narrative in Contemporary Historical Theory." *History and Theory* 23.1 (1984): 1–33.

Wiegel, Sigrid. "Double Focus: On the History of Women's Writing." In *Feminist Aesthetics*. Ed. Gisela Ecker. Trans. Harriet Anderson. London: The Women's Press, 1985.

———. "Woman Begins Relating to Herself: Contemporary German Women's Literature, Part One." *New German Critique* 31 (1984): 53–94.

Yaeger, Patricia. *Honey-Mad Women: Emancipatory Strategies in Women's Writings*. New York: Columbia University Press, 1988.

Zancan, Marina. "La donna." In *Letteratura italiana*. Ed. A.A. Rosa. Vol. 5. Turin: Einaudi, 1986.

Zuffa, Grazia. "Tra libertà e necessità: A proposito di *Non credere di avere dei diritti*." *Reti* 1 (1987): 51–53.

Index

This book was set in Baskerville and Eras typefaces. Baskerville was designed by John Baskerville at his private press in Birmingham, England, in the eighteenth century. The first typeface to depart from oldstyle typeface design, Baskerville has more variation between thick and thin strokes. In an effort to insure that the thick and thin strokes of his typeface reproduced well on paper, John Baskerville developed the first wove paper, the surface of which was much smoother than the laid paper of the time. The development of wove paper was partly responsible for the introduction of typefaces classified as modern, which have even more contrast between thick and thin strokes.

Eras was designed in 1969 by Studio Hollenstein in Paris for the Wagner Typefoundry. A contemporary script-like version of a sans-serif typeface, the letters of Eras have a monotone stroke and are slightly inclined.

Printed on acid-free paper.